VIKING FRIENDSHIP

VIKING FRIENDSHIP

THE SOCIAL BOND IN ICELAND AND NORWAY, C. 900–1300

JÓN VIÐAR SIGURÐSSON

CORNELL UNIVERSITY PRESS

Ithaca and London

This translation has been published with the financial support of NORLA.

First published 2017 by Cornell University Press

Originally published in Norwegian 2010 as *Den vennlige vikingen: Om vennskapets makt; Norge og på Island c. 900–1300* by Pax Forlag.

Printed in the United States of America

Library of Congress Cataloging-in-Publication Data

Names: Jón Viðar Sigurðsson, 1958– author. | Translation of: Jón Viðar Sigurðsson, 1958– Vennlige vikingen.
Title: Viking friendship : the social bond in Iceland and Norway, c. 900–1300 / Jón Viðar Sigurðsson.
Other titles: Vennlige vikingen. English
Description: Ithaca : Cornell University Press, 2017. | Includes bibliographical references and index.
Identifiers: LCCN 2016039393 (print) | LCCN 2016040227 (ebook) | ISBN 9781501705779 (cloth : alk. paper) | ISBN 9781501708473 (epub/mobi) | ISBN 9781501708480 (pdf)
Subjects: LCSH: Norway—History—1030–1397. | Iceland—History—To 1262. | Friendship—Norway— History—To 1500. | Friendship—Iceland— History—To 1500. | Norway—Relations—Iceland. | Iceland—Relations—Norway.
Classification: LCC DL460 .J6513 2017 (print) | LCC DL460 (ebook) | DDC 305.3409481/09021—dc23
LC record available at https://lccn.loc.gov/2016039393

Cornell University Press strives to use environmentally responsible suppliers and materials to the fullest extent possible in the publishing of its books. Such materials include vegetable-based, low-VOC inks and acid-free papers that are recycled, totally chlorine-free, or partly composed of nonwood fibers. For further information, visit our website at www.cornellpress.cornell.edu.

CONTENTS

VIKING FRIENDSHIP

Introduction

In May 2009, I took part in a conference in England. The day after it began, my daughter phoned me from home in despair. She told me that she would be taking an exam in two days and that she should be prepared to discuss, among other things, the importance of Icelandic kin-based society (*ættesamfunn*) during the time of the Free State (the period from the establishment of the Althing in c. 930 until the year 1262, 1263, or 1264, when Iceland came under the control of the Norwegian king). She was not despondent because she had to take an exam, but rather because for many years she had heard me speak about friendship and chieftains in Iceland in the same period. She knew quite well that I objected to the very notion of a kin-based society mentioned in her textbooks and by her teacher. Instead, I spoke of a chieftain society, where the chieftains—and not kin leaders—were the most powerful individuals. Indeed, I argued that kin and kin-based relations had very little meaning, especially when compared with the vital role friends and friendship played. This, of course, put my daughter in an impossible situation: Should she follow her father or the curriculum? After I had overcome my surprise at the question, I proceeded to regale her on how "old ideas die hard," followed by a surly commentary on the lack of knowledge of my work, and finally an in-depth lecture on the meaning of friendship in the Icelandic Free State. It was not long after this conversation that I decided to write this book.[1] I should add that my daughter was eventually (and mercifully) released from having to choose between her father and the Norwegian school curriculum, having been excused from this part of the exam.

This book is about friendship in Norway and Iceland, c. 900–1300; that is, from the years Iceland was settled to the time when Norway and Iceland, entered into a union with Sweden. The basic idea behind the book is that friendship was *the most important social bond in Iceland and Norway up to middle of the thirteenth century*. It did not only shape the power game, but basically it formed the entire social structure, it was the glue that held society together.

I first became interested in the theme of friends (*vinr*) and friendship (*vinátta*) in the autumn of 1984, when I began to write my master's thesis on the political development of Iceland in the twelfth and thirteenth centuries.[2] I discovered then that the term "friend" frequently described relations between the local Icelandic chieftains (*goði*) and householders in *Sturlunga saga* (a collection of sagas which deal with the period c. 1120–1260 in Icelandic history). Some years later when I began to work on my doctorate, I continued to think about friendship and came to the conclusion that it was the most important social bond in Iceland during the Free State. Since then I have had a number of opportunities to write on the subject in both Icelandic and Norwegian contexts.

In this book, I have expanded and reassessed some of my old ideas about the meaning of friendship in Icelandic and Norwegian society. Previously I have focused on friendship between chieftains and householders in Iceland, but now I have included friendship between kings, chieftains, and householders; friendship ties between householders; and women's possibilities to enter into friendship. I also examine the religious side of friendship in Old Norse society: how friendship was used among the clerics; how chieftains established and maintained a friendship with Thór;[3] friendships with the saints and God; and, last but not least, the notion of friendship in Old Norse religious literature— an area which makes it possible to explore the meeting point between the traditional Old Norse and Christian ideas on friendship.

So what is friendship? Each of us probably has a clear understanding of what it means based on our own set of experiences. I have been known to say that in times of adversity we find out who our true friends are. In many of the difficult situations we face in life, blood is not necessarily a guarantee of support. Friendship can be more important than family. And family ties need not exclude friendship. The relatives we are closest with are also our friends. In today's bureaucratic society, friendship is part of the private sphere, and we like to think that it does not influence our decisions in the public arena, where instead we follow laws and rules that stand apart from the relationships we have with our friends. Unlike our ancestors in the Middle Ages, we have no public procedures for establishing friendship. The one common modern exception is Facebook friendship; on the Internet we must confirm friendship requests before the person concerned can be called our friend and we theirs. As a rule though, our Internet friends are only visible to those who have access to our Facebook profile. In contrast, in Norway and Iceland during the period covered in this book, friendship was a visible and public relationship. Everyone knew who the king's, the queen's, or the chieftains' friends were.

Friendship exists in a state of constant flux, being shaped by and shaping other personal relationships. Thus, it cannot be studied in isolation of other social relations (e.g., kinship and professional ties). In our contemporary society—at least in the Nordic countries where I live—we depend on the state both to protect and to look after us. Friendship and family ties are relatively weak. Even though we love our friends, we are not always willing to support them in all their conflicts, and I dare say we would be reluctant to sacrifice our lives for them. This notion contrasts with the situation in medieval Norway and Iceland, where friendship ties might best be compared to a contract between two parties with clear reciprocal obligations. Feelings often had little to do with it.

Friendship has been a part of human experience from the very beginning. Among the first we know of to discuss friendship systematically was the philosopher Aristotle (384–22 BCE). He argues in *Nicomachean Ethics* that friendship is the bond that holds society together and is cultivated by men who are "good, and alike in virtue."[4] Cicero (106–43 BCE), another ancient writer to reflect on friendship, emphasizes that friendship is the pillar of a good society. In his book *On Friendship*, Cicero writes that life is meaningless without friendship, at least for "a free man."[5] The friendship that Aristotle and Cicero describe involves a relationship between two men with roughly equal status and reputation—a horizontal friendship where reciprocity, good will, and devotion are key terms. Medieval scholars followed up the classical discussion about friendship. Thomas Aquinas (1225–74) argued, like Cicero, that friendship is an ideal that sensible individuals should cultivate. At the same time, he claimed it was possible for people to establish a friendship with an angel or with God.[6] Even though friendship has been an aspect of all societies since the children of Adam and Eve began to wander the Earth and its importance has been addressed (e.g., by Aristotle, Cicero, and Aquinas), it is only recently that it came on the agenda among scholars.

Until about 1970, the idea of a strong kin group was central to the discussion of Norwegian and Icelandic society in the Viking Age and the high Middle Ages. The view was that a patriarchal kin-based organization united the social, judicial, political, and religious facets of society. The kin group possessed land in common and probably took care of the "individual kin-group member's need for protection, his lawful rights and his religious needs."[7] In a conflict the kin group's honor was crucial, and it was "not unusual that a powerful kin-group would not accept a settlement with fines. This was often the case among the higher social class in Iceland, and it caused long-lasting conflict between families, with revenge among those kin groups and chaotic conditions in legal society."[8] Eventually, the increase in royal power changed the chaotic conditions in the kin-based society and reduced the kin group's influence. The title of Arne Odd Johnsen's book from 1948, *Fra ættesamfunn til statssamfunn* (From a Kin-Based Society to a State Society), demonstrates how earlier historians viewed the changes and societal shifts within this period.[9]

In about 1970, the discussion about the Icelandic Free State and Norway in Viking Age, and the High Middle Ages began to be influenced by social and cultural history and, in particular, by social anthropological perspectives. An important inspiration in this debate was the book *The Gift*, written in 1925 by Marcel Mauss. A French social anthropologist, he analyzed the nature of reciprocal exchange across various "archaic" societies. He prefaces his work with the following eight stanzas from the *Hávamál* (sayings of the high one) an Eddic poem dated to c. 1000 that includes various proverbs and instructions on the proper code of conduct for the Viking Age people:

39: I never found a generous man, nor one so hospitable with food, / that he wouldn't accept a present; / or one so well-provided with wealth / that he wouldn't take a gift if offered.

41: With weapons and clothes friends should gladden one another, / that is most obvious; / mutual givers and receivers are friends for longest, / if the friendship is going to work at all.

42: To his friend a man should be a friend / and repay gifts with gifts; / laughter a man should give for laughter / and repay treachery with lies.

44: You know, if you've a friend whom you really trust, / and from whom you want nothing but good, / you should mix your soul with his and exchange gifts, / go and see him often.

45: If you've another, whom you don't trust, / but from whom you want nothing but good, / speak fairly to him but think falsely / and repay treachery with lies.

46: Again, concerning the one whom you don't trust, / and whose mind you suspect: / you should laugh with him and disguise your thoughts, / a gift should be repaid with a like one.

48: Generous and brave men live the best, / seldom do they harbour anxiety; / but the cowardly man is afraid of everything, / the miser always sighs when he gets gifts.

145: Better not to pray, than to sacrifice too much, / one gift always calls for another; / better not dispatched than to slaughter too much. / So Thund carved before the history of nations, / where he rose up, when he came back.[10]

Mauss used these stanzas to call attention to the idea that "such gifts are voluntary but in fact they are given and repaid under obligation."[11] This consisted of the duty to give, receive, and reciprocate. Mauss tried to explain the strong obligations attached to gifts and countergifts with *hau*, or "the spirit" of the gift.[12] Despite a special focus on the strong relations created by gift exchange, Mauss did not explicitly discuss friendship in his book. In fact, he drops the most important stanza on friendship in the quotation just given from *Hávamál*. Stanza 43 reads: "To his friend a man should be a friend / and to his friend's friend too; / but a friend no man should be / to the friend of his enemy."[13] In other words, one was obliged to support or to give aid to friends of a friend.

The debate about the role of friendship in Iceland and Norway started in the 1980s.[14] Jesse Byock then claimed that it was "often" used to form political alliances, and such pacts "extended a person's sphere of influence beyond kinship" and the standard chieftain-householder relationship. Most friendship was expected to bring "political or financial gain to both parties to the agreement."[15] Later he called this a contractual friendship which "complemented" the kin and chieftain-assemblyman "obligations and put individuals in a position to demand reciprocity."[16] These friendship ties were established between men of unequal status and between men of the same status. Byock stresses that "contractual political friendship" allowed "leaders to achieve the collaboration necessary for social control."[17]

For Byock and others, for example William Ian Miller, who discussed friendship,[18] the focus was on the assemblyman (*þingmaðr*) ties between the householders and the chieftains and how they were described in Grágás, law code of the Icelandic Free State. According to the law code, it was the duty of each farmer to serve as an assemblyman for one of the chieftains of the quarter in which he lived; Iceland was divided into quarters c. 965: the western quarter, the southern quarter, the eastern quarter, and the northern quarter. If a farmer became dissatisfied with his chieftain, he was allowed to change his choice once a year. If the chieftain accepted the farmer as his assemblyman, the farmer had to acknowledge his support of the chieftain in front of witnesses. In so doing, he also automatically bound his entire household to the chieftain.[19] For Byock and Miller, friendship was thus an addition to the assemblyman ties. They did not ask the fundamental question: How was the loyalty between the assemblymen and chieftains established? A question I have discussed in my research. I am willing to claim that friendship was more important than assemblyman ties, a topic we will return to later in this book.

Over time there has been a shift in the debate in Iceland and Norway, from a focus on the kin-based society and the political institutions described in the law codes, toward the political culture and the role friendship played. The same tendencies can be seen in the European discussion.[20] In spite of the shift in the debate, there has been no book-length work exploring the importance of friendship in Norwegian and Icelandic society during the Viking Age and high Middle Ages. We shall try to remedy that situation in this book.

Norway (c. 900–c. 1300)

At the battle of Hafrsfjord at Jæren in North Rogaland (southwestern Norway), probably in the 880s, Harald Fairhair (Hárfagri) (c. 865–930) conquered the chieftains from western Norway.[21] Since then he has been hailed as the founder of the Kingdom of Norway, though he ruled western Norway only. After the battle of Hafrsfjord, we can roughly divide Norway into three main political areas: Viken (from Lindesnes to Göta älv) was under Danish control, the western part was ruled by Harald Fairhair, and Trøndelag and north Norway was ruled by the Earl of Hlaðir. Ólaf Tryggvason (c. 995–1000) continued to build the kingdom by placing Trøndelag, and probably also Viken under more direct royal control. Ólaf Haraldsson (1015–28) took the consolidation of Norway a step further. He secured real power for himself in Trøndelag and in Viken, but it was Harald Sigurdsson (1045–66) who secured the kingdom's control over the Uplands, Trøndelag, and Viken. This is partly because the Danish royal power was greatly weakened by the death of Cnut the Great (1017–35). As king of both Denmark and England, he had included Norway in his Northern Sea Empire. Disputes concerning succession to the throne followed after Cnut's death in Denmark, and this relieved the pressure in Norway. However, as soon as the situation had calmed in Denmark, the Danish kings once more claimed the command of Viken. Valdemar Valdemarsson succeeded the throne in Denmark in 1202 and remained until 1241. It was not until after his death and the following disputes concerning succession that Norway managed to pull out of the "Danish force field" and the Norwegian kings finally took control of the eastern part of the country.[22]

After the death of Sigurd the Crusader (Jórsalfari) in 1130, a one hundred-year-long civil war began; it ended with total victory for Sverrir Sigurdarson

(1177–1202) family's kingdom. In 1217 Sverrir's grandson, Hákon Hákonarson (1217–63), was proclaimed king of Norway. The real ruler, however, was Skúli Bárdarson, who led the battle against the various bands of rebels, but it was Hákon himself who defeated the last one in 1225–27. Hostile relations developed between Hákon and Skúli, which culminated in Skúli's rebellion and death in 1240. The remaining decades of the thirteenth century were characterized by peace and the consolidation of the position of the monarchy. These internal power struggles in Norway and the Danish pressure restricted the Norwegian kings' possibilities for running an expansive foreign policy. When the power struggles ceased in 1240, the Norwegian kings began to execute a much more active foreign policy that included the insular societies in the west.

King Hákon died in 1263 and was replaced by his son, Magnús the Lawmender (Lagabætir). He died in 1280. His son Eirík was then just twelve years old. The secular leaders who ruled on his behalf did not accept the privileges that the Church of Norway had been given in Magnús's time, and this led to severe conflicts between the king and the church in the early 1280s, which reached their peak when Archbishop Jón the Red (rauði) and two of his bishops had to escape from the country. The archbishop died in exile in 1282. After that, relations between king and church began to normalize. Eirík died in 1299 and was succeeded by his brother Hákon who ruled to 1319.

Iceland (c. 870–c. 1300)

Around the year 800, people from Norway settled on the Faroe Islands, Shetland, and the Orkneys. The same happened on the Hebrides and Isle of Man some decades later, and around 870 Ingólf Arnason from Dalsfjord in Norway went ashore on Iceland as the first among approximately 415 settlers (landnáms-maðr).[23] There is general agreement among scholars that Ari fróði's (the learned) dating in Íslendingabók from c. 1125 of the first settlement to c. 874 is reliable. Just before the first settlers arrived, there was a volcanic eruption in Iceland, and the ash from this in Greenland's glacier has been dated to c. 871.[24] Most of the settlers were either chieftains or wealthy farmers; what most of them had in common was that they owned large enough ships to transport people and livestock to Iceland. The period between c. 870 and 930 is usually labeled landnámsöld, the settlement period. It is Ari's statement in Íslending-abók, that all land was claimed (albyggt) within sixty winters together with the foundation of an Althing, a general assembly, for the whole country c. 930, which marks the end of the settlement period and the beginning of the Free

State period. This period lasted until the year 1262, 1263, or 1264, when Iceland came under the control of the Norwegian king.

There are two main opinions in the discussion about the political development in Iceland in the period c. 930–1120. The first one is based on the view that it is the constitutional paragraphs in Grágás, and not the c. 35 Icelandic Family Sagas, which describe the Icelandic society in the period c. 930–1030; that is, the chieftaincy numbered thirty-six in 930 and thirty-nine from 965. The second opinion rejects Grágás as a source for the political system and relies on the *picture* given by the Icelandic Family Sagas. According to this view, there was at no time a fixed number of chieftains, and, moreover, their numbers were reduced from about fifty or sixty to about twenty in this period.

Regarding the period c. 1120 to 1262–64, there is a general consensus among scholars about the main features of political development. This period is characterized by the concentration of power; around 1200, seven families controlled most of the country. After 1220, the Norwegian monarchy started to interfere in the political development of Iceland, and the king's involvement resulted in the fall of the Free State. In the power struggle, Icelandic chieftains considered it advantageous to become a member of the king's *hirð* (body of retainers). The chieftains' positions in Iceland were strengthened by this membership, but they had to pay for this support by giving their chieftaincies (*goðorð*) or their permission to administrate the chieftaincies to the king. Thus, by about 1250, the king had managed to acquire control over all of the chieftaincies in the country except the eastern quarter, which were acquired in 1264. In 1271 and 1281, with the law books Járnsíða and Jónsbók, the Norwegian administrative system was implemented, which turned the chieftains' role upside down. They now got their power from the king.[25]

Christianity in Norway and Iceland

Christianity became the official religion in Norway and Iceland around the year 1000.[26] Essential characters in this Christianization process in Norway were the kings Hákon Aðalsteinsfóstri, Ólaf Tryggvason, and Ólaf Haraldsson. Christianity developed into being the kings' religion. Furthermore, with its organization and ideological character, the church was able to support the royal power. The church had to adjust to the royal power and its needs in order to prosper. Thus, a symbiotic relationship developed between the king and the church. The king protected the church and received in return an ideological foundation that legitimized his supreme position in society. The Norwegian chieftains and later chieftains on the western isles had little that could challenge the dominance of this alliance.

In Iceland, under pressure from the Norwegian king Ólaf Tryggvason, Christianity was introduced in the year 999–1000. In 1056 Skálholt bishopric was founded, and in 1106 Hólar see, which included the northern quarter, was established. Until 1104, Iceland and the rest of Scandinavia belonged to the archdiocese of Hamburg/Bremen, and from 1104 to 1152–53 that of Lund. In 1152–53 the archbishopric in Nidaros (Trondheim), which included Norway and its five bishoprics and the six bishoprics on the islands in the West, was founded. The archbishopric came to have major consequences for the development of a Norse community, both religiously and politically. Its most important task was to implement the church's reform laws and to reshape the Norse church to fit in with the European church. In connection to the incidents in 1152–53, the Norwegian kings accepted the church's demand for reform in order to proceed with the foundation of the archbishopric. Among other things, the church demanded the right to appoint all ecclesiastical offices and to control their own property. Hence, the archbishop was able to concentrate on the restructuring of dioceses in the North Atlantic, which he succeeded in doing around 1300.

The Icelandic chieftains had firm control over the church in most of the Free State period. For example, up to 1190, it was common that chieftains were also priests. In a register of the forty three most powerful priests dating from around 1143, some thirteen were chieftains. During this same period, there were only about twenty-seven chieftains in the whole country.[27] The close connection between religion and secular power can also be seen in the farms the chieftains used as their places of residence. In the twelfth and thirteenth centuries, almost all the farms used as chieftains' residences were the wealthiest parish churches in the country. Control over these churches was important for the subjugation of the population, and at the same time it symbolized the power of the chieftains and their links with higher authorities. In 1297, after a lengthy dispute, a compromise was reached between the Icelandic church and the chieftains that secured for the church control over the majority of the largest and wealthiest churches in the country.

Demographic Changes in Norway and Iceland

The increase of population was vital for the political, social, and economic development during the whole period. The results were not only geographical expansion of the settlement; it also changed the relationship between regions. For instance, the eastern part of Norway, which had been relatively sparsely populated in the early Viking Age, developed into a key area of importance at the end of the thirteenth century. When our history commenced around the year 900, there was probably a population of about one hundred and fifty thousand in Norway and ten thousand in Iceland. Around the year 1300, about four hundred fifty thousand were living in Norway (Båhuslen, Jemtland, and Herjedalen included) and about fifty thousand were living on Iceland.[28]

The single farm was the main feature of the settlement in Norway and Iceland, and this feature is probably one of the most important that differentiate it from the rest of Europe. The number of farms c. 900 was probably about fifteen thousand in both countries; four hundred years later, the number had increased to about eighty thousand.[29] Each farm was led by a householder; only he could participate in the assembly activities, and he had to protect his household. In the Norse world, market places were numerous in the Viking Age, but in the eleventh and twelfth centuries their numbers were reduced. In Iceland, which did not have any towns, three or four of these market places became the most important. In Norway the towns became the focal point for trading. In the period c. 1000–1300, fifteen towns were established, most if not all by the kings.[30]

Let us now return to the main content of this book: power of friendship. We start our journey in Iceland, by discussing the significance of friendship in the relationships between householders and chieftains; here we also have a look at the friendship between householders and women's ability to establish friendships, we then address the friendship between chieftains. Because of the poor survival of sources for Norway, the results from this part of the book on Iceland form a model for how we conceive the same ties in Norway. When we transition to Norway, we discuss how the kings and chieftains made use of friendship to secure their positions of power. An examination of relations of friendship among clerics follows this section, before we tackle Christian thoughts on friendship. This topic includes various "supernatural" friendships, including how people in Norway and Iceland tried to use friendship to secure support from the Old Norse gods, from the saints, and from God. We then study the relationship between friendship and kinship, before finally addressing how the political development changed the political culture and reduced the importance of friendship.

CHAPTER 1

Friendship

The Most Important Social Bond in Iceland in the Free State Period

In 1197, the chieftains Gudmund Thorvaldsson and Kolbein Tumason attacked the chieftain Önund Thorkelsson and killed him by burning down his farmhouse. In the fire Galmur Grímsson also died. He was a friend of all three chieftains and "particularly" with Kolbein. Galmur was present at the farm and tried to negotiate with Kolbein and Gudmund before the fire grew too large. He asked them to leave and promised them all his property—he was a very wealthy man and owned a large farm. In return, Kolbein replied that he would give Galmur all the wealth he wanted if he left the farm. Galmur answered, "You have often laughed at me because I like to take a steam bath and that I drink too much. Now I can see that I can take a bath, but I'm not so certain about the drink of mead afterwards." He did not leave the burning farm.[1] As a friend of all the contending parties, Galmur's choices were limited. He could not desert a friend in such a crisis. To do so would have been deeply dishonorable. Death was preferable to continuing a life lived in shame.

There is little doubt that friendship was the most important social bond between chieftains and householders in Iceland during the period from about 870, when the first settlers disembarked on the newly discovered island, until the years 1262–64. These friendships included strong reciprocal demands. The chieftains were to protect the householders and their households, organize feasts for them, and give them gifts. In return, the chieftains received the householders' support in their conflicts. However, it was not simply the householders and chieftains who established friendships with each other. Chieftains established friendships among themselves, as did the householders. Friendship was the fundamental bond that tied society together. By the 1260s friendship would lose much of its significance in Iceland, being replaced by other societal relations when the Norwegian administrative system was brought in, a topic we will return to in chapter 7 of this book. Before we consider the role of friendship between chieftains and householders in Icelandic society, we must first look at the advice Odin gives in the poem *Hávamál* about how friendship should be cultivated.

Odin's Advice

Hávamál consists mainly of didactic and gnomic matter, first and foremost of a secular character. This anonymous poem dates to about the year 1000, and therefore gives us a relatively good impression of the notion of friendship toward the end of the Viking period.[2] The first stanza of *Hávamál* tells of the traveler who comes from far away. "All the entrance, before you walk forward, / you should look at, / you should spy out; / for you can't know for certain where enemies (*óvinir*) are sitting / ahead in the hall."[3] The traveler is urged to be careful when he comes to an unknown farm where he does not know the householder and to be on the lookout for enemies.[4] It is unlikely that the danger from an enemy's attack was great. Guests were under the protection of the householder while they remained under his roof. An attack on a traveler would therefore be an insult to the host and a violation of his hospitality. Rather, the guest needed to be on the lookout for possible enemies because their presence would influence how he would conduct and express himself about people and matters of current significance.

 Hávamál emphasizes that the miserly man dreads receiving a gift because he knows he must reciprocate. The generous man, on the other hand, shares his riches with others. Nonetheless, he has a motive for his actions: he desires a countergift. *Hávamál* stresses generosity. He who is liberal with food is magnanimous.[5] The poem states at the outset that many would invite "me" home if "I" do not need food. The loyal friend does not think like this; he shares his food with his friends.[6] A man wins friends with his fortune, but wealth is an insecure friend and can abandon one when it is most inconvenient. It is therefore wise to have good friends. They will provide support in bad times. However, friendship is not only about exchange and gifts. It is also about trust. A man should entrust his friends with his worries and thoughts, otherwise anxiety will gnaw at his heart. Friends will seek to alleviate this anxiety and give as good advice as possible.[7]

Above all, reciprocity between equals characterizes the relations of friendship described in *Hávamál*. The poem emphasizes that if a man has a good friend that he can rely on and who desires his support, he should exchange gifts (e.g., weapons and clothes) with him and visit him often. This makes for a lasting friendship. In addition, gifts and gift exchange make the friendship outwardly visible. The gift exchange can never cease; the friendship must continually be renewed with new gifts.[8] It is not always necessary to give large gifts to gain a friend. Sometimes it can be "half a slice of bread" and "a half-empty tankard."[9] It is not the size of the gift that is crucial, but the will to share.[10]

Laughter among friends is also valued by the *Hávamál* author. This is probably the type of laughter occurring while in festive surroundings or at celebrations and is certainly not the laughter of ridicule or mockery.[11] According to *Hávamál*, the fool believes that all who laugh with him are his friends. He does not understand that laughter and friendly words do not necessarily create a sense of obligation. The fool will realize this when he comes to the assembly or a meeting and there are few who plead his case.[12] *Hávamál* emphasizes that wisdom is one's most loyal friend; it ensures that a man conducts himself well and assesses each situation correctly.[13]

In stanza 52 of *Hávamál*, the term *félagi* is used in connection with those who exchange gifts. It is unclear how *félagi* should be interpreted, does it mean a partner, a friend, or both? In the *Ordbog over det gamle norske Sprog* (A Dictionary of Old Norse Prose), the word can be translated as either a person who jointly holds property together with another, or a companion, friend, or a person with whom one lives.[14] We can disregard the first option because the poem does not refer to financial partnerships. It is probable, therefore, that the word *félagi* in this case means a friend.[15] Such an interpretation is also supported by the fact that generally the giving of gifts resulted in the establishment of a friendship.

Hávamál describes two types of friends: the good and the bad. The differences are loyalty, the will to provide help, and the extent of the gift exchange. The poem stresses this by pointing out that the geographical distance to a bad friend feels long, even if he lives on the main road, but it is short to a good friend's home, though he lives a long way off.[16] And if a man should go to war, he should make certain that he stands by an old, loyal friend for he will not flee.[17] One should, however, use the disloyal friend as a pawn in one's power games: exploit him, speak fairly to him, but think the opposite. Repay disloyalty with lies and return his "gifts" with comparable countergifts. One should not associate with a bad friend for long, for peace will eventually subside and the friendship could worsen. In other words, a man should cultivate all his friendships, but make use of bad friends for his own purpose. Regardless of whether a friendship is good or bad, a man should never be the one to end it.[18] Friendship bonds thus created a social security net, and in the precariousness of everyday life in the Viking Age, they provided an element of predictability. It was better to have a bad friend than none at all. After all, even a bad friend had to provide help in a crisis or else appear dishonorable.

Stanza 43 in *Hávamál* is probably the most important stanza about friendship. It stresses that a man should be a friend to his friend, as well as to his friend's friends, but he should not enter into a friendship with his enemies' friends.[19] In other words, relations of friendship extended beyond the relationship between the two individuals. This meant that a friend's friends could be drawn into a potential crisis. In return, one was also bound to support them. Thus the establishment of a friendship could have far-reaching consequences and created endlessly overlapping circles of friendship.

Hávamál gives most weight to horizontal friendship—friendship between two equal parties from the highest social rank in society.[20] To establish this kind of friendship, gifts of equal worth must be exchanged, which guarantees that neither friend ends up in a subordinate position to the other, and an equal exchange of gifts, visits, laughter, and advice must be maintained. The obligations in this relationship were clear; friends should help each other. But the foundation of friendship involved also the duty to help one's friends' friends, a requirement that made it difficult to foresee one's own obligations. Relations of friendship are characterized by pragmatism in *Hávamál*. Good friends are loyal, reliable, and helpful. Nonetheless, a man cannot blindly rely on his friends. He must first see what their intention is with the friendship. *Hávamál's* dichotomy between good and bad friends reveals that there are different degrees of friendship, and friends should be treated accordingly. A friendship with the good and faithful friend should be cultivated, but the bad friend should be exploited as a tool in the political game. Moreover, *Hávamál* does not explain how a friendship should be ended; the poem only mentions that a man should not be the one to end a friendship. Even though *Hávamál* does not give any ideal description of friendship, the poem stresses that "Generous and brave men live the best, / seldom do they harbour anxiety; / but the cowardly man is afraid of everything, / the miser always sighs when he gets gifts."[21]

Let us now move on from *Hávamál* to see how people in Iceland followed Odin's advice in practice.

Protection

It was through protection and magnanimity, expressed through gifts and feast-ing, that the chieftains established and maintained friendships.[22] Protection was probably the most important element in relations of friendship between the householders and the chieftains.[23] In return for protection, feasts, and gifts, the householders were to support the chieftains in their struggles. Since there was no king who ruled over the Icelandic Free State, the chieftains wielded the power, and only they could provide protection. However, in order to do this, the chieftains had to build up a power base, and the most important ele-ment in this was the householders. Therefore, between the householders and the chieftains arose a strong mutual dependency.

Householders who ended up in conflicts had to seek support from their chieftain. Only he was able to provide or mobilize effective help, whether defensive or offensive. The chieftain Páll Jónsson (d. 1211) supported his "as-semblymen in all appropriate cases" such that they never lost their case.[24] Generally, it was of secondary importance whether the case was good or what the original circumstances were. I have only recorded one such instance where a chieftain refused to assist his friend. In 1198 a conflict arose between Markús Skeggjason, who was a friend and assemblyman of the chieftain Sæmund Jóns-son, and Ketil Eyjólfsson and his son, Ljót. A dispute led to Markús killing Ketil and wounding Ljót. Their family then went to the chieftain Sighvat Sturluson, who took over the case. The chieftain Thórd Sturluson, Sighvat's brother, was a friend of Sæmund. Sæmund followed his advice in this case, and gave no support to Markús because he thought Markús was "of little worth" according to *Íslendinga saga*. The agreement between Sæmund and Sighvat at the assembly was that Markús was to go to Norway and "never re-turn."[25] The reason why Sæmund did not help Markús was not simply that he thought Markús unimportant but also that Sæmund was in a dilemma him-self. He could not please both friends. He had to choose between taking Thórd's advice or helping Markús. The deciding factor for Sæmund was that his own interests and those of his friends would be best served by sacrificing Markús and holding onto Thórd's friendship. If a chieftain refused to assist his friend in a conflict, it was a signal to his other friends that they might not nec-essarily be able to count on his full support in future disputes. As a result, the chieftain might be unsure of the support he could get at a later date. Thus supporting one's friends was crucial for chieftains.[26]

In Iceland, the household was under the householder's protection (*grið*). As a rule, he could not provide protection without help from the chieftain. Gener-ally, only the householders could befriend the chieftains; this group constituted from fifteen to twenty percent of the population. Thus the household was indirectly affected by relations of friendship between the chieftain and the householder, and as a consequence the members of the household, usually the men, also had to support the chieftain.[27]

Besides protecting their friends, the chieftains also had to maintain and preserve the peace within their sphere of influence and settle matters between their friends. In disputes between these friends, a chieftain had to satisfy both parties, otherwise he might lose one of them. A chieftain who maintained orderly relationships created trust and support among the householders. If he failed, he risked losing prestige, and his friends began to look for another chieftain. A good case here is that of chieftain Einar Thorgilsson, who was the younger son of Thorgils Oddason. It was Oddi, the older son, who was due to take over the position of power from their father and was brought up on the Oddi, the estate of Oddaverjar chieftain's Sæmund Sigfússon, and who became a wise man. Einar, however, was brought up by the farmer Thorgeir Sveinsson at Brunná. When Thorgils entered a monastery in 1150, the brothers took over the chieftaincy jointly, with Oddi in charge, but he died that same winter. It was a great loss, according to *Sturlu saga*, because he was a very able man and left no heir. Einar then inherited the estate and the chieftaincy, and became a chieftain. He was a bad leader who alienated his friends. The inadequacy of his leadership is shown most clearly in the saga's description of how much the government of the district had changed since his father's time: "men thought there was quite different way of governing the district from that which Thorgils used."[28] This caused some of the wealthier farmers to move away. If farmers were dissatisfied with their chieftain, according to Grágás, they could choose a new one once a year. Being an assemblyman—which we will discuss in more detail later in this chapter—was a private matter between the chieftain and the farmer. If the chieftain accepted the farmer as his assemblyman, for it to become binding, both parties had to choose witnesses and the assemblyman had to say "he is joining [t]his assembly group along with [his] household people and his household stock and that the [chieftain] accepts him."[29] But not all farmers were entitled to participate in the assembly activity, only the "assembly tax–paying householder" (*þingfararkaupsbóndi*). To achieve this status, one had to own a property of a certain size, based on the number of people living on the farm.[30] We do not have information about the number of chieftains in Iceland during the period of settlement (c. 870–930). Most scholars, as mentioned, who have discussed the political development of Iceland believe that when the Althing was founded about 930, a political system was created which consisted of thirty-six chieftaincies. In about 965, when the country was divided into quarters, three new chieftaincies were established in the northern quarter so that the total number of chieftains in the country went from thirty-six to thirty-nine. Those who ascribe to this view also claim that the number of chieftains remained stable from this point until about 1120.[31] The most important arguments for the notion of the thirty-six to thirty-nine chieftaincies are the regulations in the *Konungsbók* version of the law code Grágás from c. 1250 and an account in *Íslendingabók* from c. 1125. Grágás is preserved in two main manuscripts, *Konungsbók*, which was written down after the middle of the thirteenth century, and *Staðarhólsbók*, written around 1270. These two manuscripts are very different, as *Konungsbók* contains sections that are not found in *Staðarhólsbók* (e.g., *Þingskapaþáttr, Lögréttuþáttr, Lögsögumannsþáttr,* and *Baugatal*). The reason for the absence of the constitutional provisions from *Staðarhólsbók* is likely that it was written down after the country had received a new constitution in the form of Járnsíða in 1271. *Staðarhólsbók*, on the other hand, has paragraphs missing from *Konungsbók*, and is in general more comprehensive. Moreover, there are differences in the formulation of those paragraphs that are found in both manuscripts, and they often have different arrangements of sections and provisions. Scholars have thus come to the conclusion that there was no direct connection between the two main manuscripts, but rather that both descend from the same archetype. Scholars also agree that Grágás does not represent an official collection of laws, rather either a private collection of laws adopted by the Law Council, written down by individuals, or a "rights" book, containing notes on legal provisions that may not necessarily have been adopted as law.[32]

The Icelandic Family Sagas, which deal with the period c. 930–1030, provide a different picture of the political situation than the one we find in Grágás. Not only is the number of chieftains higher, perhaps fifty to sixty, but the political system was also quite unstable. Old chieftain families disappeared, most of the chieftaincies mentioned in the Icelandic Family Sagas only lasted for two or three generations, and new chieftain families could come onto the political scene. This instability led to a reduction in the number of chieftains from the saga period (c. 930–1030) until c. 1120, from about fifty or sixty chieftains to about thirty.[33]

However, all scholars who have discussed the political development of Iceland are in agreement that a concentration of power occurred after 1120. By the 1200s, the number of chieftains was reduced to about seven and remained at this level until the country became a tributary land of the Norwegian king in the years 1262–64.

The political development of Iceland during the Free State period was characterized by the transition from chieftaincies to domains (*ríki*). Administration of the Icelandic chieftaincies entailed control over people (*mannaforráð*) and not specific geographical areas, and thus friends of different chieftains could live side by side. In contrast, domains were larger areas of power with more or less clear geographical borders and control over all those who lived within the limits of the domain. This transition began about 1100, when the Haukdælir, Ásbirningar, Svínfellingar, Oddaverjar, and Austfirðingar families formed their domains. The development of these domains continued in Borgarfjörður, Eyjafjörður, and Vestfirðir at the end of the twelfth century and the beginning of the thirteenth. After about 1220, the struggle for power in Iceland was a matter of control over domains rather than chieftaincies. Until the middle of the eleventh century, farmers throughout the country had the freedom to choose their own chieftain. When the domains emerged the institution of assemblymen changed, the opportunities for farmers to choose their own chieftains then disappeared. All who lived within the boundaries of a domain became the assemblymen of the chieftain of that domain, and they had to submit to his rule.[34]

Gifts

The chieftains and their sons were under great pressure to show their generosity. A good example is the story of Brand, the chieftain's son, nicknamed ǫrvi (the magnanimous). He sailed his ship to Nidaros in Norway. There the skald Thjódólf, Brand's friend, told King Harald Hardrule about Brand and how distinguished a man he was, and that no one in Iceland was as well suited to be king as he was on account of his ǫrleiki (generosity) and stórmennska (prominence). The king wished to put Brand's magnanimity to the test and ordered Thjódólf to go to Brand and request his cloak. Thjódólf did as the king commanded and went to where Brand was working, and related that the king wanted his cloak. Brand did not stop working, but he allowed the cloak to fall to the ground. Thjódólf took it up and brought it to the king. The king asked how it had all taken place, and Thjódólf informed him that Brand had not uttered a word when he presented the gift. The king answered that this was a magnanimous man since he did not comment on the king's request. Then the king sent Thjódólf again to Brand with the message that he now wanted Brand's gold-inlaid axe. At first Thjódólf protested against going, but ultimately he had to yield to the king's will. He went to Brand and repeated the king's wish. Brand presented the axe to Thjódólf, again without saying a single word. Thjódólf returned to the king with the weapon. The king told Thjódólf to go back to Brand once more and this time ask for the tunic Brand was wearing. Thjódólf again objected, but as before he had to obey the king. He went back to Brand and said the king now wanted his tunic. Brand finished working, but before he presented the tunic to Thjódólf, he undid the seam on one sleeve and threw the tunic on the ground. Thjódólf picked it up, went back to the king and showed him the tunic with the missing sleeve. The king looked at this and said, "This man is both wise and generous. There is no question about why he has removed the sleeve. He believes that I own the one arm and still took all the same, always taking and not giving back. Go now and fetch him hither."[35] This was done, and Brand went to the king and received great honor and gifts from him.[36]

The story must be characterized as a moral account, where the central theme is Brand's magnanimity. He had a reputation to live up to, and if it had become known that he had refused the king's requests, he would have lost honor. An important aspect of this story is that the king is the one who requests the gifts. He could only make the requests because of his superior social position. It would have been unthinkable for Brand or other chieftains' sons or chieftains, Icelandic or Norwegian, to demand gifts from the king in this way. This would have been perceived as an insult to the king and possibly have led to death. However, when he returned home to Iceland, Brand could behave like the king and request things from the householders, in his future chieftaincy.

Gifts were an important tool in the political arena. Those who wanted to establish their power base gave gifts to those who were not able or willing to give a countergift. Those who received a gift must earn the gifts in one way or another. They were under a debt of honor to the giver until they had repaid the gift in the form of service. It was countergifts and repayment via service that secured rights of ownership and disposal over the gift. The strong obligation to return the gift is evident from both Grágás and Gulating's law of Western Norway.[37] The gift was important to maintain balanced social contracts and alliances, or to "buy" friends, power, or honor. A gift was rarely refused, for to do so was a great insult. It would be the same as refusing friendship. The duty to receive was as strong as the duty to give or to reciprocate.[38] Ownership and control over resources was the main basis for a position of leadership. Thus the chieftains' economic resources were crucial in determining how large their group of friends could be.[39]

Gifts in Iceland consisted of weapons, horses, axes, jewelry, food, and clothes. This fits well with what we know from other "primitive" societies. Some of these gifts, especially weapons and jewelry, circulated as a kind of constant in the economy. They were passed from man to man and from generation to generation.[40] There were clear rules about which objects could be used in this gift-giving process, and when a potential countergift should be reciprocated. We saw with *Hávamál* the recommendation that a friendship should be maintained with an exchange of gifts, and we know from stories that chieftains exchanged weapons with each other. As a rule, though, weapons were passed downwards in the social hierarchy, from a king to a chieftain or retainer, or from a chieftain to a householder. It is therefore strange in the story about Brand that the king asked Brand to give him his weapon. This signals that the king stood lower in the social hierarchy than Brand. We must, however, not forget this story was addressed to an Icelandic audience. It should show that Brand had all the necessary qualities to be king of Iceland. In the end, the gift-giving process was a matter of who was able to take the initiative to give gifts and thus establish friendships. Here the rule was clear: it was those who occupied the superior social position.

Between the chieftains there was fierce competition about who could give the greatest gifts. *Þórðar saga kakala* relates that Thórd kakali Sighvatsson gave Bárd Thorkelsson a number of gifts, including the farm Svefneyjar at Breiðafjörður valued to 45 hundreds (equivalent to 45 cows), in 1243.[41] In 1695 Svefneyjar was valued to 40 hundreds, while the farm Bárd previously lived on, Sandar, was valuated to 12 hundreds, an average farm in Iceland being valued at 20 hundreds.[42] Bárd was a tenant and when Thórd returned to Iceland in 1242, Bárd supported him, gave him permission to manage his farm, and accompanied him on his first campaign. For Thórd this was very important. To be able to participate in the power game in Iceland, he had to be a householder. Soon after, when he had established a power base, Thórd gave Bárd the farm Svefneyjar. Even though the help Thórd received was of great significance for him, the gift was exceptional, and Bárd apparently became completely subject to Thórd's will—those who accepted land entered into a service relationship as a subordinate of the giver as long as both lived.[43] Thórd's gift to Bárd is probably the largest from a chieftain to a householder in the history of the Free State. Thórd's generosity here must have been well known all over the country. This was a great advertisement for Thórd, and consequently more householders wished to become his friend.

Three actors took part in the gift-giving process: the giver, the receiver, and those who witnessed the transaction. The eyewitnesses were perhaps the most important. It was these people who would relate the news of the gift, and thus of the giver's generosity and the newly established friendship. We can also add to the group of witnesses the men and women who later saw the gift which the receiver had been given. According to *Hávamál*, friendship should be visible. Gift-giving took place on a "stage," and for the chieftains it was important that as many people as possible monitored the event and heard about it or saw the actual gift. This was the best form of publicity. We see this illustrated in the description of Brand Kolbeinsson (d. 1246), the chieftain of Skagafjörður, who was said to be "an extremely generous man, and therefore he had a good reputation."[44]

In the process of formation of domains, marriage and concubinage was important. In the year 1197, the Icelandic chieftain Sighvat Sturluson asked for Halldóra Tumadóttir's hand in marriage. The chieftain Sigurd Ormsson and his wife, Thuríd Gissurardóttir from the Haukdælir family, who was Halldóra's mother, were the ones who had the right to respond to the enquiry. Earlier, Thuríd had been married to the now-deceased chieftain Tumi Kolbeinsson from the Ásbirningar family and had by him Halldóra and another daughter, Álfheid. Thuríd's answer to the request was to say that she loved Halldóra more than Álfheid and wanted her to be married to a man of the same social status. Thus she was married to Sighvat Sturluson. Álfheid, however, was to be married to a man who could care for her satisfactorily.[45] Later she was married to the householder Ingimund Grímsson.

For Sighvat, this marriage was especially important. In fact, it was crucial to his ability to build up a domain that stretched across Eyjafjörður and Þingeyjarþing. The chieftain Gudmund dýri Thorvaldsson controlled two chieftaincies in Eyjafjörður in 1188. Nine years later, when he burned his main rival in his farm, he acquired a third chieftaincy, and it is likely that he also had control over a fourth chieftaincy in the area at that time. In about 1200, when Gudmund entered a monastery, besides his son Thorvald, there were only two other chieftains in Eyjafjörður and Þingeyjarþing. Thorvald gave all his chieftaincies to Sigurd Ormsson, who in turn gave them to Tumi Sighvatsson, his wife's grandson who had been named for his maternal grandfather. But because of Tumi's young age, his father Sighvat took control of these chieftaincies. In 1209, Sighvat gained control of two additional chieftaincies, and two years later a third one when he had his friend, the important householder Kálf Guttormsson, kill the last chieftain in that part of the country. In 1215, three years after this event, Sighvat moved to Grund in Eyjafjörður.[46]

Sighvat's marriage to Halldóra was the key to his advancement. Through the gift from Sigurd Ormsson to his son Tumi, Sighvat was able to enter the power struggle in Eyjafjörður. Additionally, his marriage ensured that the most powerful family on the eastern border of Sighvat's domain, headed by Sigurd Ormsson, did not interfere in his plans. And since Halldóra belonged to the powerful Ásbirningar family, who controlled the area of land west of Sighvat's domain, he was secure from any troubles from them. His area of power was bounded on the north by the sea, and on the south by uninhabited inland. In other words, Sighvat's marriage literally ensured that he had allies on the two sides that were potentially troublesome.

After the number of chieftains declined and the areas of power became larger and took on a clearer geographical character. The chieftains probably established friendships primarily with the most influential householders in local society through, among other means, concubinage relationships with their daughters. In the period from the end of the 1100s until 1262–64, the vast majority of chieftains had relationships with several concubines at the same time. These relationships were entered into with the consent of the girls' families. Concubinage was advantageous for all the parties involved. The girls secured their position in society. It was better to be the mistress of a chieftain than to be married to a poor householder. Also, this relationship gave the concubines' families extra protection, and if sons were born who later became chieftains, this would add luster, and possibly riches, to the concubines' families. Through this relationship, the chieftains secured loyal support for themselves from important local actors. The chieftains could marry a different woman and send the concubines home without ending the bonds of friendship between the chieftain and the woman's family—and the women could still be married later to other men.[47]

Feasts

Right from the beginning of Iceland's colonization around 870, communal drinking was used to build up one's power position. Such social gatherings were expensive. Only those who owned or controlled a large amount of property could organize such celebrations and make use of them to build up their position of power. A competition took place between chieftains about who could organize the biggest and most lavish feast—and thereby follow *Hávamál's* advice about sharing food with friends. The number of guests at these drinking parties not only signaled the chieftains' wealth but also their power. He who arranged the biggest feasts was the richest and most powerful. He had the most friends; he was thus *vinsæll* (powerful, lit. "had many friends").[48]

In a number of cases, especially during the 1200s, chieftains began to establish themselves in areas they had not originally controlled. It was essential for them to establish friendship relations with the householders and begin the process of gift giving as quickly as possible. When Thorgils Bödvarsson became a chieftain in Skagafjörður and Húnaþing in 1255, he had to build up his power base. Now, Thorgils had proclaimed a sheep tax; all the householders in the region he controlled had to give him one sheep. Afterward, he held a great feast for the most distinguished householders in the area and gave them generous (*stórar*) gifts when they departed. The saga about Thorgils relates that after the feast the householders were particularly pleased that they had gained such a chieftain and thought that Kolbein ungi Arnórsson, the most powerful chieftain in the region in the first half of the 1200s and who died in 1245, "had returned and was reborn," a chieftain they had "longed for."[49] In the winter, the majority of Thorgils's guests invited Thorgils to their homes and gave him "modest" (*sæmiligstu*) gifts.[50] This implies the gifts from Thorgils were more valuable than those from the householders. The householders almost immediately got back a great deal of what they were forced to part with. In the long run, they probably made a small profit. The chieftains always had to give bigger gifts than they received, and in addition, they had to organize feasts. Thus it can be claimed the chieftains partly subsidized the running of the householders' households. Gifts were also used in connection with feasts to maintain friendship. In 1243, Thórd kakali Sighvatsson held a feast at Mýrar in Dýrafjörður, and when the guests were preparing to go home, he gave many of them gifts. Thus they were all "greater friends with him than before."[51] These householders supported Thórd in his struggle with the chieftain Kolbein ungi Arnórsson, and when Þórður took up his father's position of power, which Kolbein had controlled, and three years later obtained the property, he again gave his supporters substantial gifts.[52]

A chieftain's death was dramatic for the householders, his entire social network disintegrated, and his friends found themselves without protection. If the chieftain had a son or sons, on many occasions they organized an *erfi* (funeral feast) to commemorate their father and to establish friendship with his former friends.

> Hjalti, the son of Thórd skálpur, came to Iceland and settled at Hjaltadalur after consulting with Kolbein and lived at Hof. His sons were Thorvald and Thórd, both men of great renown. The funeral feast (*erfi*) which they held for their father was the finest in Iceland. There guests numbered over twelve long hundreds (approximately 1,500), and all of the most noble among them received gifts when they departed.[53]

In this story from *Landnámabók*, book of settlement, about the biggest funeral feast in Iceland's history, "all" of the most distinguished guests received gifts before they left the celebration. In addition to these guests—some of whom had certainly been Hjalti's friends—we can assume that all Hjalti's friends from the chieftaincy he had control over were invited. For Hjalti's sons, Thorvald and Thórd, it was crucial to take over their father's friendships with these householders. This happened by inviting them to the funeral. We can assume that these householders had been particularly pleased with the extent of the feast and the grandiose gift giving. This signaled Thorvald's and Thórd's ambitions for power while adding luster to their friends. Another function of the feast was to provide Hjalti's friends with the opportunity to take leave of a beloved leader. Thus a funeral had a variety of functions and was an important arena for the chieftain's sons to demonstrate their ambition.

Probably at some point in the eleventh century, after the introduction of Christianity and maybe because of the introduction of new burial customs, the sons began to automatically take over their father's bonds of friendship.[54] Thus an impressive funeral was superfluous. In the year 1151, Einar Thorgilsson took over his father's and brother's positions of power. He had a great deal of support from "kinsmen and in-laws [men married to women in his family] and friends," whom Thorgils, his father, had gained.[55] Not all chieftains had sons as enterprising as Hjalti's, or even any sons at all. In such circumstances the chieftains' friends had to look for a new chieftain when their chieftain died. Indeed, the problem of "producing" good sons who could take over their father's position of power was an important reason for power in Iceland becoming concentrated in fewer and fewer hands during the course of the Free State.

Food and feasting has become an important topic among archeologists, anthropologists, and historians in recent years. A number of studies have demonstrated that groups established identity through "customs related to food." Feasts were used to show power and power relations; the sharing of a meal strengthened the social ties and the "political commitments."[56] We can distinguish between three types of feasts. The first of these, the entrepreneurial feast, revolves around competing leaders who use "commensal hospitality" as a way of creating a bond of debt between themselves and their guests. The goal of such banquets is to produce symbolic capital, which can then be converted into political power and can be used by the host to influence a group into accepting his decisions. Entrepreneurial feasts are thus intended to create a reciprocal relation and consolidate a social hierarchy.[57]

The second type of feast is the patron-role feast, used to "legitimize institutionalized relations of unequal social power." The idea underlying these two types of feasts is to create reciprocity through hospitality. "In this case, however, the expectation of equal reciprocation is no longer maintained. Rather, the acceptance of continually unequal patterns of hospitality symbolically expresses the formalization of unequal relations of status and power, and this acceptance ideologically naturalizes the formalization through repetition of an event that induces sentiments of social debt." There was thus a clear distinction between those who are always hosts and those who are always guests, and that it is to be expected, given that it is invariably the role of the leader to hold feasts.[58] The third type of feast, the diacritical feast, is discussed in chapter 7.

The feasts the chieftains organized for their friends in the Free State society fit well into the first two feast models. The chieftains were usually the hosts, and they used the feasts to maintain their friendship with the householders. These feasts reaffirmed the social hierarchy and created an identity among the participants—they were the friends of the chieftain. We have no information about how often the chieftains organized such feasts for their friends, but there is reason to think they were held regularly.

The seating order was an important aspect of every feast, as it "recreated" the social hierarchy. In the Icelandic Family Sagas, there are episodes when seating a person in the "wrong" place caused problems because it was interpreted as an insult. In most cases these incidents involve women. It is hard to explain why women should feature so prominently in these scenes, but certainly women in the Icelandic Family Sagas played a more noticeable role in the power game (often by goading their male family members into action). It should be stressed that these episodes from the Icelandic Family Sagas were related to weddings and feasts where householders were inviting one another. The notion that the chieftain's friends, in most cases men, would protest about their allocated seating is highly unlikely. If they did so, they would insult the host and run the risk that he would not support them in their disputes. The overall impression given by the sagas is that feasting in Old Norse society was "civilized"; scholarly discussion about feasting has too often focused on the small number of cases in which something went wrong.[59]

Feasting, gift giving, and protection to gain political support in return could never cease. If the chieftains stopped arranging feasts or failed to fulfill their obligations, relations of friendship came to an end and the householders looked for a new chieftain. For the protection, feasting, and gifts the householders received, they were to support the chieftains in their conflicts, possibly by providing advice or effecting settlements with other chieftains. If a chieftain had to pay a high fine in a case, he sometimes received help from both his friends and his relatives.[60] After friendship was established between the chieftains and the householders, it was difficult for the householders to refuse if their chieftain asked them to carry out a task for them. This is clear in an incident between the chieftain Brodd-Helgi Thorgilsson and Ketil. The chieftain entered into a friendship with Ketil. Afterwards, Brodd-Helgi wanted Ketil to go to Thorleif the Christian and summon him for not paying his temple tax. Ketil was dissatisfied with this and said that he would not have begun a friendship with Brodd-Helgi if he had known his plans. All the same, he went to

Thorleif and summoned him. Because the weather forecast was bad, Thorleif invited Ketil and his followers to stay overnight. Ketil refused, but the bad weather forced them to turn back and stay overnight with Thorleif for two days. When they departed, Ketil said that he would repay Thorleif's hospitality by letting the case drop and becoming his friend. Thorleif thanked Ketil for his friendship, but when Brodd-Helgi found out, he ended his friendship with Ketil.[61] This is one of the few cases in the sagas where a chieftain establishes a friendship with so clear an intention in mind. Although it was nigh impossible for a householder to refuse the chieftain's task, usually chieftains did not ask their friends to do the "dirty work" for them.

Loyalty

As we saw at the outset of this chapter when Galmur chose to die with his friend Önund, the sagas sometimes tell of cases of extreme loyalty where friends sacrificed their lives for their chieftain in his struggle. There are even stories about chieftains' friends who took their own lives when they heard their leader was dead. Eyvind was a friend of the chieftain Ingimund Thorsteinsson. When he heard that Ingimund was dead, he said to his foster son:

> "Go and tell my friend Gauti what I have done, and that I would value him doing the same." Then he put his short sword under his cloak and let himself fall on it. And when Gauti heard this, he said, "What is life to Ingimund's friends without him? I will follow my good friend Eyvind's deed." And he then put his large knife against his chest and took his own life.[62]

Such stories are exceptional, and there is no reason to place too much weight on them. Nevertheless, they emphasize the ideological importance of a strong loyalty within the friendships between chieftains and householders. The instability of power relationships made loyalty both an honorable and a worthy quality.[63]

Most householders were friends with only one chieftain. For them, there was no doubt about where their loyalty should lie. In a number of conflicts, we hear about a group of householders referred to as *beggja vinir*. These men were friends with both of the conflicting chieftains. Householders who were friends with two chieftains at the same time were an important buffer in conflicts between chieftains. As friends of both the chieftains involved, they could not support one friend against the other. Therefore, it was their task to mediate. It could be advantageous for householders to be friends with two chieftains simultaneously. In this way, they secured their own interests, and if someone tried to violate their rights, they could seek support from both men. However, the drawback was the householders might encounter a conflict of loyalty if their chieftain friends had a dispute. Nonetheless, for society as a whole, it was greatly beneficial for the overlap between the groups of chieftains' friends to be as large as possible. Their role as mediators aided in keeping the peace, and this is the main reason why the Icelandic Free State society was so peaceful.[64]

We can assume that in the period c. 930–1030, when the number of chieftains was comparatively high and they lived a relatively short distance from each other, a portion of the householders were friends with two chieftains at the same time. Gradually, as the number of chieftains was reduced in the twelfth and thirteenth centuries and the population grew, the spheres of power increased in size. It is probable then that the chieftains established friendships primarily with the most influential and richest householders. An average-sized farm in Iceland was about 20 hundreds. We regard those who lived on farms larger than 30 hundreds as large householders, and they amounted to roughly one-fifth of the total number of householders.[65]

At the same time as they were developing their domains, the chieftains tried to prevent other chieftains from establishing friendships with their friends within the boundary of their sphere of influence. This resulted in a decrease in the overlapping between groups of friends, and the confrontations between chieftains grew harsher and bloodier. However, because it was impossible to refuse a gift, it was very difficult for chieftains to prevent their friends from entering into friendship with other chieftains. The majority of large householders in south Iceland and in many other places in Iceland were friends with Gissur Thorvaldsson (1209–1268), who was the country's most powerful chieftain after 1240.[66]

In violation of the advice from *Hávamál*, the chieftains often attempted to establish friendships with their adversaries' friends, thus neutralizing them and undermining their enemies' power in individual disputes. The householders also established friendships with their chieftain's rivals in order to reach a settlement. When Kolbein ungi held Sturla Thórdarson prisoner in 1242, he received a message from Sturla's in-laws saying that they would be his friends if he released Sturla. At first, Kolbein refused and wanted Sturla to go to Norway, but then he changed his mind and sent a message to Sturla's in-laws stating that he would be their friend. They, and many other men from west Iceland, then went to meet Kolbein and became his friends.[67] As friends of both Sturla and Kolbein, these householders formed a buffer which prevented the outbreak of open conflict between the two chieftains. Those who were friends of both Sturla Thórdarson and Kolbein ungi would not have supported a chieftain who would attack them. And for Kolbein's part, by establishing a friendship with Sturla's friends, he also placed an effective end to the help that they were able to give Sturla's kin in their fight against him. Additionally, these friends had to support Kolbein in his conflicts with other adversaries.

We can divide the chieftains' friends into two groups with respect to their relationship with the chieftain: Those who were his friends only, and those who were friends with other chieftains as well. It was the former faction that the chieftain relied on in all disputes and that probably accounted for the majority of his friends. Support from the latter faction, these *beggja vinir*, could vary from case to case according to who the adversary was. The chieftain himself controlled the recruitment into his group of friends, and the friends did not necessarily have anything in common to hold them together other than friendship with the chieftain. It was primarily the chieftains' personal goals which characterized the groups, and these also influenced recruitment. Thus, within the friend groups there could be opposing interests, even conflicts. As mentioned, Galmur Grímsson is the only householder we know about who was friends with three chieftains simultaneously. This indicates that these circumstances were exceptional. However, it is difficult to explain why the boundary was set at two chieftains. Perhaps the chieftains did not regard it as expedient to establish a friendship with a farmer who was already friends with two other chieftains. He had too many ties to consider. There would be too many conflicts in which his loyalty would be divided.

It is difficult to ascertain how durable friendship relations between the chieftains and the householders were. If both parties fulfilled their obligations, the friendship was probably lifelong. When, however, a chieftain died or withdrew by entering a monastery, the bonds of friendship ended and the chieftain's friend group ceased to exist, unless there was an heir who was able and willing to take over the bonds of friendship. When a householder died, it is likely that the person who took over his farm also "inherited" his friendship with the chieftain.

It is debatable who had the most to win from these friendships: the chieftains or the householders. I would argue friendship was more important for the householders. They needed protection; without it, their situation was precarious. It was therefore important for the chieftains to maintain a certain level of disorder. In a society without conflict, chieftains were unnecessary.

Friends or Assemblymen?

The assembly organization (*þing*) was an integral part of Old Norse society. In Norway, local assemblies were held in specific places at fixed times in most regions in the ninth and tenth centuries. These assemblies were likely general assemblies, meetings that all free householders within the area of that assembly had a duty to attend.[68] The assembly was a holy place. It was forbidden to bear weapons there. Thus it was a good and useful place to discuss common concerns. There is no reason to presume that in this period, or later, the assembly was particularly democratic. It was power that ruled. A short time after the first Norsemen settled Iceland, they began to organize local assemblies, and in 930 the Althing for the entire country was founded.

In 965 Iceland was divided into quarters and, according to the standard view, also divided into thirteen spring assemblies (*várþing*). The western quarter, the southern quarter, and the eastern quarter had three spring assemblies each, while the northern quarter had four. As the name suggests, these assemblies should take place in the spring. Three chieftains were in charge of each of these assemblies and its court. Any cases that had not been concluded at the Spring Assembly courts were to be taken to the quarter courts and then to the Fifth Court at the Althing, founded in c. 1005. In the autumn, the three chieftains who were to organize the Spring Assembly, together held an assembly to inform of new laws and other important messages from the recently concluded Althing.

According to Grágás, all householders, tenants, and landowners who did not manage their own farms had to be assemblymen of a chieftain in the quarter in which they lived. There were two exceptions to this rule. The first was for those who lived in Hrútafjörður, the boundary between the western quarter and the northern quarter. These householders did not need to change their assembly membership, that is, their attachment to a chieftain and assembly, even if they moved to the other side of the fjord. The second was that the Althing enabled chieftains to have assemblymen outside the quarter in which they lived. According to the law, if assemblymen were not satisfied with the chieftain they had, once a year they could choose another. To become an assemblyman was, as mentioned, a matter between the householders and the chieftains and should be established by both parties by appointing witnesses.[69]

If an assemblyman was injured or killed, the chieftain should take up the case at the local assembly. The chieftain should also *handsala* for his assemblymen, which is the authority to take over their cases and represent them at the assembly. Assemblymen had to follow their chieftain and support him if he needed help. All householders had to come or send a representative to the Spring Assembly. Every ninth householder required to pay the assembly tax had to travel together with his chieftain to the Althing. These householders should stay in the chieftain's booth at the Althing.[70] Primarily men were assemblymen, but women could also be assemblymen if they were the head of a household. For example, the widow Jórunn audga (the Wealthy) was in assembly with the chieftain Magnús Gudmundarson.[71] However, we do not know how many widows were heads of households. There is little reason to think that there were many.

Much is unclear about the Icelandic assembly organization. The problem we face is that we hardly find any evidence in the sagas (either in the Icelandic Family Sagas or in *Sturlunga saga*) for the model presented to us in Grágás. The sagas mention a good deal more spring assemblies than Grágás called for, and they tell us that these assemblies were often held irregularly. *Eyrbyggja saga* relates that the Rauðmelingar chieftaincy was removed from Þórsnesþing, the Spring Assembly at Snæfellsnes, on account of a disagreement between the chieftain who owned the assembly and another more powerful chieftain. The chieftain of Rauðmelingar then established a new assembly.[72]

The unstable political situation and concentration of power meant that it was not possible to organize spring or autumn assemblies on a permanent basis at fixed locations. The only assembly which continued every year during the entire period of the Free State was the Althing at Þingvellir. The Althing played an especially important role in the development of the country. At Þingvellir, new alliances could be formed and old ones renewed. Chieftains and householders could find spouses for their children there. The Althing was also the country's most important information center. Only there was it possible to obtain information about what happened within the country and abroad. Not least, the Althing was a forum where conflicts could be resolved for there it was possible to exert pressure on warring parties to reach a solution they could live with. The Althing at Þingvellir was the central institution in Icelandic society, and the peace that held sway during most of the Free State period was for the most part created there.

Every householder in the country was probably an assemblyman of a chieftain. But how was loyalty in the relationship between the assemblymen and the chieftains ensured? Through friendship. Hrólfur from Skálmarnes under Múli was a "good friend of Thorgils Oddason and his assemblyman."[73] In most instances, assemblymen were also a chieftain's friends. This is clear from the following narrative from *Íslendinga saga*. Thórd Bödvarsson of Gardur had assemblymen at Akranes and many up in the region [Borgarfjörður]. He thought that his nephew Thórd Sturluson oppressed those assemblymen closest to him. He therefore gave Snorri [Sturluson] half of the Lundar-menn chieftaincy so that Snorri might protect his assemblymen against Thórd Sturluson and others who wanted to control them. But when Snorri had taken over the assemblymen, Thórd Bödvarsson thought that Snorri tried to control his friends to an even greater degree than his brother Thórd Sturluson had.[74]

Here the concepts of assemblyman (þingmaðr) and friend (vinr) are used synonymously.[75] However, not all assemblymen were also the chieftain's friends, and if a dispute arose between two assemblymen of one and the same chieftain, and one was that chieftain's friend and the other was not, the chieftain would support his friend. This is seen in the conflict between Álf Örnólfsson and Thorvald and his son Kjartan, dated about 1173. Álf sought the help of Einar Thorgilsson, but Einar supported Thorvald and Kjartan, because they were his "friends and assemblymen." Álf then turned to the chieftain Hvamm-Sturla, who took up Álf's case. Hvamm-Sturla reached a settlement in the case, and Álf then became his assemblyman.[76]

The problem with relationships between the chieftains and the assembly-men was ambiguous loyalty. Therefore, it was important for both chieftains and householders to establish friendships, and when the chieftains' power bases are described, it is the friends who are emphasized. "Höskuld was soon vinsæll because many supported him, both kin and friends, whom Koll, his father, had gained as supporters."[77] We never hear about assemblymen in such narra-tives. When the chieftains gathered their forces, they always sent word to their friends and often their kin.[78] I have only found two instances in the sagas where assemblymen are mentioned in this context.[79]

Gunnar and Njál: The World's Best Friends?

The sagas tell us little about friendship between householders. The only such friendship described in detail is that between Gunnar Hámundarson and Njál Thorgeirsson, Brennu-Njáls saga's two main protagonists. According to Brennu-Njáls saga, Gunnar Hámundarson was an excellent warrior, in addition to being helpful with good advice, compassionate, even-tempered, loyal to his friends, and careful in his choice of them. He was also well-to-do. One of Gun-nar's female relations, Unn, asked him for help in a difficult case, which Gunnar reluctantly took on himself to resolve. Unn suggested that he ask Njál for advice, because they were good friends. A short time later Gunnar traveled to Bergþórshvoll and told Njál about the situation. Njál answered that many of his friends were worthy of his advice, but none as worthy as Gunnar. Njál then gave Gunnar some advice that led to Gunnar winning the case for Unn. A short time later, Gunnar traveled abroad. Before he left, he asked Njál to assist his mother with the running of the farm while he was away, which Njál was willing to do. Gunnar then transferred all his property into Njál's hands, such that Njál had formal responsibility for it. When Gunnar returned, he gave Njál good gifts for his help. Gunnar then married Hallgerd. During the marriage negotiations, he learned that she was not always to be trusted. When Njál heard of Gunnar's marriage plans, he told Gunnar outright that much malice would follow this marriage to Hallgerd. Gunnar replied that she would never destroy their friendship.[80]

Gunnar and Njál had the habit of visiting each other alternately each winter. After Gunnar married, it was his turn to visit Njál. He traveled with his wife and followers to Bergþórshvoll. However, the visit was short-lived because Hallgerd insulted their host, forcing Gunnar to leave with her and his followers. The summer afterward Gunnar traveled to the Althing, and before he left, he ordered his wife not to be aggressive toward his friends. "The trolls take your friends" was her reply. Shortly thereafter, she got one of her servants, Kolur, to kill one of Njál and his wife Bergthóra's servants. Hallgerd then sent a man to the Althing to inform Gunnar about what had occurred. Gunnar went to Njál, who was also at the Althing, and gave him self-judgment (*sjálfdæmi*) in the case, that is, he alone should decide the outcome of the conflict. Njál decided that Gunnar should pay twelve ounces of silver, while also requesting that if something similar should befall Gunnar, he should remember this compensation. The next summer, when Gunnar and Njál had both gone to the Althing, Bergthóra got one of her servants, Atli, to kill Kolur. When Njál learned of this, he sought out Gunnar at the Althing and told him that he alone should decide the size of the fine. Gunnar demanded the same amount of compensation as Njál had been paid the year before. Njál then presented Gunnar with the same silver that Gunnar had given him. Hallgerd and Bergthóra continued with their "game" for two more rounds, each having two more men killed in the other's household. Their husbands cleaned up after them. The conflict between Hallgerd and Bergthóra did not influence the good friendship between Gunnar and Njál, and at the regional assembly for the part of the country in which they lived, they proclaimed that they would always come to terms in all cases between them. They kept to this and were *jafnan vinir* (always friends).[81]

An economic crisis befell south Iceland, and consequently many men turned to Gunnar for help. Gunnar assisted them all. Eventually he had neither hay nor food remaining. He tried to buy foodstuffs and hay from the householder Otkell, but Otkell refused to sell or give Gunnar what he required. When this news reached Bergþórshvoll, Bergthóra urged Njál to give Gunnar what he needed. Njál and his sons took the gift to Hlíðarendi. Njál informed Gunnar that he should not go to anyone else if he needed help. "Góðar eru gjafir þínar" (your gifts are good), said Gunnar, "en meira þykki mér vert vinfengi þitt ok sona þinna" (but I place a greater price on your friendship and that of your sons).[82]

Gunnar, the great warrior and hero, ended up in a series of conflicts, and in all of them he turned to Njál for advice. Njál's guidance contributed to Gunnar coming out of these conflicts with his honor intact. But in the last conflict, Gunnar did not follow the advice he was given, and it resulted in his death.

Hávamál places great weight on loyalty, reciprocity, and generosity in friendship. The loyalty between Gunnar and Njál is strong in the saga. It survives their wives allowing the repeated killing of men in their households. In all other cases, this would have led to hostility. Also remarkable is the apparent lack of balance in the friendship between the two. It is Njál who gives advice to and supports Gunnar, and never the other way around. It may be that Njál, as he is portrayed in Brennu-Njáls saga, occupies a position halfway between a chieftain and a householder. He speaks about himself as a höfðingi (chieftain), but in the saga it is nevertheless clear that Njál was not.[83] Gunnar and Njál were guest friends—they visited each other's homes, until Gunnar married Hallgerd, and from this point of view, the relationship was in balance.

Earlier we suggested that those who only received were placed in a subordinate position in relation to the giver. But that does not seem to be the case here. Gunnar did not lose status. He is the saga's great tragic hero. It is probably this which saves his reputation in relation to Njál. Gunnar's hero status casts a glow over his friends and gave them honor, especially his best friend: Njál. If we accept such an argument, it can be asserted that the relationship between Gunnar and Njál was, in fact, balanced.

The sagas tell us very little about the friendship between householders, but the little information we do have shows that they provided advice and help to each other during conflicts. They also received support from their friends' friends at every opportunity. If a friend refused to help, the friendship ended. The householders' friendships varied in duration, from some lasting mere days or weeks to others being lifelong. Like friendship between chieftains and householders, friendship between householders was similarly maintained with gifts and feasts.[84] How common was friendship between the householders? It was the householders' wealth that limited the extent of their friendships. Thus, it is probable that it was primarily the more prosperous householders who were able to enter into such alliances; only they had enough resources to organize feasts and give gifts—such as Gunnar and Njál.

Women and Friendship

In some of the Icelandic Family Sagas, we hear about female friends, for example, Thóra Thorgrímsdóttir in *Finnboga saga*. She was the friend of both the saga's heroes, Finnbogi Ásbjarnarson and Jökul Ingimundarson, who considered marrying her or making her his concubine.[85] The reason Finnbogi refers to Thóra as his friend might be because she had accepted that she should marry Jökul, and Finnbogi has promised her his friendship in return.[86] In some tough situations, women could force the establishment of friendship. Probably in the year 1170, the chieftains and brothers Páll Thórdarson and Snorri Thórdarson from Vatnsfjörður went to Helgafell with their followers and abducted Hallgerd, who was the daughter of the priest Runólf and the wife of Ólaf Sölvason. She was not only beautiful but said to be accomplished and exceptional in every way. Runólf, Ólaf, and his brother, the chieftain Páll Sölvason of Reykholt, sought the assistance of the chieftain Jón Loftsson at the Althing the next summer and told him how they had been dishonored. Jón was a "great friend" of the brothers Ólaf and Páll, while Runólf was his kinsman. Jón was therefore duty-bound to support them in their case. At this time, Jón was by far the most powerful man in the country; in fact, none of the Icelandic chieftains had ever held a similar position in society as he did. Jón's position was in part due to his ability to solve conflicts. After he took on the case, he summoned Hallgerd. Jón asked her to abandon Páll and go back to her husband, and if she did this, in future she would be able to seek his help if she got into trouble. Hallgerd accepted this offer, and the saga tells us that she wanted to be counted among Jón's friends, that is, under his protection.[87] Hallgerd used this friendship a short time later when her own daughter was abducted by a chieftain's son, Svein Sturluson.[88]

The only narrative I have found in the sagas where two women enter into friendship is in *Laxdæla saga*. This saga reports that Aud was Thorgerd Egilsdóttir's *vinkona*.[89] What their friendship meant is not discussed. Thorgerd was a widow and Aud was divorced. They both probably ran their own farms, and as heads of their households, they could enter into relations of friendship with chieftains, bishops, and abbots and could become assemblymen.[90] The position of widows was special. If a woman lost her husband while the children were still minors and she took over the running of the household, she became a "man" in the eyes of society and acquired nearly all the rights that a male head of household possessed, including the right to become a chieftain's assemblyman, establish friendships, and participate in the business of the assemblies.[91]

It has been argued that if we read between the lines in the sagas, we will see that women's friendships are perceived as self-evident and thus not mentioned.[92] I do not agree with this view. The relations of friendship we have discussed were mainly linked to heads of households, both large and small, and individuals from the highest ranks in society. These friendships functioned within the political sphere, from which women were generally excluded. That women could influence their husbands is another matter entirely.

Friendship was of vital importance for both chieftains and householders—and their households. It was the tie that bound them together and provided certain predictability for both parties: the householders getting protection, and the chieftains support. It is important to emphasize that in this relationship loyalty was strong, and to betray a friend resulted in the loss of honor. This relationship of friendship between chieftains and householders is identical to the so-called patron-client relationships we find in almost all societies in all periods.

The patron-client association is an alliance between two people with different status, power, and wealth. Each finds it beneficial to ally himself with the other, and both have something to give: the client loyal support and respect, the patron protection and help. Patrons and clients are obliged to support each other, and it is the patron who decides his duty to the client. The patron-client relationship has two prerequisites. First, the patron has something that the client lacks and is interested in acquiring or receiving (e.g., protection or food). Second, the client is willing to do the patron's bidding in exchange for access to a portion of resources (that the patron controls). Therefore, the client provides the patron with the tangible or nontangible equivalent of that which the client has received from the patron.[93] The relationship between a patron and a client is characterized as an asymmetrical reciprocal alliance. It gives the patron great power over the client, especially if the relationship includes a strong form of protection. These relationships are unstable, and the disintegration of one client group can lead to others increasing and becoming more complex, as was the case with the chieftains' groups of friends.

Ancient Rome is a good example of a society where patron-client relationships played an important role. In Roman society, a politician's power was based on how many clients he had. As mentioned, patrons should protect and clients support. This relationship was called *fides*. This term was also used to describe relations with the gods. The Romans asked their gods for support in the same way as clients asked their patrons for help.[94] To become a client, one often had to take an oath of loyalty. The Romans called the favors the patron provided to his clients beneficence (*beneficia*), and he who had rendered a good deed had a moral claim to a return favor (*officia*). He who received a good deed was bound by gratitude (*gratia*). Gratitude was an important virtue in Roman society, for those who were ungrateful were "everyone's enemy."[95] To show his gratitude, the client was to vote for his patron or his patron's candidate in elections, and the client should assist his patron if he had to pay out huge expenses. The client also had to consult with his patron when he wanted to marry his daughter. If a patron was deceitful and did not protect his client, the client could end the relationship and seek protection with another patron, who thereby became more powerful. A client could have two patrons, but the client's position and wealth were at stake if his patrons came into conflict with each other.[96]

The Roman patron-client relationship had many elements in common with the chieftain-householder relationship in Iceland. The biggest difference—if we ignore the obvious differences such as the size of the two societies—was that in Iceland or in Norway, terms denoting *fides*, *beneficia*, *officia*, and *gratia* did not exist. Yet, the different aspects of the patron-client relationship these words describe were all characteristic of Old Norse friendship.

The vertical friendship between the chieftains and the householders in Iceland, as discussed in this chapter, has little in common with the horizontal friendship we have seen in *Hávamál*. To study this latter type of relationship, we must look at friendship between the Icelandic chieftains.

CHAPTER 2

Friendship between Chieftains

"To His Friend a Man Should Be a Friend, and Repay Gifts with Gifts"

In Iceland from the time of the settlement (c. 870–930) until the end of the Free State power slowly became concentrated in fewer and fewer hands. In the whole of this period, friendships between chieftains played a decisive role in the power game. They used friendship to enter into alliances with each other and in attempts to neutralize and outdo their rivals. Because of the exceptionally good written source situation, this chapter focuses on the relations of friendship between the Icelandic chieftains in the Sturlung Age, the time between 1220 and 1262–64. During this period, a new player entered the political game: the Norwegian king. His goal was the subjugation of Iceland to Norway. To accomplish this, King Hákon Hákonarson and Earl Skúli Bárdarson (who ruled the country when King Hákon was a minor), used a goal-orientated strategy. They bound the Icelandic chieftains to them as royal retainers and friends. After this, it was only a matter of time before the country became a Norwegian tributary land. This occurred as mentioned in the years 1262, 1263, and 1264. The Norwegian king's entry into Icelandic politics changed the political game; there was now a player more powerful than the Icelandic chieftains, even though in the beginning he had no formal power. For the Icelandic chieftains, it was important to gain support from this new player because doing so might strengthen their own position of power in Iceland. Snorri Sturluson and his career illustrate this point. His political career took off after he established a friendship around 1220 with Earl Skúli.

Selfishness

Early in the thirteenth century, Snorri Sturluson gained control over the majority of the chieftaincies in Borgarfjörður and established his domain.[1] Snorri's career began in 1197, when he married Herdís Bersadóttir of Borg and thereby gained control over the Mýramenn chieftaincy. In 1202, he received half of the Lundarmenn chieftaincy as a gift, and three or four years later he acquired the Reykhyltingar chieftaincy. Snorri probably also obtained the Jöklamenn chieftaincy, and likely half of the Allsherjar chieftaincy. In the end, his domain stretched across what is today Mýrarsýsla, Borgarfjarðarsýsla, and also to a certain extent Kjósarsýsla and Gullbringusýsla.

In 1218, Snorri traveled to Norway. Right before he left Iceland, a conflict arose between the powerful Oddaverjar family and some Norwegian merchants, with killings on both sides. The merchants complained to Earl Skúli, who planned an attack on Iceland. Snorri strongly opposed these plans, and "said that his advice would be to make friends with the best men in Iceland, and [he] claimed that as soon as he could reach them with his advice, his countrymen would think it best to turn to obedience for Norwegian rulers."[2] Snorri went back to Iceland in 1220, with the mission from King Hákon and Skúli to bring the country under the king's rule. Before he left Norway, Skúli gave Snorri a ship and fifteen other expensive gifts.[3]

During the years c. 1223–28, Snorri became Iceland's most powerful chieftain. This was due to his wealth, his friendship with Earl Skúli, and his friendships with Icelandic chieftains.[4] Until 1222 Sæmund Jónsson from the Oddaverjar family was Iceland's most powerful chieftain. His death that year created a power vacuum in the politics of the Free State. His sons could not agree which of them should take over after him, and thus the Oddaverjar lost their national position of power. This created opportunities for other chieftains.

In 1223, Sturla Sighvatsson and Thorvald Vatnsfirdingur entered into a friendship. Thorvald promised to support Sturla against all his opponents in Iceland. Sturla promised in return to help Thorvald in his conflict with Snorri Sturluson. To show their friendship, they sent the priest Torfi Gudmundarson to the Althing with formal control over both their chieftaincies for the short time during which the Althing was held. At the Althing Snorri Sturluson had Thorvald declared an outlaw. A few months later Sighvat Sturla's father tried to effect a reconciliation between Thorvald and Snorri, such that both Snorri and Sturla could gain honor from the case. Sighvat managed this, and Snorri received self-judgment. After the reconciliation, Sighvat and Sturla gave Thorvald good gifts, and Thorvald promised to be as good a friend to Sighvat as he was with Sturla. However, the alliance between Thorvald, Sturla, and Sighvat did not last long. In the winter of 1223–24, Thorvald Vatnsfirdingur sent friendly words to Snorri about creating an in-law relationship and an alliance. Snorri accepted on the condition that Thorvald should "undertake whatever Snorri might ask of him, no matter against whom."⁵ In 1224 Thórdís Snorradóttir married Thorvald Vatnsfirdingur.⁶

When debates about the content of friendship pacts occur, the sagas use the terms alliance (*samband*) and talk about friendship (*mæla til vináttu* or *vináttumál*), words which emphasize that the parties have spoken together or intend to. However, only rarely do we know the content of the actual deliberations. One of the few exceptions is the discussion between the householder Björn Arngeirsson and the chieftain Thorstein Kuggason, from *Bjarnar saga Hítdælakappa*. Björn is reported to have said,

> "We have [previously] spoken about becoming friends; I decided to subscribe to this and be your friend. But we are both in conflict with others. I now want us to promise each other that the one who lives the longest will avenge the other, if we were to lose our life to a weapon or through violence." Thorstein said they were worthy of each other's friendship in every way, and he again offered: "and when you speak about revenge, let us tread a little carefully, because people now understand better than ever what to do. I want both of us to require self-judgment for the other, or outlawry [*sekð*], or compensation, but not avenge each other. This is more suitable for Christian men." They then promised each other with binding agreements that they would avenge each other or bring a case as if they were relatives. Then the herd of unruly horses was brought forth again, and Thorstein now accepted the gift with thanks. The horses remained there in the winter and the following summer without being fetched, and in the autumn Björn was to send them westward. Björn gave Thorfinna a gold ring and a well-woven kirtle, which King Olav [Haraldsson] had given Thórd Kolbeinsson and which he awarded to Björn after the robbery at Brennøyene. And so they parted as good friends and each went to his own home.⁷

The friendship pact between Björn and Thorstein has clear reciprocal duties. As Christian men, these two were not to avenge each other through killing, but to seek monetary compensation, which was the common term for outlawry or three years' exile, the Free State's two harshest penalties. What gave rise to this friendship pact was that Thorstein had been asked by Björn's enemies to assist them in their struggles against him. To consolidate their plans of friendship, Thorstein was invited to a Christmas feast by one of Björn's enemies.[8] On the way there, Thorstein and his followers ended up in a storm and were forced to request accommodation with Björn, and eventually the unintended visit turned into a feast. This resulted in Thorstein and his men staying with Björn for some days. When Thorstein was about to leave, Björn wanted to give Thorstein a herd of unruly horses.[9] Thorstein would not accept the gift because he had not repaid Björn for the feast. Therefore, he proposed that he should mediate in the conflict between Björn and his enemies. Björn accepted this proposal, and a reconciliation meeting was called. Because of the negative attitude of Björn's enemies—those who Thorstein had originally considered entering into friendship with—the meeting did not result in a settlement. Thorstein saw this as an insult against himself. He then went to Björn and accepted the horses.[10] A gift required a countergift, but it was important that time passed before the countergift was presented, and that it was not identical to the gift. The pace of the gift-giving process was therefore charged with meaning, and changes in it could produce significant consequences.[11] In addition, it was important to establish a balance in friendships, as *Hávamál* emphasizes. Thus, Thorstein could not accept a feast first and then a gift immediately afterwards. This would have placed him, as a chieftain, in a clear subordinate and dependent position. The reconciliation meeting was Thorstein's countergift for the feast, and after this he accepted the horses to enter into friendship with Björn. Thorstein was a chieftain; it was therefore important for Björn to secure his friendship. Not only would it strengthen his case, but at the same time it would reduce the effectiveness of his enemies. But let us now return to Snorri.

The same year Snorri's daughter Thórdís married Thorvald Vatnsfirdingur, Snorri and Thorvald Gissurarson, a friend of Snorri's brother Sighvat Sturluson, "bound their friendship" through Thorvald's son Gissur marrying Snorri's daughter Ingibjörg. Later that same year, Snorri and Loftur, the son of Bishop Páll Jónsson, established a friendship.[12] In 1224, Snorri also sent a communiqué to his brother Thórd, who had been one of Sæmund's friends, that they should put down "all their differences and to pledge again an affectionate kinship."[13] Another of Snorri's daughters, Hallbera, who had married the chieftain Árni Magnússon in 1218 and divorced him in 1224, was married a second time in the winter of 1227–28, this time to Kolbein ungi Arnórsson from the Ásbirningar family.[14] This marriage was hastily conducted, for Snorri thought it important to establish an alliance with Kolbein. After the wedding, which took place at Snorri's farm, Snorri's son-in-law went home to his own farm without taking his new wife with him; Snorri sent her to Kolbein some months later.

In about 1220, not only was Snorri a powerful chieftain who had three daughters he could use to create alliances but he was also friends with Norway's most powerful man, Earl Skúli. All of this gave him a great advantage over the other chieftains in the country. During the period from 1223 to 1228, Snorri managed to establish friendships with most of the country's chieftains, according to his agreement with the Norwegian monarchy. However, Snorri was not very interested in getting the Icelandic chieftains to obey the Norwegian king, as he himself had suggested. First and foremost, Snorri was concerned with expanding his own position of power.

Toward the end of the 1220s, Snorri's power began to lessen, and over the course of the 1230s, he was outplayed in the Free State's power struggles. Sturla Sighvatsson had Thorvald Vatnsfirdingur killed in 1228.[15] Hallbera died in 1231, and with her death the alliance between Snorri and Kolbein ungi came to an end. Kolbein then married Helga, daughter of Sæmund Jónsson of the Oddaverjar family. The Oddaverjar were also related by marriage to the Sturlungar, but they could support either them or the Ásbirningar family in their struggles in the 1230s. In 1231, Gissur and Ingibjörg divorced. In 1232, Snorri prepared a case against Kolbein ungi concerning Hallbera's inheritance. He invited his brother Thórd, his son Bödvar, and Sturla Sighvatsson to a feast because he wanted to ensure solidarity among his friends in this matter.[16] In 1232, Snorri Sturluson and Kolbein ungi reached an agreement concerning Hallbera's inheritance and the chieftaincies in northern Iceland. Part of the settlement included the promise that Snorri should receive half the chieftaincies that Kolbein owned, but Kolbein would continue to administer them and give Snorri support at the Althing. Kolbein should marry his sister to Snorri's son Óraekja and give her a dowry of 60 hundreds. For his part, Snorri was to give Óraekja 240 hundreds, the farm Melur in Midfjördur, and the *Hafliðanautr* chieftaincy; and the brothers-in-law were to manage Húnaþing jointly.[17] After the agreement between Snorri and Kolbein, Sturla Thórdarson, the author of *Íslendinga saga*, relates that his father the chieftain Thórd had said, "I have a suspicion that Snorri, my brother, has swapped his friends and sold his friendship with Sighvat (Snorri and Thórd's brother) and Sturla (Sighvat's son), but received Kolbein's friendship."[18]

In 1234, a new confrontation arose between Snorri and Kolbein ungi. This time Snorri received help from the chieftain Thorleif Thórdarson and Árni Magnússon. But the chieftains from the Svínfellingar family, Ormur Jónsson Svínfellingur and Thórarin Jónsson, supported Kolbein; they had become his good friends.[19] In 1237 Snorri's nephew, Sturla Sighvatsson, forced Snorri and Óraekja to go to Norway. Sturla arrived in Iceland in 1235, with a plan that King Hákon and he had devised whereby Sturla was to try and bring the country under the rule of the king. Within a short space of time, Sturla managed to gain control of the areas governed by Snorri and his son, Óraekja, and forced them to go to Norway, but before Snorri left, he renewed his friendship with his brother Thórd.[20]

Sturla Sighvatsson was killed in the battle at Örlygsstaðir in 1238, the year after Snorri and Óraekja returned to Iceland, and they immediately regained their earlier positions of power in Borgarfjörður and Vestfirðir. Before Snorri left Norway, he became involved in Earl Skúli's uprising against King Hákon. Snorri had been explicitly forbidden by the king to leave Norway but departed nevertheless. According to Hirðskrá (the law of the king's retainers), vassals who leave Norway against the king's wishes are traitors and should lose their rights and fortunes.[21] The provisions in Hirðskrá were later to be King Hákon's authorization for claiming Snorri's property and chieftaincies. In 1240, Kolbein ungi and Gissur Thorvaldsson received letters from the king ordering them to make Snorri leave the country, with or without his consent, or failing that, to kill him. On the night of 23 September 1241, Gissur and his men attacked Snorri in Reykholt and killed him, without trying to make him leave the country.

Snorri's network in the 1220s was the biggest in the Free State and included nearly all of the country's chieftains. His alliances can be divided into two groups. The "nucleus" consisted of the chieftains Thorleif Thórdarson and Árni Magnússon, who apparently supported him in the majority of his conflicts. However, these two were relatively weak chieftains. The other group in Snorri's network included his son, his brothers and their sons, and Kolbein ungi Arnórsson, Thorvald Gissurarson, Gissur Thorvaldsson, Thorvald Vatnsfirdingur, Ormur Jónsson, and Loftur Pálsson. It was the antagonism between these men at the end of the 1220s and the beginning of the 1230s that led to the disintegration of Snorri's friendship network. Snorri lost his position of power because he did not manage to fulfill all his political obligations. The dissension between, for example, Snorri and his brothers and Snorri and his son Óraekja led to the Sturlungar being split into factions.[22] The biggest weakness with Snorri's network was its extent. It was too large to be able to function effectively. Another important reason why Snorri lost his position of power in Iceland in the 1230s was that his daughters' marriages ceased to function to his advantage: Hallbera died in 1231; Ingibjörg and Gissur were divorced the same year; and Thórdís, after becoming a widow in 1228, refused to obey her father and took over her son's household. This meant that Snorri could no longer use his daughters to establish friendships with other Icelandic chieftains.

Snorri's policy toward the Norwegian rulers also failed. For the chieftains and other Icelanders, it was very important to be friends with the kings and earls of Norway. This meant that they gained a higher status and greater prestige in Iceland. Around 1220, Earl Skúli was Norway's most powerful man, but in the following years King Hákon took over more and more of the governance of the country. The relationship between the two steadily worsened, and finally Skúli rebelled against Hákon and was killed in 1240. When Snorri came to Iceland in 1220, he was Skúli's man. After Snorri had to flee Iceland in 1237, he went to his friend Skúli, and in 1239 Snorri returned to Iceland, probably with the title of earl.[23] He openly gambled everything on Skúli defeating King Hákon. Snorri found himself in an untenable political situation in Iceland. Only a change of king in Norway could save him. With Skúli as king, Snorri would again become Iceland's most powerful man.

As a result of the small number of chieftains in the thirteenth century and the overlapping of their friendships, a chieftain could not rely on all his allies in his conflicts. Therefore, a chieftain's alliance could be weak in one conflict and strong in another, depending on who the opponent was and whom he was allied with. Friendships were established to achieve the political goals of individual chieftains. Alliances between the chieftains rarely worked together to achieve a common goal. Each individual chieftain wanted the greatest amount of power possible. Therefore, these men could not cooperate for long. Snorri Sturluson was a sought-after partner as long as his power continued to increase in Iceland and while he had a good relationship with the Norwegian rulers. When he began to show signs of weakening, he lost his value as an ally for the other chieftains, and they began to withdraw from their friendships with him. The system was built on chieftains having political support to offer each other. When the chieftains lost their political weight, it led to fewer being willing to be their friends, and as a result the chieftains' alliances were unstable. Thus there was little loyalty between the parties. An exception to these short-lived friendships was the friendship between the Haukdælir and the Ásbirningar, an alliance that dominated politics in Iceland for a large part of the period 1180–1246.[24]

Disputes, Friendship, and Peace

The establishment of friendship among chieftains was also useful in creating peace and bringing about reconciliation. *Brennu-Njáls saga* relates that the lawspeaker and chieftain Thórarin Ólafsson went to the chieftain Höskuld Kollsson to ask for compensation for the killing of his brother, Glúm. Glúm had been married to Hallgerd, Höskuld's daughter, and was killed by a man who Hallgerd persuaded her husband to accept as a member of their household. When Hallgerd learned of the killing, she sent the killer to her father's brother, Hrút, who killed him. When Thórarin came to Höskuld, he did not have a case, since the killer was already dead. However, to allow Thórarin to gain honor from his visit and to show their magnanimity, Höskuld and Hrút gave Thórarin gifts and entered into friendship with him: "give him gifts, and it would make him our friend for life."[25] The brothers Höskuld and Hrút used the situation to ensure support for themselves from the lawspeaker and chieftain Thórarin, while showing their greatness and generosity to the whole of society.

Paradoxically, conflicts between chieftains often resulted in the establishment of friendship between them.[26] To bring disputes between chieftains to an end, arbitration was used. It was the most effective and secure way to end a conflict. When a dispute went to arbitration, the contending parties would agree on appointing the same number of arbitrators—private judges who would issue an award or a settlement. The arbitrators were not bound by formal rules of evidence; they would issue their judgment based on their discretion. Chieftains were generally chosen to make the award. Thus, arbitrators were men at least as powerful as or more influential than those involved. Most arbitrators were also the friends or relatives of the parties they represented.

According to Grágás, arbitrators should only punish with fines. It was also possible to punish with outlawry (skóggangr), three years' exile (fjörbaugsgarðr) or loss of land and chieftaincies if the parties agreed on such a punishment beforehand.[27] The Free State's harshest punishment was outlawry. It entailed a lifelong banishment from the law. The outlaw lost all rights that protected him under the law, and his property was confiscated. It was forbidden to help him. Anyone could kill him with impunity, without any claim for damages from his kin. He could not be buried in consecrated ground, and children born to him after his sentencing could not inherit. Fjörbaugsgarðr was milder than outlawry; it entailed exile from Iceland for three years and the confiscation of property. The convicted had three years in which to leave Iceland. In this period, he had sanctuary in the immediate area around his farm and on his way to the ship. If he did not manage to get away from Iceland in this period, he became an outlaw.[28] Before the fines were determined by the arbitrators, it was usual to compare the injuries of those involved; the differences should be

compensated for. The fines varied from case to case. There were no set crite-
ria for fines for the different types of wounds or insults. Each individual case
was discretionary, and often the damages were dependent on how much prestige the parties placed on the case. Therefore, in trivial cases, the fines were
low. In cases of prestige, however, they could be quite high.

The arbitrators were under pressure, not only because they were friends
or relatives of those involved but also because it was important in the political game of the Icelandic Free State to reach a settlement both parties could
accept and not interpret as an insult. The arbitrators could expect that in any
future cases in which they were involved the roles would be reversed, and
then they could risk facing the same punishment. At the same time, it was important that the parties in the conflict did not go against an arbitrator's decision. That was perceived as an insult, which could develop into enmity with
the arbitrator.

It was of great importance for any chieftain to be successful in their claims.
It increased prestige, and in his next case a chieftain would appear stronger
with this higher status, and more householders would want to become his
friends. Arbitration and direct negotiation between the parties was the best
means to reach a lasting settlement in a dispute. The advantage of settling a
conflict in this way was that it usually took place in a quick and safe manner,
which, in most instances, satisfied the parties involved. Arbitration made it
possible for the parties to withdraw from a critical situation with their honor
intact.

The use of gifts in connection with the settlement of small conflicts rarely
occurred. In large conflicts, it was more common for gifts to be used to
secure the peace, thus establishing friendship between the parties. One example is in the dispute between Thorgils and Haflidi around 1120. After Thorgils
had paid the fine to Haflidi, he gave him

> honorable gifts, five stud-horses together, a gold finger-ring and a sheep-
> skin cloak . . . Haflidi then said: "Now I see that you mean to respect
> our agreement and from now on we shall be more on our guard against
> quarrelling." And they fulfilled that, for as long as they lived they were
> always of one mind in important cases.[29]

The agreement took place in a social context. It defined or redefined the status
and duties of those involved and their supporters. After conflicts, new alliances were often formed, such as the one between Thorgils and Haflidi.
Those who were enemies previously might become friends. This strengthened
the chieftains' positions of power and meant their friends could feel more

secure against claims from other householders and their chieftains; such new alliances also arose after the conclusion of conflicts between chieftains and bishops.[30]

The chieftains primarily used political support and advice to maintain friendships and to show their counterpart the interest he had in the relationship. The purpose of this exchange was also to outwardly show the alliance's strength. It was a signal to other chieftains that those involved were desirable as allies, and thus it encouraged others to approach them. Another goal of friendship pacts was to frighten potential opponents and to signal to them that they must fight two chieftains rather than just one. However, a chieftain might enter into a friendship with another chieftain to prevent him from giving support to rival chieftains. Friendships between chieftains was easy to establish and easy to end. Therefore, they were good tools for the chieftains to use to achieve their goals. They could plan their own strategy and establish alliances with those it was beneficial to have on their side, depending on the goal they wanted to achieve. This did make the political situation frequently unclear.

According to *Hávamál*, good friendship consisted of two equal parties who were loyal and generous to each other. It is not easy to find such friendships among the Icelandic chieftains in the thirteenth century. It is also unlikely that the situation had changed radically from the period of settlement. The chieftains were, first and foremost, preoccupied with their own power and honor. They were willing to sacrifice a weak friend for a more powerful one if the opportunity arose. That is not to say that the advice in *Hávamál* was not useful. The poem also instructs one how to use bad friends to achieve one's political goals. On this point, there is good reason to argue that the Icelandic chieftains followed the poem's advice.

CHAPTER 3

Kings and Their Friends

Friendship played an important role in Norwegian politics in the period c. 900–1300. But the situation outlined in Norway was more complex than the one we saw in Iceland, because Norwegian society was bigger and more complex, which was not at all due to royal power. There was a level of power over and above the local chieftain level. The Norwegian kings used friendship to the highest degree to secure support for themselves from local chieftains and householders. However, in the long run friendship was unsuitable as a political foundation for the kings' power. In accordance with a new ideology that developed at the end of the twelfth century and in the first half of the thirteenth, friendship was replaced with obedience (*hlýðni*) and service (*þjónusta*).[1] To put it simply, a transition occurred from bilateral to unilateral relationships. After these changes, the king no longer needed to establish friendships with the householders. They had become his subjects to rule. However, the king continued to use friendship to secure the loyalty of the most central persons in the royal administration.

The emergence and development of royal power in Norway reduced the chieftains' positions and changed the character of the aristocracy; the old family elites with local power bases were replaced by an aristocracy whose position in society was founded on participation in the royal administrative system.[2] These changes resulted in the weakening of the presumably strong bonds of friendship between the chieftains and the householders, and they were replaced with an even greater local collaboration, which we will discuss in chapter 7. In the following, we first examine friendship relations between the king and the householders, and afterward, friendship between the king and the Norwegian aristocracy. We then consider the relationship between the king and his retainers in the *hirð*, before we finally discuss friendships and foreign policy.

Kings and Householders

The first paragraph in Gulating's law from around 1160 states:

> The first in our laws is that we shall bow toward the east and pray to the Holy Christ for peace and a fruitful harvest, and that we may keep our country settled and our sovereign lord complete; may he be our friend and we his, and may God be a friend to us all.[3]

Loyalty between the king and the people who participated in the assembly— the householders and the chieftains—was ensured through friendship. At the same time, God was implored to befriend all who entered the earthly friendship pact, that is, the Almighty should protect the king and the assembly participants.

The importance of the householders' friendship for the kings can be seen in a number of saga episodes. Soon after King Ólaf Kyrre's death in 1093, his son Magnús Barefoot became king in Viken. When the people of Oppland heard the news about the king's death, they made Magnús's cousin, Hákon Magnússon Thórisfóstri, king. Hákon and his men then went to Nidaros and summoned the Øyratinget. There, Hákon was accepted as king. *Heimskringla* (a collection of sagas about the Norwegian kings up to 1177, written by Snorri Sturluson) tells us that in order to secure the friendship of the householders, Hákon abolished the land tax for Trøndelag and gave the people of Trøndelag "many other legal amendments [royal decrees about changes to the current law]. He also freed them from the obligation to give the king Christmas gifts. At that point, all the people of Trøndelag joined with King Hákon in friendship." Afterward, the king went back to Oppland where he gave "the Opplanders all the same legal amendments as the people from Trøndelag. They all became his complete friends." In the autumn of 1093, King Magnús Barefoot traveled to Nidaros, and it is reported that he disliked all "the great gifts which King Hákon had given the householders to win their friendship." Magnús believed what Hákon had given away was also Magnús's property.[4]

Hákon Thórisfóstri used the kingdom's resources and legal amendments to secure the householders' friendship. It is therefore easy to understand Magnús's frustration. In theory, the kingdom's property was something he and Hákon should either manage together or divide between them such that each had control over their part of the realm and its revenue. If Magnús was to secure the householders' support, he had to be able to give the householders bigger gifts and better laws than Hákon. He could not do this. There was, however, a limit to how far the kings could go. This story illustrates how vital it was for kings to take the initiative in the struggle for power and to secure the householders' friendship.

When Hákon heard that Magnús had gone to Nidaros, he returned there. The situation was tense while the two kings stayed in the town. After Magnús left, Hákon decided to do the same and go south to Viken, probably to secure support from the people there. Before he left Nidaros, he held a meeting and asked "the people for their friendship and promised them all his friendship. He said that he was not properly assured what Magnús, his kinsman, would do. . . . All men promised him friendship with good will and a retinue, if he needed it."[5]

Townsmen were another group that the kings needed to establish friendships with. After the victory over Magnús Erlingsson in the battle of Fimreite in 1184, King Sverrir traveled to Bergen where he called a meeting with the people of Bergen. Hávard, one of the king's *lendr maðr* (royal vassals) opened with a short speech. [6] In it, he supposedly said Sverrir would be "gracious to all who served him without deception" and posed a rhetorical question to the townsmen: Was it not better to seek Sverrir's "friendship" than to fight with those who stood against his will?[7] The king then took the stage and gave a passionate speech where he accused the son and father, Magnús and Erling skakki Kyrpinga-Ormsson, of killing his kinsmen and usurping a position of power that was not theirs. Finally, Sverrir asked Magnús's men to abandon the town and thanked all his and God's friends for their attendance.[8] The entire meeting was framed by the notion of friendship. Friendship with Sverrir was emphasized first and last on friendship with God. The two relationships were linked together. God's friends, or those who wanted to be, were also Sverrir's friends.

For the kings, the friendship of the householders and the townsmen was important. It would guarantee their support. Friendships, however, between the king and the householders encountered a significant problem: the local chieftains. The little information we have about the relationship between them and the householders indicates it was of a similar nature to that between the chieftains and the householders in Iceland.[9]

The Norwegian householders maintained friendships with both chieftains and kings. Nevertheless, there is little doubt who the real local leaders were—the chieftains. They had an established position of power in local society that they had held for a long time. It was more important for the householders to support the local chieftain than the king. Chieftains were the primary protectors for day-to-day life, and there is little doubt that the householders' loyalty lay essentially with the chieftains and not with the king. In order to rule the country, the king had to establish a friendship with the local chieftains.

The Opportunistic Chieftain

About the year 900, the population of Norway was probably in excess of one hundred and fifty thousand people, spanning several dozen chieftaincies. Even if the majority of the chieftaincies were small, they were well organized and could mobilize people and resources for huge tasks. This is indicated most clearly by the large burial grounds. To build these it was necessary to have, in addition to the know-how, control over people and materials.

The unification of Norway, as mentioned, began at the end of the ninth century. To ensure their control over the country, the kings could either remove the chieftains from their positions of power and put in their own men or they could establish friendship with the chieftains. The chieftains who fought against the king risked not only their lives but also the confiscation of their property. Chieftains with whom the king established friendship had to accept him as their overlord. Yet because the kings were dependent on support from the local chieftains and because there were often kings and claimants to the throne, the chieftains could play them off against each other. Compared with their European contemporaries, the Norwegian aristocracy was poor. They were therefore dependent on the kingdom's resources. It was of great importance to the chieftains to establish good relations with the most important king in the country. This was the only way they could gain access to the wealth distributed by the king and thereby secure their position of power on the local level.

These friendships between the king and the chieftains were characterized by instability. As a rule, the chieftains supported the most generous king. Once the king's finances worsened and gifts became fewer (i.e., when the king was not able to uphold his friendship obligations), the chieftains began to look for a new and more generous king. The classic example of this situation was when Cnut the Great secured control over Norway.

Cnut was crowned king of England in 1017. Two years later he became king of Denmark. In the beginning of his career, Cnut had to secure control over the English and the Danish kingdoms. After this was done, he wanted to expand his area of power in the North Sea and the Baltic regions. To resist him, King Ólaf Haraldsson, the Swedish king Ólaf Eiríksson, and King Jaroslav of Russia established an alliance. In 1019, Ólaf and Jaroslav each married a daughter of the Swedish king. Early in the 1020s, Cnut went to the Baltic with a large fleet, and in 1025 or 1026, Ólaf Haraldsson and Önund, Ólaf Eiríksson's son, attacked the Danes. Cnut won the battle, and in 1028 he came to Norway and was made king over the entire country. Ólaf Haraldsson escaped to Russia. He tried to win the country back, but as is well known, he died at the battle of Stiklestad in 1030.

An important reason why Ólaf lost the battle of Stiklestad was that Cnut had established friendships with the most influential chieftains in Norway:

> When Erlingur Skjalgsson travelled to Norway with his followers in the autumn [probably in 1027], he received magnificent gifts from King Cnut. Together with Erlingur, envoys travelled from King Cnut north to Norway, and they took a large quantity of gold and silver. In the winter, the envoys went around the country and dispersed the money King Cnut had promised the people in the autumn if they would accept him as their leader; they also gave to many others whom they paid to show friendship to King Cnut. They had support from Erlingur when he travelled around. So many men went on to become King Cnut's friends and promised him their service, as well as promised to oppose King Ólaf; some did this openly, but many more kept it secret from the common people.[10]

It is worth noting that in *Heimskringla* Snorri does not criticize the chieftains' actions, even though Ólaf after these events became the most popular saint in Scandinavia. As we have seen, Snorri himself was well aware of the rules of the political game. He was clear that Ólaf Haraldsson had defaulted on his obligations to his friends. He had not given them gifts, as Cnut had. It was therefore legitimate for Ólaf's earlier friends to establish friendship with Cnut and to abandon their friendships with Ólaf.

However, even when the kings upheld their part of the friendship bargain, it might happen that their supporters would try to protect themselves against a possible change of king. In the beginning, King Magnús Erlingsson was popular and supported by most of the chieftains in the country, especially in eastern and western Norway.[11] But when things began to turn sour and King Sverrir's power grew, all of Magnús's royal vassals sent a letter to Sverrir to enquire about the likelihood of obtaining his protection and friendship.[12] It is likely that *Sverris saga* exaggerates the number of supporters who turned to Sverrir. Nevertheless, this account clearly shows how the royal vassals were thinking. In such circumstances, it can hardly have been easy for the kings to build up an effective method of governing. As long as there were claimants to the throne or other kings who competed for power, the local aristocracy was able to play the rivals off against each other and use them to their own advantage. The existence of the term *vinhollr* (to be loyal to your friends) suggests rather that loyalty in many friendships could be weak.[13] Perhaps because of this, not all kings were equally concerned with acquiring the greatest number of friends possible. It was said that King Sverrir was *vinvandr*; that is, he carefully selected whom he would establish a friendship with.[14] Having a few loyal friends was better than having many disloyal ones. It also meant there was less pressure to continually give gifts, and thus fewer obligations. It was not necessarily the number of friends one had that was crucial, but the support one could count on from them.

In the struggle for power in Norway, friendship played an important role in calming tensions between the kings. *Heimskringla* tells us that the most loyal friends of King Magnús Ólásson arranged a meeting regarding the sharing of the country between him and Harald Hardrule. At this point in time, Harald was in Denmark, and he sailed to Norway in order to meet Magnús.[15] After Harald arrived in Norway, Magnús invited him to a feast. In the afternoon, Magnús went into Harald's tent and he distributed weapons, clothes, and gold to Harald's men, making them also his friends. Finally, he came to Harald:

> He [Magnús] had two branches in his hands, and said to him [Harald]: "Which of these two sticks do you want?" Harald answered: "The one which is closest to me." Then King Magnús said: "With this stick I give you half of the kingdom of Norway, together with all taxes and all property which belong to it, with the agreement that you shall reign everywhere in Norway with the same rights as I have."[16]

The morning after, Magnús publicly proclaimed at an assembly the gift he had given to his kinsman Harald, and Steigar-Thórir Thórdarson gave Harald the name of a king (*konungsnafn*). The same day, Harald invited Magnús to a feast, and, as a countergift, he gave Magnús half the enormous wealth he had gained abroad, including in Byzantium.[17] The agreement between the two was assured with the exchanging of gifts—Magnús gave half of his realm and, in return, received half of Harald's gold. It was Magnús who initiated the gift exchange because he was, after all, the king of Norway and the superior in his relationship with Harald. The opposite would have been a clear break with custom. The term "friendship" was not used here to describe the relationship between the two kings. It is unnecessary; the extensive gift giving makes it clear. At the feast Harald also gave Steigar-Thórir Thórdarson good gifts:

> a bowl made of birch encircled by a silver ring and a silver strap across it, both gilt; and it was full to the top with money of pure silver. There were also two gold rings which weighed a total of a mark. The king also gave Steigar-Thórir his cloak, made of dark purple with white fur, and he promised him great honor and his friendship.[18]

There is little doubt the costly gifts Steigar-Thórir received were good publicity for the king and increased expectations of him.

Kings in Norway and chieftains in Iceland did not use objects alone to become popular, but also made use of good marriages. After his victory over King Magnús in the battle of Fimreite in Sogn in 1184, King Sverrir married many of his men to the widows of his fallen adversaries.[19] This was a good tactic for the king, who could have confiscated all their property. By arranging these marriages, he not only secured wealth for his men but he also showed willingness for reconciliation. None of the widows had to leave their farms, and they and their families retained their position in society. With the limited resources in both Norway and Iceland, a good marriage was often the only possibility to gain wealth and a good social position. It was important for the kings and Icelandic chieftains to be able to influence or control the marriage market among the higher social ranks; marriage to either a rich widow or a girl who was sole heir to a large fortune was a valuable prospect. In this way, the kings and chieftains could acquire needed support.

As discussed in chapter 2, which focuses on the Icelandic chieftains, the gift-giving process had very clear rules about who was able to take the initiative in giving gifts and thereby establish friendships. Only people in the superior social position could take the first step. In a narrative about Harald Fairhair, it states that he would not receive a gift from Ásgrím Úlfsson, because he wanted to rule alone.[20] The king had difficulty accepting gifts from chieftains and householders. If he did so, he would then lose control over recruitment to his network, and others could begin to pull him into their own political plans against his will.

In *Króka-Refs saga*, one of the Icelandic Family Sagas, we find one of the few stories where a householder starts the gift-giving process with a king. It relates that Bárd presented King Harald Hardrule with many good objects from one of the most distinguished men in Greenland, Gunnar. Included among the gifts was a board game, an object worthy of giving to a king—there were clear rules about which objects one could use for such gifts to a king (*konungsgjöf*), the most usual being ship sails, horses, and falcons.[21] Bárd said Gunnar did not want to be paid for the board game, but would rather have the king's friendship. The king accepted the gift. Bárd continued to give the king gifts from Gunnar throughout the winter. Eventually Harald became suspicious and wondered if something other than a desire for his friendship lay behind the gifts. Bárd answered what Gunnar wanted was the king's friendship and advice in a conflict in Greenland.[22] Even though the historical accuracy of the story in *Króka-Refs saga* is extremely doubtful, it shows us that a gift required a countergift, even for the king. In this instance, it was his advice. *Heimskringla* stresses, as a rule, that the king was the wisest of all men and therefore should be able to find good solutions for his friends.[23]

Claimants to the throne could enter into agreements about establishing friendship if they came to power. The Icelandic chieftain Thórir Skeggjason had established a good relationship with Ólaf Haraldsson soon after he arrived in Norway. After a short stay there, Thórir returned to Iceland. When he learned that Ólaf had become king, he wanted to confirm Ólaf's promise of friendship and so sent his two sons to Norway in the hope they would become the king's liege men.[24] In this instance, the sons can almost be regarded as a gift from Thórir to the king. At the same time, the journey was a part of the boys' upbringing. For them, and for other ambitious Icelanders, it was important to gain honor abroad and eventually come home to Iceland with the king's friendship. This would increase their esteem in the eyes of Icelandic society.

Another way to become the king's friend was to support him in battle. Eyvind úrarhorn fought with his men for Ólaf Haraldsson in the battle of Nesjar on Palm Sunday, 25 March 1016. When the two men parted company after the battle, the king promised Eyvind his friendship, and Eyvind assured the king in return he would support him "however he wished." The next winter, Eyvind was with the king at his Christmas feast, and the king gave Eyvind *góðar gjafar* (good gifts).[25] Such rewards were an important incentive for leaders like Eyvind to fight for the king. These men secured wealth for themselves with which they could expand their own positions of power, and, equally important, they had the king's support in their conflicts in Norway.

Did all the kings' friends receive gifts from him? In the saga about Harald Hardrule, we read that he was inordinately greedy of power and of valuable possessions and that he was "very generous with those of his friends that he thought much of."[26] This cannot be interpreted to mean that the king's friends did not receive gifts. Rather, all of them did receive gifts, but his closest friends received the finest gifts. Harald, like all other kings, must have valued his friends differently, from those who stood closest to him and with whom he probably consulted in difficult cases, to those whom he did not have any strong personal ties with.

Promises of friendship were important tools in the struggle for power in the country and could be used to expose potential enemies. In the saga about King Magnús Erlingsson (1161–84), we are told about the Danish pilgrims who came to Nidaros, where the relics of Saint Ólaf Haraldsson were kept, and met with many of the Trøndelag chieftains. The pilgrims informed the chieftains they were really envoys from King Valdimar of Denmark, and he had sent them to ask the men of Trøndelag for their friendship. If they would receive him should he come to the country, he promised to give them both power and money. To prove their case, the envoys presented the letter and seal from Valdimar, and then they asked the men of Trøndelag to send a letter in return with their seal on it—which they did. Some months later, the men of Trøndelag got an unexpected visit from Erling skakki, the most powerful man in the country and King Magnús's father. He called an assembly where he accused the men of Trøndelag of

> treason against the king and himself. . . . [The men of Trøndelag] an-
> swered by denying the accusation. Then Erlingur's chaplain stood up
> and held up many letters and seals, and asked if they recognized their
> seals there on the letters they had sent to the Danish king in the spring.
> The Danish men who had travelled with the letter in the winter were
> also with Erlingur, who had put them up to it. They then told everyone
> the very words which each one of them [the Trøndelag chieftains] had
> said. . . . There was then no way out other than to allow Erlingur self-
> judgment for the entire case. He immediately took a great many goods
> from many men, but all those who were killed as a part of the judgment
> should not been compensated for. And then he travelled south again to
> Bergen.[27]

It can safely be said that Erling's strategy was cunning. He not only lured his greatest opponents in Trøndelag out into the open and confiscated a large part of their property, but he also created great uncertainty among them. Whom could they trust?

We have seen that in Iceland there was a group of householders who were friends with two chieftains (*beggja vinir*) and had to mediate in potential conflicts between them. In Norway, there were a number of chieftains who were friends with two kings at once while remaining friends with other chieftains. In disputes between their friends, either between kings or between kings and chieftains, these chieftains had to mediate.[28] We can see this clearly in the conflict between Harald Hardrule and Einar Thambarskelfir

Eindridason—the most powerful chieftain in Trøndelag. A thief, who earlier had been Einar's man, was taken in Nidaros. The king was at the meeting where the thief's case was to be heard, and, according to *Heimskringla*, Einar was worried about the king punishing the man. Einar thus collected his followers and freed the thief. As a result of his actions, Einar had insulted the king. Those who were friends with both the king and Einar stepped in and tried to reconcile them. The king agreed to meet Einar at the palace, but against all convention he let his men kill Einar and his son.[29]

The kings' friend groups, like those of the chieftains in Iceland, were not homogenous; what held them together was friendship with the king. We can assume that among the kings' friends, clashes were often great, and it was important for the king to solve potential disputes between his friends; otherwise, he risked alienating one party.[30]

In the introduction to this chapter, we discussed the aristocracy's dependence on the crown's resources. This tendency became stronger throughout the twelfth century. In 1130, Sigurd the Crusader died. His son, Magnús, and the Irish-born Harald Gille became joint kings of the country. They reigned together for four years, but after that they began to fight for power. This conflict gave rise to a period of strife lasting a hundred years, which was later known as the civil war period in Norwegian history. This ended with Skúli Bárdarson's rebellion against King Hákon Hákonarson in 1239 and his defeat in 1240.

The hard fighting in the civil wars, especially in the period c. 1177–1208, testifies to an aristocracy in a resource crisis. A financial profit was necessary for the aristocracy to maintain their lifestyle and to mark the social differences that set them apart from the householders. The crisis was due to several different factors: the subsiding of the Viking raids after the middle of the eleventh century, the church coming to own a large portion of the land in the country, and the crown securing a large landed estate, through confiscation. In a way, the civil wars were a solution to the resource crisis. They led to a reduction in the number of aristocrats while the aristocracy closed ranks around the crown. A strong king would be able to provide lucrative offices and bestowment of fiefs from the royal property. The aristocracy's landed wealth was not very large. Thus they were dependent on royal estates to be able to maintain their position in society, and if the aristocracy wanted to prevent others from gaining these properties during the king's reign, they had to constantly ingratiate themselves with the king.[31] It was therefore important for rebels to ensure that their candidates became king because only then could they gain access to the kingdom's resources. To crown a claimant king was seen along the same lines as giving a gift. Friendship was established between the giver and the receiver, and it was important for the king to give a countergift to his friends (e.g., a royal office) and thereby provide them access to the kingdom's wealth.

In 1184, a decisive battle took place between the kings Magnús Erlingsson and Sverrir Sigurdarson at Fimreite in Sogn. In many ways, this battle marked a turning point in the unification of the country. A large part of the old aristocracy, who supported Magnús Erlingsson, was wiped out and replaced by King Sverrir's supporters. As a rule, the latter had either a weak or no local power base and were therefore more loyal to the crown than the old aristocracy had been. In addition, the new aristocracy had less landed wealth than the old; thus they were dependent on the king to an even greater degree for enfeoffment and positions within the royal administration.[32]

The sagas place a great deal of emphasis on the generosity and wealth of kings and chieftains. Gifts and feasts were used to create or renew ties of friendship, and it was through friendship that secular leaders built up their power base. Strong obligations of loyalty were associated with friendship; therefore, it was the only means secular leaders had to ensure support. If the recipient could not afford to give a gift in return, the gift was to be paid for by rendering services; otherwise it could be taken back, and it was the service or a countergift that ensured the right to own or dispose of the gift. Because of the strong obligation to reciprocate, gifts were a good instrument by which secular leaders could bind supporters to themselves. Laxdæla saga narrates that after a swimming contest with Kjartan Óláfsson, King Ólaf Tryggvason gave him a cloak. Kjartan's men were not happy that he had accepted the gift and thought he had "put himself too much under the king's power."[33]

In both Norway and Iceland, powerful secular leaders were described as vinsælir; that is, a person rich in friends. Generous leaders achieved great honor and consequently more individuals wished to become their friends. The generosity of the kings, earls, and chieftains was usually expressed in the distribution of wealth downwards in society; however, the kings usually gave gifts to chieftains in Norway, whereas the earls and chieftains gave gifts to householders. The gift-giving process could not stop: if the secular leaders did not continue to arrange feasts and give gifts, their friends would start looking for other, more generous leaders. The powerbase was therefore highly unstable and boiled down to the economy of the leaders. "Reciprocity" was a key word in the relationship between the king and his friends. In the saga about Harald Hardrule, we hear that, in return for vægð ok vináttu (grace and friendship), one could gain the king's traust ok trúnað (defense and protection).[34] The first expression implies that one should accept the king's superior position, be faithful, support him in his fight, and perform tasks on his behalf. In return, the king would protect his friends and be loyal to them. Neglecting to perform this duty meant the king could not expect his friends' support at a later point.

When discussing friendship in Norway and Iceland, it is important to stress the differences between the kings and the chieftains. When comparing the description of the chieftains with portrayals of the kings, one clear difference emerges: the kings, who were at top of the social hierarchy in the Old Norse society, are not only depicted with more personal abilities than other secular leaders but also their virtues are more extravagant than other rulers and are depicted in greater detail. The kings are bigger and stronger, more beautiful, wiser, more just/righteous, more generous, and more victorious than other rulers. Icelandic chieftains are usually portrayed with only two-thirds of the above-mentioned qualities. It is thus the number of personal abilities and the qualities linked to those virtues that separate leaders in the Old Norse society.[35]

It was also crucial for the king to secure complete control over the fleet (*leiðangr*) in the twelfth and thirteenth centuries. Although professional warriors played an important role for the secular leaders, whether they were kings, earls, or chieftains, it was the householders who constituted the greatest part of their armies. The military significance of the householders can be seen particularly well with the *leiðangr* in Norway. The *leiðangr* was a naval organization under the leadership of the king. The householders provided the ships, crew, and weapons and bore the cost. The *leiðangr* could be used both to defend and to attack, within the kingdom as well as abroad. It was probably first used in western Norway around the middle of the tenth century. In the beginning, it was the local chieftains who, by all accounts, were in charge of the organization. For the most part, they took with them their own men, but after their local positions of power weakened, the householders and the crown took over the organization. It took a while for the *leiðangr* organization to become permanently established, and it probably was not until the twelfth and thirteenth centuries that a nationwide *leiðangr* organization became a reality under the leadership of the king.[36]

The Retainer: King's Friend?

As a Christmas gift King Ólaf Haraldsson gave Brynjólf a *gullbúit sverð* (gold-inlaid sword) and the *hǫfuðbær* (manor) Vetteland. Brynjólf composed a stanza about the gifts, the end of which has been preserved: "The king gave me / a blade and Vetteland." Afterward, Ólaf named Brynjólf a royal vassal, and he was "always among the king's best friends."[37] Brynjólf first received the sword, then the farm, and in the end was made a royal vassal, each gift being an increasing honor. The presentation of the sword symbolized that Ólaf was the superior in the friendship. Vetteland was, by all accounts, a farm that was part of the royal demesne lands, so Brynjólf could only live there as long as Ólaf wished it or as long as Ólaf was alive.[38] This permission to live at Vetteland also signaled the relation of power between the giver and the receiver. As mentioned previously, those who accepted land entered a service relationship as a subordinate of the giver as long as both lived.[39] Being made a *lendr maðr* was a great demonstration of honor on the king's part toward Brynjólf. At the same time, it very clearly showed who was superior in power between the two men. The story emphasizes the power dynamic between Ólaf and Brynjólf three times with the gifts before finally stressing the friendship between the two men. In this relationship there was no doubt about who gave the orders and who carried them out.

Royal vassals were usually of high birth and in many instances had an inherited position of local power. Brynjólf is a good example; he came from a distinguished family and acted as a leader of the householders when Ólaf wanted to become king over Ranrike. Brynjólf supported the king's case. After Ólaf was accepted as king, Brynjólf was invited to the king's feast, and *Heimskringla* tells us that they spoke for a long time during the feast in private—perhaps the saga author is indicating that they negotiated the content of their friendship pact during this meeting.[40] A short time later, Brynjólf was made a royal vassal, and as such he could be used as Ólaf's agent. Such a mixture of roles was natural for the king and the local aristocracy.

However, Brynjólf was not only Ólaf's friend; he was also a part of his *hirð* and thus had to obey the laws of the *hirð*. We do not know when the first *hirð* laws were introduced, but it could have been as early as the tenth or eleventh century. In the preserved Hirðskrá from about 1277, we find rules for the *hirð* men. For example, they could not leave the country without the king's consent. If they did, they were traitors and outlaws, and their property was forfeit.[41] The king's *hirð* was the focal point of Old Norse society, and all men with ambition joined.[42] The greatest feasts occurred where the king and his *hirð* were staying; the king owned many large estates all over the country and residences in and close to the cities and traveled between these with his *hirð*. The king's household without a doubt was the largest in the country and also the largest center of consumption. The goal of the banquets was not only to entertain the *hirð*, but also to produce symbolic capital that could be converted into political power. These feasts, best labeled as entrepreneurial or patron-role feasts, made it possible for the king to influence the *hirð* to make certain decisions or take actions in accordance with his wishes. These feasts thus created a reciprocal relationship and a social hierarchy.[43]

The political changes that occurred from about 900 until the end of the thirteenth century changed the mentality of the *hirð*: it became more "civilized." In the tenth and eleventh centuries, the focus was on war, warlike activities, and drinking. Later in the thirteenth century this was replaced with "discipline and hierarchy" and focus on courtly behavior.[44] The king, through the creation of the ideal courtly ruler, gained status not only from power and strength in war but also from his refinement.

The *hirð* was the most important tool for the crown's exercise of power in the period c. 900–1300. It was divided into two parts: those men dining at the king's table, and those living on their farms. After having served the king for a period, the *hirð* men were allowed to travel back to their farms. At that time, they were often given one or more demesne farms from the king, and they could be used as his representative agents. The emergence of the king's system of governance was also linked to the development of the *hirð*. In about 900, we hear of the *merkismaðr* (standard bearer), who was to look after the king's banner in war. In times of peace, the *merkismaðr* was probably an adviser. The king's *stallari* (marshal) is mentioned in the sources that describe the period around the year 1000. He was probably, like the *merkismaðr*, also someone who gave advice, and the *hirð*'s spokesman to the king. Early in the eleventh century, the *hirð* was divided into *hirð* men and *gestir* (guests). The difference between these groups was that the *hirð* men usually came from good families and were used for peaceful missions in times of peace, whereas the *gestir* were of low rank and were used as a kind of police force.

From the start, kings as we have seen had personal advisers around them. Beginning about the year 1260, the king's council took on a more formal quality. Select members of the secular aristocracy, bishops, and some officials sat on it. The daily central administration of the country lay with the king and a small circle of courtiers, primarily the *stallari*, the *merkismaðr*, the *féhirðir* (royal treasurer), and the *kannslari* (chancellor). The last of these men and his clerk were probably the most important officials in about 1250, with responsibilities that included the issuing of letters and looking after the realm's archive. The most important local link between the king's central administration and local communities was the *sýslumaðr* (district governor). The position of *sýslumaðr* emerged in the second half of the twelfth century. When a king subjugated a part of the country, he appointed a *sýslumaðr* to be in charge of the area. The *sýslumenn* (district governors) always had a military background and belonged to the highest rank in the *hirð*, and, as a rule, they had responsibility for a group of warriors. After the end of the civil wars, the *sýslumenn* became

key people in the local administration, with a particular responsibility for pros-
ecuting and carrying out sentences.

In Europe the oath of allegiance (*juramentum fidelitatis*) was used to secure
loyalty and to confirm legal agreements and duties of a secular and ecclesiastical nature.[45] The duty to keep the oath was binding; nobody had any wish
to be an oath breaker. Furthermore, the punishment for breaking an oath was
harsh, both in ecclesiastical and secular law. In Norway, the use of the oath of
allegiance is demonstrated most clearly in the provisions in Hirðskrá concerning who had the right to demand the oath of allegiance. Hirðskrá states
that the householders in the country and the *hirð* men should take an oath of
loyalty to the king—apart from the king, only dukes and earls could claim an
oath of loyalty. "Now, whereas all the people of the country owe a great deal
of allegiance to the crown, this applies to an even greater extent to those of
us who are his liegemen and who are thus chosen from among all the people
to guard the king and serve him personally . . . serve him with complete and
unbroken loyalty."[46] There are different oaths for the different members of
the *hirð*: including the *hertogi* (duke), the *jarl* (earl), *lendr maðr*, *kannslari*, and
gestir. The *hertogi* and the *jarl* should lay their hand on reliquaries and say: "I
shall be loyal and faithful to my lord N, king of Norway, both secretly and in
the open . . . I will show him all the obedience which a good duke or earl owes
a good king."[47]

But were the king's *hirð* men also his friends? When King Ingi Bárdarson
lay on his deathbed in 1217, his "friends and *hirð*" spoke together.[48] This might
be said to indicate that the *hirð* men were not the king's friends. Rather, this
probably emphasizes that not all of the king's friends were his *hirð* men; for
example, the archbishop and the bishops, whom we will discuss later. We can
assume that all the king's advisers and men in central positions in his administration were also his friends. This is supported by an undated amendment
of King Eirík Magnússon (1280–99) and Duke Hákon Magnússon (king from
1299–1319), which mentions the *sýslumenn* and the *handgengnir menn* (vassals)
as their friends.[49] There is good reason to assume that the districts given to
the *sýslumenn* by the king and the duke were seen as "gifts" that they could
manage for as long as the king wished it.

Hirðskrá tells us that, "according to advice from his friends," the king should
choose two from among his *skutilsveinar* (table servants) to become a *dróttseti*
(master of the royal household) and a *skjenkari* (cupbearer) "who seem most
suitable, both with respect to their lineage and their conduct."[50] Unfortunately,
we do not get to find out who these friends are, but Hirðskrá adds that, in
"most countries," it is the most powerful noblemen who choose men for these
tasks. Thus we can assume that these advice-giving "friends" were high-born

hirð men. There is much to suggest, therefore, that the king established friend-ships with the most central men in his administration. It can thus be asserted that the most central actors in the king's government had a double duty of loyalty to the king—duty through friendship and duty through the oath of allegiance—and that relations of friendship were used to tie the aristocracy even more tightly to the crown. But in the relationships between the king and the householders, the oath of allegiance took precedence over friendship, de-spite the earlier necessity of friendship with the householders on the king's part. The paragraph in Gulating's law about the king being "our friend and we his" was not repeated in Landslög (Norwegian National Law) in 1274. In line with a new ideology that emerged at the end of the twelfth century and in the first half of the thirteenth, the king now got his power from God. In *Konungs skuggsiá* (*The King's Mirror*) from the middle of the thirteenth century, we read that

> the king is exalted and highly revered on earth, and all yield to him as they do to God, because the king is a sign of God's own worth. For he bears God's own name and sits in the highest seat of judgment on the earth, and even when a man honors the king for the sake of the name which he has from God, it must be regarded as the man honoring God.[51]

In his superior position, the king could now require obedience and loyalty from his subjects. The loyalty that the king could demand can be characterized as an absolute loyalty, in opposition to the relative or the rational.[52] The differ-ence between these two forms lies in the power relationship. The first type builds on an understanding of a clear hierarchy structure with the king as so-ciety's sovereign leader who can demand loyalty from his subjects, at least in theory. The second form of loyalty is more closely linked to reciprocity, for example, between chieftains and householders. Both parties must show their loyalty to each other.

Friendship and Foreign Policy

Friendship between kings was often established in order to create alliances against common enemies. According to *Heimskringla*, Cnut the Great wanted to secure control over Norway. Therefore, he sent men to King Önund Ólafsson of Sweden with "great gifts and promises of friendship." The envoys told him that he did not need to interfere in the struggle between Cnut and Ólaf Haraldsson. The saga also tells us Önund was not particularly enthusiastic about the visit, "and the envoys thought they noticed that King Önund was most disposed to establish friendship with King Ólaf. They travelled back and told King Cnut how things had gone with the errand, and they said furthermore that he should not expect any friendship from King Önund."[53] A short time later, Önund and Ólaf met at Konghelle. The first thing they did at this meeting was to give each other promises of friendship. Then they spoke together privately. And when they parted, they exchanged gifts and left the meeting as friends.[54]

Önund did not want to establish friendship with Cnut likely because he would then have to accept being the subordinate party. This would have resulted in a loss of honor: a king could not serve another king. It was therefore better in such circumstances to enter into a pact with another king and ally himself with him. Together Önund and Ólaf might stop Cnut's expansion. This is a pattern we often find in Scandinavian history. When one of the kings became too powerful, usually the Danish, the two other kings often established an alliance in an attempt to create a balance of power in Scandinavia.

This symbolism linked to gift giving and the difficulty of saying no to a gift regardless of the recipient enabled some political players to take advantage of the process. King Æthelstan of England was said to have sent a man to Harald Fairhair. This man went to the king with a sword "adorned with a gold hilt and handle, and the whole sheath was also adorned with gold and silver and inlaid with precious stones." The envoy held the hilt out to the king and said, "Here is a sword, which King Æthelstan said you should have." The king took it by the hilt, at which point the envoy said, "Now you have taken the sword as our king wished, and now you will be his subject, since you accepted his sword."[55] In order to balance things out, Harald sent his envoy to Æthelstan. The envoy tricked Æthelstan into fostering King Harald's son, Hákon. Snorri adds this information: "For people used to say that one who fosters another's child is beneath the foster child's parent in rank."[56] There is no reason to place too much weight on the veracity of these stories. Nevertheless, they demonstrate the games that might accompany the establishment and maintenance of friendship and how difficult it was to say no to a gift.

Kings, like chieftains, arranged marriages for their children and family members. The purpose was to establish friendships with secular leaders. In Norway, we can trace a clear change in the marriage strategies of the kings. The increasing consolidation of power around the king, especially in the second half of thirteenth century, and a new ideology linked with his office, led to the king being elevated in relation to the rest of society. This also applied to his family. The king ceased to marry his children and closest kin with the Norwegian chieftains. Now, they could only marry members of other royal families.[57]

Marriage alliances were entered into not only to expand and ensure positions of power, but also to create peace between political enemies. In many instances, however, the conflicts continued, and this created problems, in particular for the women. Should they support their husbands or their own kin? Margrét Skúladóttir's situation is probably the most famous example of this kind of conflict of loyalty. In 1217, the thirteen-year-old Hákon Hákonarson was proclaimed king of Norway. However, it was Skúli Bárdarson who was the real ruler of the kingdom. In fact, he had also been one of the candidates for the throne. Because Hákon was so young, Skúli took over ruling the country. To ensure friendship between the king and Skúli, Skúli's daughter Margrét was betrothed to Hákon in 1219. This was to ensure that the earl loved the king as a son, and in 1225 Margrét and Hákon were married.[58] While Hákon was young, Skúli led the struggle against the different groups of rebels who fought against Hákon for power in the country. After a while, Hákon began to act more and more on his own, and in the 1230s, the relationship between Hákon and Skúli developed into open conflict. In 1239, Skúli allowed himself to be proclaimed king at Øyratinget in Nidaros and started a rebellion against Hákon. The rebellion was crushed, and in 1240 Skúli was killed by Hákon's men. The friendship between Hákon and Skúli had deteriorated into real enmity. We do not know what Margrét thought about the conflict between her husband and her father, but she probably supported her husband. Before Skúli began his rebellion, Hákon and Margrét had two sons, and if Skúli's plans had ended with Hákon's death, it would likely have meant that neither of her sons would have become king, and in the worse-case scenario, they could have been killed.

It is well established that kings' daughters were important tools in the power game; good examples include the daughters of King Harald Gille (1130–36)—Brigida, Maria, and Margrét. Brigida was first married to the Swedish king Ingi Hallsteinsson, then to Earl Karl Sónason, and later to the Swedish king Magnús. "Finally, she married the earl Birgir Brosa. . . . Maria was the name of another daughter of Harald Gille; she married Símon skálpur. . . . Margrét was the third daughter of Harald Gille; she was married to Jón Hallkjellsson, brother of Símon."[59] Brigida was married four times in all, in each case to a Swedish man. She was married so often because she lost her first three husbands after a short marriage. Daughters of rulers, like Brigida and her sisters, were important objects in the marriage market and were actively used by their fathers and guardians to establish friendships with desirable political partners. It is interesting to note that Brigida, unlike her sisters, was married to foreign rulers. This may indicate that she was viewed as the best of the sisters, or simply that she was liked the most. Parents and guardians treated their children differently, which could have had implications for whom they were married to.

Some women from the highest ranks could establish friendships without necessarily heading their own household. One of these was Ástríd, Saint Ólaf's widow. Her stepson Magnús Óláfsson sought her out in Sweden to seek her support. At that point, she called a meeting, at which she spoke and promised her friendship to all the men who helped Magnús in his fight for control over Norway.[60] Brigida Haraldsdóttir promised her friendship, together with her husband Birgir Brosa, to the royal heir, Eystein Eysteinsson Meyla.[61] It is difficult to explain how these women were able to establish friendships. It could be due to their wealth and their personal characteristics. Nonetheless, it must be emphasized that we rarely hear about such women.

The influential householder Ólaf from Store-Dal in Åmord had two children, a son Hákon and a daughter Borghild. Borghild was considered beautiful, wise, and knowledgeable. Ólaf and his family were in Sarpsborg at the same time as King Eystein Magnússon (1103–23). Borghild was constantly talking to the king, and people began to murmur about their friendship. After Ólaf and his family left the town, Borghild heard the slanderous rumors about her friendship with the king. At that point, she returned to Sarpsborg and she underwent the ordeal. This meant that she had to either hold or walk across red-hot iron. Three days later the wound would be examined, and if it had healed like a normal wound, God's judgment would show that she had done nothing improper. This was the case in this ordeal. When Eystein's brother, King Sigurd the Crusader, heard this, he went with all speed to Ólaf in Store-Dal and took Borghild as his concubine. Their son was King Magnús the Blind.[62]

It is problematic to interpret these stories. The alleged rumors about the friendship between King Eystein and Borghild and their conversations were surely about her being the king's lover. Nevertheless, after Borghild underwent the ordeal and passed it, Sigurd came to Store-Dal and took Borghild as his concubine. This meant that Borghild's father and the king entered into an agreement about this relationship, and in contrast to wives, concubines did not bring dowries with them to the relationship or receive a bride price.

The kings' relations of friendship were a crucial aspect of foreign policy throughout the period between about 900 and 1300.[63] The best example of this is with Hákon Hákonarson. In his saga, we are told that he had many friends abroad, including the German emperor Frederick II (1220–50).[64] Furthermore, we are told the emperor sent men to Norway with gifts for King Hákon and for Earl Skúli. Hákon sent back gifts that were difficult for the emperor to get. It is tempting in this context to imagine that the gifts which the emperor received were the white falcons from Greenland. These birds were highly sought after throughout all of Europe and were used by secular and ecclesiastical leaders in Norway to establish friendships with foreign princes. In other words, the Norwegian king had at his disposal an important resource which few other kings had. The kings who received these falcons could pass them on to high-ranking secular leaders to secure their support.[65] The gift exchange between King Hákon and the emperor Frederick was extensive and took place over a long period. Hákon even had a man whose only job was to carry gifts to and from the emperor. This gift exchange resulted in a "great friendship" developing between Hákon and Frederick.[66] For the king and the emperor, this friendship was important. It increased their prestige and gained each of them supporters in the struggle for political power in northern Europe, while neutralizing their possible enemies. Yet, as in the story about Harald Hardrule and the Greenlander Gunnar in *Króka-Refs saga*, these two good friends never actually met each other. With friendships between kings, this was not unusual.[67]

An interesting aspect of King Hákon Hákonarson's foreign policy was that he was said to have established friendship with the trading organization of Lübeck.[68] So far, we have seen that friendship concerned relations between individuals. Was it possible to establish a friendship with an organization? Hardly. In this instance, friendship was established between the king and the men administrating Lübeck. Most agreements in the Middle Ages were made between individuals and not institutions.

In the fight for control over the seas around northern Scotland, King Alexander III of Scotland gave Jón of the Hebrides a promise of friendship and protection if he stopped supporting King Hákon Hákonarson. Jón, however, wanted to honor his oath to Hákon and therefore did not change sides.[69] King Hákon and Earl Birgir of Sweden agreed to a peace between them and strengthened the agreement through the betrothal of Hákon's son Hákon to Birgir's daughter.[70] The friendship between Hákon and Birgir grew stronger after a while, and this was an important reason for the good relationship between Norway and Sweden in this period.[71] Additionally, King Hákon Hákonarson and the Danish king Kristoffer I (1252–59) held a meeting of reconciliation in Copenhagen in 1257. At this meeting, they sealed their friendship with the condition that they should support each other if the need arose. Then they exchanged gifts, and Kristoffer was able to choose between the large Mariasuden ship or three other ships.[72] For the author of the saga about Hákon, it was important to emphasize these friendships that underlined the king's international status for posterity.

The important role friendship played in foreign politics can be clearly seen in how the Norwegian kings secured control over Jämtland and Iceland. According to *Heimskringla*, King Eystein

sent a message to the wisest and most powerful men in Jämtland and invited them to his court. He welcomed all who came with great affection, and when they departed he gave them friendship gifts; and thus led them into friendship with himself. Many of them got into the habit of travelling to the king and receiving gifts from him, and he sent gifts to many men because they could not come, he entered into full friendship with all those who ruled the country. Later, he spoke to them and said that the people of Jämtland had done wrong when they turned away from the Norwegian kings in obedience or in tributary gifts (*skattgjǫfum*). He pointed out that the people of Jämtland had been subjugated by King Hákon, foster son of King Æthelstan, and then they were ruled for a long time by the Norwegian kings. He also mentioned how many essential things they could obtain from Norway, or how troublesome it was for them to look to the Swedish king for the things they needed. His speeches made such an impression that the men of Jämtland offered to yield their alliances to King Eystein. First, the leading men took oaths of allegiance for the whole people. Then, they went to King Eystein and swore the country over to him, and it has remained like this ever since. King Eystein won Jämtland with wisdom and not by force as some of his ancestors has done.[73]

Hákon Hákonarson used a similar tactic when he subjugated Iceland.[74] A bloody conflict emerged between the Icelandic chieftain family, the Oddaverjar, and Norwegian merchants in 1215. This quickly developed into a trade war, and in 1219 no ships came to Iceland from Norway. In the summer of 1220, Earl Skúli prepared a military expedition to Iceland. Snorri Sturluson who was in Norway at the time, managed to persuade the earl and the king to solve the conflict by peaceful means. Snorri suggested that he himself go to Iceland to obtain peace for the Norwegian merchants and to get Iceland to recognize the king as overlord. He was to do this by establishing friendships with the Icelandic chieftains. Before Snorri left Norway, he became the king's retainer, and the earl gave him great gifts.[75] As discussed previously, Snorri tried to establish friendships with the most important chieftains in Iceland during the 1220s. He showed less interest, however, in getting the country to accept the Norwegian king as overlord. This led to King Hákon establishing a friendship with Sturla Sighvatsson and setting him the task of securing control over Iceland. Sturla failed and died in 1238 during the largest battle in Iceland's history.[76]

From about 1240, the Icelandic chieftains began to present or give their chieftaincies to the king and then receive them back from him. Through this practice, friendships were established between the king and these chieftains. These relationships strengthened the chieftains' positions in Iceland, while increasing King Hákon's influence over the power struggles in the country. Around 1250, he owned or had secured control over all the chieftaincies in three of the country's four quarters.[77] By this time, there was no doubt about who was the most powerful actor in Icelandic politics, and it was only a question of time before the country became a part of the Norwegian realm. In 1247 Thórd kakali Sighvatsson, brother of Sturla Sighvatsson, was sent to Iceland with Bishop Heinrek, and they were instructed that "they should try to persuade the people to accept Hákon as their king and such *skattgiafir* (tribute gifts) as they agreed upon."[78] Thórd's first action after coming to Iceland was to subjugate Snorri Sturluson's domain in Borgarfjörður. Then he conquered the entire western and northern quarters without meeting any opposition. The king, however, was not satisfied with the way Thórd was going about things. He thought Thórd was trying to achieve personal control of the country. He therefore summoned Thórd to Norway in 1249. As a royal retainer, Thórd was obliged to obey the summons.

It was Gissur Thorvaldsson who finally managed to get the Icelanders to pay tax. He became the earl of Iceland in 1258, and as a result received a number of large gifts from the king.[79] We can thus say the king established friendship with the earl. However, the king was not convinced of Gissur's loyalty. So he sent trusted men to Iceland to examine whether Gissur was fulfilling his mission.[80] The king's doubt was justified. Gissur showed more interest in advancing his own political agenda than the king's. In the end, however, the king managed to force Gissur to obey his orders and get the Icelanders to take an oath of loyalty to King Hákon as their overlord.

In the years 1262, 1263, and 1264, Icelanders were subjugated to the kings of Norway, and the so-called Gizurarsáttmáli was made. *Hákonar saga Hákonarsonar* recounts that the terms of the submission in 1262 were written down in a document (*bréf*).[81] We do not know whether Icelandic leaders in 1263 and 1264 agreed to the same terms as those attending the Althing did in 1262, but we can assume so. It is highly unlikely that there were different terms for the subjugation of the different parts of the country. Gizurarsáttmáli and the covenant from 1302, which was made in connection with the succession of King Hákon Magnússon (1299–1319) and contains many of the same elements as Gizurarsáttmáli, are highly problematic documents because the earliest manuscripts date to the fifteenth century.[82] The problem faced by scholars when they have tried to date these documents is that some provisions are anachronistic if they are dated to 1262, while others appear equally so if they are dated later to the beginning of the fourteenth century.[83] It has therefore been suggested by Patricia P. Boulhosa that the documents containing the Gizurarsáttmáli could potentially be "fabrications" constructed by Icelanders in the fifteenth century because they were "anxious to carry on trading freely with whomever they wished." She also claims

> that these texts were created so that Icelanders could tell the history of their submission to the Norwegian crown in the thirteenth century, which would enable them to negotiate with the Norwegian crown in the fifteenth century. Rather than being intentionally produced as fake documents, however, it seems that these texts reflect the need to record something which was either believed to be true, or should have been true, about the country's past.[84]

It is undeniable that there are variations between the different manuscripts of the covenants from 1262–64 and 1302, but these are not substantial.[85] The paragraphs that most scholars usually identify as dating from 1262–64 reflect the political situation in Iceland in the 1260s. Randi Wærdahl, in her discussion about this problem, stresses that most of the provisions from Gizurarsáttmáli can be traced back to 1262. Although the actual document of the agreement is lost, we can be reasonably sure that we know the content and that it provided a judicial foundation for the king's lordship in Iceland.[86] This is also confirmed by a letter from the Icelanders to King Magnús Eriksson (1319–55/74) dating from 1319, where they clearly state that there was no question of accepting the king unless he acceded to their demands and gave guarantees.[87] It is therefore likely that the following eight paragraphs that recur in most manuscripts of Gizurarsáttmáli was the agreement reached by Hallvard gullsko and the Icelanders in 1262:[88]

1. The people of Iceland agree to pay tax of "twenty ells," or the price of one sheep, for each householder paying attendance dues (*þingfararkaupsbœndr*).
2. In return, the king should let the Icelanders "enjoy peace and the Icelandic laws."
3. The king should guarantee a minimum number of ships sailing to Iceland *per annum*.

4. Inheritance that "falls to Icelanders in Norway is to be given to them, however long it may remain due, as soon as the rightful heirs, or their legal representatives, present themselves to claim it."
5. The land-dues (*landaurar*) in Norway are to be abolished.
6. Icelanders in Norway should have rights as advantageous as those they previously had enjoyed there.
7. Icelanders will accept the earl as their overlord as long as he is faithful to the king and keeps peace with them.
8. "We and our descendants shall keep faith with you [the king] so long as you and your descendants keep this covenant, but we shall be free of all obligations if, in the opinion of the best men, it is broken."[89]

The paragraphs in Gizurarsáttmáli can be interpreted as part of a *skattgjöf* process whose aim was to establish friendship and to ensure loyalty between Icelanders and the kings of Norway. The term *skattgjöf* derives from the Old Norse words *skattr* (scat, tribute) and *gjöf* (gift). According to the Oxford English Dictionary, "scat" means a tribute, "with reference to countries under Scandinavian rule." The same dictionary defines "tribute" as a "tax or impost paid by one prince or state to another in acknowledgement of submission or as the price of peace, security, and protection; rent or homage paid in money or an equivalent by a subject to his sovereign or a vassal to his lord."[90] The level of reciprocity between the parties paying and receiving tributes therefore depends on the power relations between them. In contrast to a scat, or tribute, a gift always required a countergift or service. However, in this instance, *skattgjöf* can be interpreted as the scat being paid as a gift in order to establish friendship and mutual ties of loyalty between the giver and the receiver. To confirm the friendship, the receiver, here the Norwegian king, had to give a countergift.

If we interpret the paragraphs in Gizurarsáttmáli as part of a scat-gift process whose aim was to establish friendship and to ensure loyalty between Icelanders and the kings of Norway, the scat of twenty ells should be seen as the Icelanders' gift. It was only the wealthiest householders in the country, the attendance dues-paying householders, who were supposed to pay it. The first and probably most important countergifts that the Icelanders expected are listed in paragraph two of the covenant. The king agreed to let the Icelanders "enjoy peace" and "Icelandic laws." Jón Jóhansson and others after him claim that this clause relates to the "internal conditions in Iceland" and how problematic it was for the Icelanders "to tolerate the constant civil unrest which had long plagued the land."[91] They were therefore eager to have the king establish peace in the country and maintain it in the future. This meant that the king's gift included a new administrative system, established through the law books Járnsíða in 1271 and Jónsbók in 1281. In the covenant, the agreement is called *sáttargerð*, meaning that it was a bilateral settlement. Jón Jóhansson argues that "although the term *sáttargerð* is employed in the text of the covenant, it is really, in its form, a unilateral agreement, as it was composed by the Icelanders alone." But he also claims that the "approval of the king's representative was obtained . . . [and] the covenant is bilateral in content in that it takes into account both the responsibilities undertaken by Icelanders and the rights they stipulated in exchange for their commitments."[92]

Gizurarsáttmáli was established through negotiations in what I have labeled as the scat-gift process. Its aim was to establish friendship between the king on the one side and the Icelandic people on the other. For the kings of Norway the best way to gain and maintain control over a new territory over which legally they had no historical claim to rule was through negotiations. A military conquest of Iceland was not an option for Hákon and his son Magnús; such a course of action would not have given them the legal rights they were looking for. The first step in the king's strategy to subjugate Iceland was to acquire control over the chieftaincies, and in the 1240s King Hákon achieved control over most of the chieftaincies in the country. Therefore, in 1247, King Hákon could send his retainer, Thórd kakali, and Bishop Heinrek to Iceland to try to persuade the Icelanders to accept him as "their king and such tribute gifts as they agreed upon."[93] Hákon now had legal right on his side: he was the most powerful "chieftain" in Iceland. Nevertheless, he had to negotiate with the Icelanders and become their friend, because that was the only means he had to ensure their loyalty and to gain control over Iceland. After Iceland became a *skattland* (tribute land), the negotiations between the kings of Norway and Icelanders had to take place every time a new king took the throne.

Norwegian foreign policy revolved around personal relationships between the Norwegian kings and the neighboring kings and chieftains. The kings used envoys in many cases to establish these ties. It has been claimed that the king's envoys changed from being "missions of friendship" expressed partly through the exchange of gifts and promises of mutual support, to envoys being equipped as proxies with different levels of specifications. Such emissaries had the authority to negotiate and conclude on the king's behalf, and a series of letters of authorization are extant from the middle of the thirteenth century.[94] This view underestimates the strong continuity of friendship as the main key in conducting foreign policy in the Middle Ages.

CHAPTER 4

Clerics and Friendship

Bishop Árni Thorláksson of Skálholt (d. 1298) "often held feasts at the bishop's residence with many guests invited. The feasts were held with great zeal and generosity, since he was happy to receive much from others while being very willing to do much for others. Due to these and similar circumstances, he was exceedingly highly regarded and sought out by the common people."[1] In other words, it was not only the secular leaders who organized large feasts and gave great gifts. It was as important for bishops as for kings and chieftains to secure political support. While bonds of friendship played an ever decreasing role in secular circles throughout the thirteenth century, they did not lose their importance among the church's leaders.

Christianity became the official religion in Iceland from about the year 1000, and about twenty years later in Norway. It grew slowly in the beginning, but during the second half of the twelfth century, it gained a secure foothold. Until 1104, as mentioned, Iceland and Scandinavia were part of the archdiocese of Hamburg-Bremen, and till 1152–53 they belonged to the archdiocese of Lund. In about 1070, Norway was divided into three bishoprics, and about thirty years later each of these three acquired a permanent see in the country's three largest towns: Nidaros, Bergen, and Oslo. Two new bishoprics were founded in Norway in the twelfth century: the bishopric of Stavanger was separated from that of Bergen in 1125, and Hamar from Oslo in connection with the establishment of the archbishopric at Nidaros in 1152–53. The bishopric of Skálholt was founded in 1056 and was Iceland's only bishopric until Hólar was established in 1106. Otherwise, it was the rate of church building and foundation of monasteries that was a decisive factor in the proliferation of Christianity. In about 1300, there were thirty-one monasteries in Norway and ten in Iceland, and approximately 1,600 parish churches in these two countries, around 1,300 in Norway and around 300 in Iceland. In addition, there were an unknown number of places of worship with a lower rank than parish churches. It is unknown how many clergy there were, but they probably accounted for about .5–1 percent of the total population.[2]

Before we start discussing the clerics and their friendships, it is important to stress that the source situation is not good and as usual the best sources are from Iceland in the sagas about the bishops (*biskupasögur*). In the following we will start at the top of North Atlantic church hierarchy, by looking at the archbishop before we discuss the bishops and their friends. Finally, we will turn to friendship among the cloisters' residents.

Friends of the Archbishop

The establishment of the archbishopric at Nidaros in 1152–53 had significant consequences for the development of Norwegian and Icelandic society, both religiously and politically. The archbishops, who were also the bishops of Trøndelag and northern Norway, spearheaded the church's struggle for independence and managed to gain support for this cause during the second half of the twelfth century and the thirteenth century. An important basis for the archbishops' success can be found in the bonds of friendship that they established, especially with the kings of Norway.

The second archbishop of Nidaros, Eystein Erlendsson (1161–88), was well received by the people of Trøndelag when he became bishop because most of the "great men in Trøndelag were bound by kinship or by marriage" to him and "all of them were his friends."[3] *Heimskringla* tells us that a short time later, Eystein went to Trondheim and called a meeting with the householders. At this meeting he mentioned

> first that the diocese needed wealth, and then that it needed a great deal of assistance, at a time when it should be kept more seemly than before, since it was now more eminent in rank after being elevated to an archbishopric. He demanded that the householders should pay fines to him in silver coins, but earlier he was given current coin such as was paid the king for mulct; the difference between these monetary values was

that the silver coins he wanted were worth twice as much as the others. The archbishop put this into effect with help from relatives and friends; and since he himself worked very hard on this case, men judged that it should be allowed in the whole of Trøndelag, and it was adopted in the dioceses which constituted the archbishopric.[4]

This story emphasizes clearly the importance of friendship, without which it would have been more difficult, if not impossible, for the archbishop to gain acceptance for his demands. Eystein was the most powerful archbishop of Nidaros in the Middle Ages. However, it was not only his friendship with the people of Trøndelag that made this possible, but also his close friendships with Erling skakki Ormsson (d. 1179) and his son King Magnús (1161–84).[5]

Cooperation between the archbishop and Erling resulted in Magnús Erlingsson being the first king of Norway to be officially crowned. This occurred in 1163. After the coronation, a new law of succession was passed. According to this law, it was the king's oldest legitimate son who was rightful heir with first claim to the throne. Thus St. Ólaf's law, which held that all sons of earlier kings—both legitimate and illegitimate—could become king, was abolished. In other words, the new law of succession provided legal protection for Magnús Erlingsson's kingdom; only his sons could become king. And to be on the safe side, Erling killed as many people as possible who potentially posed a threat, including his stepson Harald, who was the son of King Sigurd Haraldsson and Kristín, Magnús's mother and Erling's wife. The law of succession from 1163 not only provided legal protection for Magnús Erlingsson, but it was also an attempt to stop the bloody fighting for the throne. In return for supporting Magnús, the concessions that the church received in connection with the founding of the archbishopric were implemented.[6]

The friendship between the archbishop and the king was of great import for them both. In Norwegian society, no one could oppose their common will. Norwegian historians have emphasized the effective cooperation between King Hákon Hákonarson and the church during his reign, 1217–63.[7] During this period, there were six archbishops of Nidaros. The first was Guttorm (1215–24). At first, he was King Hákon's "enemy," but they sorted things out between them, and the archbishop promised the king complete loyalty.[8] The second was Pétur of Husastad (1225–26). He was handpicked by the king and Bishop Nikulás of Oslo and was called the king's friend.[9] The third was Thórir (1227–30). Nothing is known about his relationship with the king. The fourth was Sigurd Eindridason (1231–52). He and the king exchanged gifts; in addition, he was the son of one of the leaders in King Sverrir's *hirð*.[10] The fifth was Sörli (1253–54). We are told nothing about his personal relationship with the king.

The sixth was Einar (1255–63). He was King Hákon's friend, and he was also a dear friend of the king's son, Hákon ungi (the young).[11] Later, Einar exchanged gifts with King Magnús Lagabætir (Lawmender).[12] Of these six archbishops from the reign of King Hákon, I would characterize four of them as the king's friends: Guttorm, Pétur, Sigurd, and Einar. Hákon's friendship with Sigurd was, without doubt, the most important for him; Sigurd was archbishop for over twenty years. The good cooperation between crown and church during King Hákon's reign was due to the friendships between the king and the archbishops.

The most important conflict between the crown and the church in thirteenth-century Norway concluded with the Tønsberg Concord in 1277. The traditional view taken of this conflict has been that the two important powers could not agree about who should make the Christian legislation.[13] Magnús Lagabætir (1263–80) believed that the crown and the church should jointly handle the making of these laws. The church's standpoint was that the Christian laws were exclusively the church's domain. In connection with the revision of Gulating's law in 1267 and Eidsiva and Borgarting's law in 1268, the Christian laws were included in line with the king's desire. When Magnús initiated the revision of Frostating's law, which was to follow the same template as the previous revision of the other two provincial laws, he met strong opposition from Archbishop Jón the Red (1268–82). The archbishop started working on his own Christian law for Trøndelag, a law more in keeping with the spirit of the church. As a result of the conflict between the king and archbishop, the revised version of Frostating's law has no Christian law section. When Magnús initiated work on Landslög (Norwegian National Law), the strife between the king and the archbishop continued, so the Landslög of 1274 does not have a Christian law section either. After many years of negotiation between the crown and the church, the Tønsberg Concord was concluded in 1277. In this agreement, King Magnús Lagabætir and Archbishop Jón the Red defined the border between their spheres of power. One result of this agreement was that the church would not interfere in royal elections, nor the king in episcopal nominations. The church was to have jurisdiction in lawsuits against the clergy in a number of cases concerning violations of the commandments about adultery and marriage, and its tax exemption was extended.

For us, the political content of the concord is not central; rather, it is the way in which the conflict was resolved. The king and the archbishop agreed on a "friendly settlement," that is, they established friendship between themselves. The settlement was written in Latin and then translated into Old Norse under the heading *"sættar gerð"* (sometimes spelled *sáttargerð*), a bilateral settlement, of King Magnús and Archbishop Jón. In the Latin version, the terms used to describe the agreement are "amicabiliter componendum" and "composicionem amicabilem," while the Old Norse uses the words "vinattuliga samsátt" and "vinattuliga samsætt," literally meaning "friendly settlement."[14] As noted earlier, the establishment of friendship was the best method for securing peace between high-ranking leaders. The Tønsberg Concord is probably the first written pact of friendship in Norway. As both the king and the archbishop knew, it was difficult for them to bind the hands of their successors, especially for the king, who could not apportion privileges which lasted beyond his reign. Thus, the concord concluded with the attestation of six clergy, including the bishops of Oslo and Stavanger, and eight of the kingdom's barons (Magnús Lagabætir gave the nobles the title of baron in 1277), and these men strengthened the agreement with a mutual oath, so that it would remain valid forever.

The settlement between Magnús Lagabætir and Jón the Red lasted until the king's death in 1280. After his death, Magnús's twelve-year-old son Eirík became king. Because of his young age, the barons ruled on his behalf, and they were not willing to accept the privileges the church had secured in the agreement from 1277. This led to harsh conflicts, and Archbishop Jón the Red finally had to flee the country, together with two of his bishops. He died in exile in 1282.[15] We can speculate that the conflict between the crown and the church flared up again after 1280 because of the lack of friendship between the new king and the archbishop, and that the barons hindered any establishment of such a relationship. We do not know of any lower age limit for entering into a friendship. Erling skakki, for example, bound the Norwegian aristocracy in friendship to his son, even though then he was only a child.

It was not only the archbishop of Norway who was an important ally for the Norwegian kings, but also foreign archbishops. King Sverrir's conflict with the church and his excommunication is well known. In his struggle against Pope Innocent III, Sverrir tried to secure foreign clerical support, including the archbishop of Canterbury's. We do not know the circumstances of this contact, other than that Sverrir sent the archbishop gifts. The pope heard about it, and in the year 1200 he wrote a letter to the archbishop of Canterbury stating that if he did not break off all contact with Sverrir, he would be excommunicated himself.[16] Undoubtedly the archbishop must have known of Sverrir's excommunication. Yet the archbishop could not refuse to accept a gift, even when it came from an excommunicated king. This clearly indicates how strong the obligation was to accept gifts, while demonstrating how useful a tool gifts were in the political game. Through his gift, Sverrir forced the archbishop of Canterbury to become his friend, and thus indirectly signaled to Christian Europe that his excommunication was unlawful. It was on account of this that the pope reacted so strongly—he had to maintain order in his own house.

The archbishop had, at least in theory, overall responsibility for the administration of the archdiocese. However, because canon law was unclear about his authority over the bishops themselves, the archbishop was dependent on their support if he wanted to get his own cases through.[17] The diocese formed the nucleus of the church organization: "The Catholic church was and is a diocesan church, the bishops being seen as successors of the apostles who demand[ed] everyone's obedience."[18] The bishop led the clergy, and in his hands was the triple authority given under canon law: the authority to teach, the authority to ordain and legislate, and administrative and judicial authority.

As a rule, the first meeting the bishops had with the archbishop was in connection with their episcopal ordination. Thus the Icelandic candidates for the bishopric, and probably the Norwegian candidates as well, generally spent some time at Nidaros and spoke with the archbishop about their duties and how they should act on the issues of the day. After Árni Thorláksson was ordained bishop of Skálholt in 1269, he received as a gift a collection of canon law with glosses (*decretales cum apparatau*) from Archbishop Jón the Red.[19] This was a symbolic gift that clearly emphasized which cases Árni should work on, while signaling a relation of friendship between the two men.

In Iceland at the end of the twelfth century, a conflict emerged over who was to control church property, the church itself or the family of the person who had founded the church. When a church was established, its patron saint generally received the property that accompanied the foundation, and it was the saint who was the official owner of the gifts and other property that the church acquired—through this gift giving a friendship was established with the saint. The founder gave his property to the saint with specific conditions attached: he and his family were to manage the gifts for all eternity on behalf of the saint.[20]

In Iceland, we find two types of main churches (*alkirkjur*), *staðir* and *bændakirkjur*, which were also parish churches. If a church owned the entire farm on which it was erected, it was a *staðr*, or local ecclesiastical institution; if it owned less, it was called a *bændakirkja*, or farmer church. The main difference between these two types of churches was that *staðir* were usually wealthier than farmer churches. Those who governed the churches had a great deal of freedom in the control of the church's fortunes and incomes. They received about half the tithes (probably introduced in 1097), the share belonging to the churches and the priests, and they controlled churchyard and funeral fees. The administrators of the churches also kept the profits from the management of the institutions themselves in addition to receiving the land tax from farms

owned by the institutions and rent.[21] At the end of the twelfth and during the
thirteenth century, it became common practice for the chieftains to receive
proof of authority over the *staðir*. Hvamm-Sturla's proof of authority over
Hjarðarholt in Dalir, from the 1180s, is one of the first examples of this, if not
the first.[22] Not all the *staðir* were equally important or wealthy, however, and
it was primarily the wealthiest ones that attracted the chieftains. The chieftains gradually took control over most of these *staðir*, and they became an
important element of the chieftains' finances. This system is referred to as
proprietary churches and was common in Europe in the early Middle Ages.[23]

The church reform movement proved an important impetus in the founding of a new archbishopric in Trondheim. The aim of the movement was to
free the church from secular influence and place it under the leadership of the
pope. To this end, the kings of Norway in 1152–53, and later on King Magnús
Erlingsson, made concessions in three important fields. First, the church was
to have complete authority over its clergy and the final word in the election
of bishops and the appointment of priests. Second, the church was to control
its own property and finance. Third, the church was granted jurisdiction over
its own matters and personnel.[24] The archbishop, because of his friendship
with the king, managed to get most of his demands accepted in Norway, soon
after the foundation of the archbishopric. He tried to introduce these same
demands in Iceland. To do this successfully he needed support from the Icelandic bishops. He got support from Thorlák Thórhallsson who became bishop
in Skálholt in 1178. Thorlák demanded in his visitation the same year in the
eastern quarter that all churches and their properties, especially the *staðir*,
should be handed over to the bishop. The church owners and their wardens
were not powerful enough to stop Thorlák's claim, so in almost all churches
in the quarter they accepted that it should be the bishop who controlled
the *staðir*. Afterward, Thorlák invested church owners and the wardens with
the patronage of the churches. On his way to Skálholt, Thorlák stayed on
Höfðabrekka in Mýrdalur, over which Jón Loftsson had gained control. Jón
Loftsson was leader for the Oddaverjar family in the southern quarter and the
most powerful chieftain in the country. He had built a new church on
Höfðabrekka, and now he wanted the bishop to consecrate it. The bishop refused to do this unless Jón accepted the bishop's control over the church at
Höfðabrekka. After a lengthy dispute the bishop gave up his claims, and did
not raise them again. The main reason for this shift in Thorlák's policy was a
change in the political situation in Norway. Conflicts with the king had forced
Archbishop Eystein to leave Norway in 1180. Without the archbishop's support there was little Thorlák could do on his own, and he was therefore forced
to concede. The case was put on hold by the church.[25]

This battle reemerged a century later when Árni Thorláksson returned to Iceland after his consecration in 1269. Immediately upon his return he advanced the church's demand for control over their property on behalf of Archbishop Jón the Red. After prolonged conflict, the church and the Icelandic aristocracy reached a compromise in 1297, the Treaty of Avaldsnes, which secured for the church control over the majority of the biggest and richest churches in the country.[26] The outcome of the conflict was catastrophic for the Icelandic aristocracy. They had used their positions of power to secure the right to manage these churches, and as administrators the aristocracy could then use the church's wealth in their fight for power. The Treaty of Avaldsnes therefore weakened the chieftains' economic foundation.

Árni was a capable and powerful politician, and his friendship with the archbishop and the Norwegian kings Magnús Lagabætir and Eirík Magnússon (1280–99) made it possible for him to implement his policies in Iceland. Friendship with the kings was crucial in this context. The Icelandic aristocracy was a part of the king's *hirð* and thus had to accept the king's decisions. As bishop, Árni had a higher and more prominent role than the secular aristocracy in Iceland. It was easier for him to establish friendship with the king on a more equal basis. This gave him a stronger position to influence the king.[27] Bishop Árni entered also into friendship with many secular leaders in Iceland, for example, with Ásgrím Thorsteinsson. This friendship was so strong that it was said no one could accomplish anything other than what the two men wanted when they were in agreement.[28] Later when the friendship came to an end, the saga mentions that Ásgrím only then realized how much he stood to lose.[29] We do not know anything about how the relations of friendship between the Norwegian bishops and the Norwegian aristocracy developed. Nevertheless, it is reasonable to believe that establishing alliances with the key players in their dioceses in order to gain support for their policies was as important for bishops in Norway as it was in Iceland.

The archbishop's relationship with the bishops of Iceland demonstrates clearly how dependent he was on support from the bishops in order to gain approval for his plans. It was impossible for the archbishop to force changes in the Icelandic church structure without the support of the bishops there, but it was just as problematic for the Icelandic bishops to push through changes without the archbishop's help. However, the archbishop's level of engagement in the church's fight for independence in Iceland was determined by the political situation in Norway. If he was involved in conflicts in Norway, especially with the crown, he could not engage in the struggles in Iceland. Therefore, the political situation in Norway and a strong friendship between the king and the archbishop were critical for the development of church politics in Iceland.

The Bishop and His Friends

The Norwegian kings had bishops in their *hirð* since the eleventh century. In fact, they were usually referred to as *hirð* bishops. It is likely they were both his friends and liege men and therefore had to obey the laws of the *hirð*. As mentioned in the introduction to this chapter, it was not until the end of the eleventh century that bishoprics were established in the country. The first three sees were set up around 1100 in the country's three largest towns: Nidaros, Bergen, and Oslo. By c. 1150, the number of bishoprics in Norway had increased to five, with another see established in Stavanger in 1125, and finally one in Hamar about twenty-five years later. In Iceland, there are two bishoprics: Skálholt, established in 1056, and Hólar, established a half century later in 1106.

The bishops were important political actors, and it was important for the king and the chieftains to establish friendship with them. More than any other king, King Sverrir experienced firsthand how difficult it was to rule the country in opposition to the bishops. One of Sverrir's main opponents was Bishop Nikulás Árnason of Oslo. He was a kinsman of King Magnús Erlingsson and had fought on Magnús's and the Baglar's side in the conflict with Sverrir. When Magnús was killed in 1184, Nikulás stepped back from politics to devote himself to the church. Sverrir prevented Nikulás from becoming Bishop of Stavanger in 1189, but the next year the king allowed himself to be persuaded by his Queen Margrét Eiríksdóttir, Nikulás's second cousin, and accepted him as Bishop of Oslo. In his struggle against King Sverrir at the end of the twelfth century, Nikulás fought alongside Ingi, who was probably Magnús Erlingsson's son.[30] The prolonged conflict between Sverrir and the bishops resulted in his excommunication, but the archbishop and two other bishops had to flee the country. As a result of the conflict with the church, King Sverrir advised his son Hákon to reconcile with its leaders. Hákon took this advice to heart, and we are told that the Norwegian bishops were his dear friends.[31]

The sources are relatively sparse concerning the extent of the bonds of friendship between bishops and kings in Norway, but there is no reason to underestimate their importance or extent.[32] As a result of the bishops' position of power, it was important for the kings to take part in their appointment, not only in Norway, but also in Iceland. King Magnús Erlingsson would not accept Thorlák Thórhallsson as bishop of Skálholt and eventually the archbishop became involved. He was able to negotiate a friendship between Thorlák, the king, and Norway's most powerful man, the king's father, Erling skakki.[33]

The events that led to Iceland becoming a part of the Norwegian realm reveal how important it was for the king to have a good relationship with the bishops. Cathedral chapters, councils that consisted of twelve canons who took part in the governance of the diocese, were established at all the episcopal sees in Norway. These councils were also supposed to choose the bishops; it was thus important for the king to establish and maintain friendship with the canons, and vice versa.[34] Because, however, there were no canons within the Icelandic sees, in 1238 the cathedral chapter at Nidaros was able to usurp the right to elect the Icelandic bishops from the Icelandic chieftains. The episcopal candidates whom the Icelanders themselves had chosen were not accepted for they were not considered legitimate in the eyes of canon law. The cathedral chapter at Nidaros made use of this opportunity to choose two Norwegians to take over the dioceses in Iceland. Because of the good relationship between Hákon and these men, and between Hákon and the archbishops, the Norwegian bishops in Iceland actively supported Hákon's plans to subjugate Iceland. The bishops had established friendships with the Icelandic chieftains who supported the king, and these friendships strengthened the chieftains' positions of power and their ability to fulfill Hákon's plans.[35]

As we saw in the introduction to this chapter, feasts and gift exchanges were an important part of the Christian tradition in the Middle Ages.[36] It is not surprising then that the bishops' sagas tell us about the Icelandic bishops' munificent gifts and magnificent feasts—which we can categorize as entrepreneurial feasts and patron-role feasts.[37] The difference between the bishops and the chieftains was not especially great in this respect. The Icelandic bishops controlled vast resources, in most cases greater than those of the chieftains, and could organize large feasts. Like Bishop Nikulás Árnason of Oslo, Bishop Páll Jónsson of Skálholt (1195–1211) was a chieftain before he was elected bishop; he was used to organizing feasts and taking care of his friends. Nothing indicates that Páll changed his conduct to any great extent after he became a bishop. When he returned to Iceland after his consecration, he held a large feast for Bishop Brand of Hólar and his other friends, and the saga adds he liked to organize feasts for his friends and kinsmen.[38]

The bishops frequently also acted like secular leaders. They supported their friends in conflicts and helped them make good marriages.[39] The saga about Bishop Árni tells us that Árni was often "used as an arbitrator, and even though he did not have secular power, like the saintly bishop Ambrose had in his time, people nevertheless wanted his assistance with their lawsuits, as long as they, and not the king's officials, handed down the decisions."[40] Árni made "friends with his enemies, since he insisted on their rights as well in cases in which his friends took part, as Jón Loftsson [d. 1197] had done in his time when he was reconciled with his enemies by means of honor and gifts."[41] In this instance, apparently, the bishop has taken to heart the Christian message about not unjustly favoring one's friends, a subject we will discuss later on. But most important of all is that, through gifts and the apportioning of honor, he made his enemies his friends, as Jón Loftsson had done. It is interesting that Jón Loftsson is mentioned in this context, since he was the most powerful chieftain in Iceland during the Free State period. The saga of Árni further tell us that people thought Árni was too

> harsh in his judgments against the clergy when they acted unlawfully towards the laity. . . . Therefore, he attached great importance to breaking them of all improper behavior, so that the Holy God's Christendom should never be dishonored by them. Many a time it happened, when the clergy gladly gave in to him, that he assigned them profitable offices or helped them in some way so that they could be satisfied with the outcome.[42]

In his saga, Bishop Árni is described essentially as a first-rate secular leader—he was wise, powerful, and beloved; furthermore, he is referred to as a friend of the law and of truth.

Even before 1297 the bishops in Iceland had control over a few of the largest *staðir* in Iceland and could give their kinsmen or friends permission to administer them. Bishop Thorlák Thórhallsson, for example, allowed his nephew Orm Jónsson to manage the church at Breiðabólstaður in Fljótshlíð, the biggest and wealthiest church the bishop had control over.[43] Besides churches, there was also the tithe itself; it was introduced c. 1097 and was divided between the bishop, the poor, the priest, and the church (controlled by the church warden). In most cases, the church warden did receive half of it—the parts for the church and the priest—and sometimes the bishops did give their parts to the churches that their friends or relatives controlled.

The bishops not only established friendships with kings and chieftains but also with others: householders, relatives, and other clergy. Because these groups' interests could be at odds, the bishops, like others in similar situations, played an important role in conflicts between their friends. This can be seen in the dispute between bishop Thorlák and Jón Loftsson in 1178, friends of both managed to find a solution.[44] We do not know who these men were, but we can assume that they belonged to the highest level among the householders in Jón's chieftaincy. Only men from this group would have had the opportunity to become Thorlák's friends.

Árni Thorláksson, like other bishops of Skálholt, entered into friendship with the bishops of Hólar.[45] It was important for the two Icelandic bishops to establish an alliance with each other in the Icelandic political game. Both gained from it. We also hear about a gift exchange between the Icelandic and Norwegian bishops.[46] These latter relations of friendship were of little direct importance for the Icelandic, and Norwegian, fight for power. However, they were significant on a symbolic level. They emphasized the bishops' reputations abroad.

Bishop Árni received a valuable Christmas gift from the king, which he later gave to Abbot Runólf of Þykkvabær.[47] Runólf was later mentioned as the bishop's dearest friend.[48] Árni could not show his friend greater honor. The king's gift had a completely special status in Norwegian and Icelandic society. They were generally larger than other gifts, but more importantly they were gifts from the king. Also, they were something everyone knew about. In return, the support Árni received from the abbot was important for the outcome of the struggle between Árni and the Icelandic aristocracy concerning control over the church's landed property. Runólf used the teaching of the monks in his monastery to argue the church's point of view in this fight.[49]

We do not know of any friendships between bishops and priests. There is, however, reason to believe that they occurred, especially between the bishops and the priests of the largest and richest churches in Norway and Iceland. The bishops' network of friends also extended to the clergy in their own administration. Like the kings, they could not take loyalty for granted. Haflidi Steinsson, who was a priest and official at Hólar, was a dear and loyal friend of Bishop Laurentius.[50] It is probable that, in many instances, the bishops distributed offices to their friends or used the offices to secure supporters. These friends then had to carry out the tasks that the bishops, or the archbishops, imposed on them. Otherwise, the bishops could threaten to withdraw their friendship, which might mean that their friend would lose their position.[51]

In the decades following Iceland's recognition of the Norwegian king as sovereign in the years 1262–64, the position of the Icelandic chieftains changed. In general, the extensive relations of friendship between them and the householders came to an end. Previously, the chieftains had a duty to protect and help their followers, but as the king's officials they were to prosecute and punish those who earlier had been their friends. In many ways, Bishop Árni was the last chieftain of the Free State in that he acted like the chieftains had acted before 1262–64. He had a large network that he used in the same way that chieftains had used theirs; he took advice from his friends and they, in turn, spied on his enemies.[52] And if Árni's friends were unwilling to carry out these tasks on his behalf, he could threaten them with his enmity.[53]

Monasteries and Friendship

In the period up to 1300, thirty-one monasteries were founded in Norway and ten in Iceland. Although there were few monasteries and they were set up relatively late—the first only at the beginning of the twelfth century—they played a key role for Christianity. They were centers of learning with strong ties to central Europe, and through these connections, new ideas and teachings were disseminated throughout Old Norse society. Contact with the church's reform movement was particularly important in this context. The clergy were divided into regular (monks) and secular (priests) clergy. The regular clergy lived in monasteries and by stricter rules than the secular clergy, while the secular clergy got their name from working most often among the common people. Primarily, it was parish priests, deans, and bishops who belonged to the second group. In practice, the boundary between the two groups was unclear. Nearly all monks were ordained priests able to minister to the laity. A few monks also held priestly offices, and men from the secular clergy could be monastic leaders. Only men could be ordained. Women could not hold a higher position within the church hierarchy than abbess.[54]

We have seen that abbots could establish friendship with bishops. In addition, abbots had other friends, both householders and priests.[55] It is probable that abbesses entered into friendships as well. The leaders of the monasteries needed to secure the position of the monastery as well as they could, and they did this in part by establishing friendships with the key political players. Monastic leaders generally came from the highest rank of society and knew well the value of such relationships.

I have only found one story of friendship between a monk and a person outside of the cloister. In the saga of Bishop Laurentius of Hólar (1324–31), we hear about the monk Laurentius, who traveled to Hólar to be reconciled with Bishop Audun. The bishop gave the monk his friendship in return for his obedience.[56] It goes without saying that the sources we have at our disposal focus very little on monks and their friendships. Nevertheless, there is no reason to assume that friendships between monks and individuals outside of the cloister were common. The nature of monastic life would have inhibited these contacts.

The first monasteries in Norway and Iceland were Benedictine. An important regulation in their Rule can be found in paragraph fifty-four, where it is stressed that a monk cannot accept a letter or any form of gifts (*munuscula / mūnusculum*) without his abbot's permission. And even when the abbot allowed a monk to receive a gift, the abbot could later give this gift to whomever of the brothers he wished, and the monk for whom it had been intended must not be dissatisfied because of this, so as not to give the devil a foothold.[57]

A number of Augustinian houses were founded in Norway and Iceland at the end of the twelfth century and during the thirteenth. Among the Augustinians, a sense of community was strong. Therefore, no one outside of the monastic communities can give their children or other close persons in the cloister a gift, whether it is clothes or other useful objects, and one must not receive such a gift in secret; rather it should be entrusted to the head of the community and made common property, and then be given to those who need it most.[58]

These rules suggest that both the Benedictines and the Augustinians tried to prevent all but the monastic leaders from entering into friendships. Even though attempts were made to hinder friendships with those outside the cloister, the monasteries called for a spiritual community between their members in order to create a unity based on friendship. A key element in a friendship within the cloister was that a friend should protect his friend's soul and take responsibility for his well-being and redemption. Friends had to know each other's inner lives, and they were bound together in spiritual brotherhood. Other important features included in these ideal friendships were that friends should be loyal to each other, and that friendship should be indissoluble.[59]

Friendship was as important for religious leaders as it was for their secular counterparts. They needed faithful supporters to enact their plans. Yet, in contrast to what we have seen in secular circles, friendship continued to play an important role among the clergy for the whole of the period from the middle of the eleventh century until the end of the thirteenth. The bishops, as the key element in the church hierarchy, were very powerful political players, not least attributable to their position within the Church hierarchy, their network of friends and connections, the wealth they controlled, and the position they held in society. Therefore, it was important for the secular leaders to control the election of bishops so that their friends and kinsmen were chosen.

CHAPTER 5

Friends of the Gods

The *Icelandic Homily Book* says that we should pray to Almighty God for mercy, lest we disappear from his sight when he calls his "friends" to the Kingdom of Heaven. In this way, we can avoid the fate of God's enemies (*óvinir*), who will end up in the eternal fires of Hell.[1] Here we are presented with a notion of redemption through friendship with God, to which there was no comparable idea in pre-Christian Norse religion. Friendship was the most important social tie in the Old Norse society; however, only a fraction of the population, mainly householders and members of the social elite, could establish such a tie. By making it possible for everyone to become God's friend, the Icelandic church broke down the traditional societal framework and made friendship an important theological concept. This openness of God's friendship was not the only area where new Christian notions differed from pre-Christian ones: another novelty was the idea that one should forgive one's enemies and treat them as well as one's friends. However, even though Christian ideas about friendship were different in some respects, the Church could not radically change the old ideas, as they were heavily intertwined with political structures.

Anthropologists and historians of religion have long tried, without success, to find a universal definition of the term "religion." In the following pages, we make use of a definition that emphasizes the dealings and communication that people had with deities; that is, the connection between the empirical or secular world in which people lived and the spiritual or sacred world, populated by gods, ancestors, and other powers.[2]

In this chapter, we first evaluate pre-Christian Norse concepts of divine-human friendship, through an investigation of the relationships people could have with the god Thór. After that, we discuss God's "best friend," Job. Then we examine the notion of friendship in the Old Norse religious literature and, finally, how the saints, as God's friends, functioned as role models.

Thór's Friends

According to *Snorra-Edda*, also known as the *Prose Edda* (written by Snorri Sturluson c. 1220), Odin is the "noblest and oldest of the Æsir. He controls everything. And even though the other gods are powerful, they all serve him as a child would serve his father."[3] Odin is presented here as the leader of the gods, and his superior position of power is highlighted in the fact that of all the gods, he alone has a warrior retinue. Nonetheless, the other gods and goddesses in the *Prose Edda* appear as independent actors who only follow their father's advice to a limited degree. The male gods are portrayed almost as householders, married to their goddesses and managing their farms and households. The gods make most of their decisions at meetings and assemblies. The *Prose Edda*, like Eddic poetry, tells us little about the relationships between and intrigues among the gods; nor is much attention devoted to the relationship between gods and humans. An exception is Odin's relationship with warriors, he "is also called Father of the Slain (Valföðr), because his favorite warriors all died on the field of battle. A place was made for them in Valhalla and Víngólf (lit., floor for friends) and they are called Fighters."[4] By giving his favorites a place in Valhalla, Odin indicates that they were also his friends, in a relationship similar to that between a king and his *hirð* men in the Viking Age.

In the pre-Christian period, people tried to establish friendship with the gods to ensure their support—this especially applied to Thór, the most popular of the gods in the Viking Age. Although originally a warrior god who could protect against all evil powers, he also ruled over wind, rain, the weather, and lightning, and during the Viking period he gradually came to be seen as a fertility god with dominion over crops and the harvest.

The Icelandic settler Thórólf had a son, Stein, whom he gave "to his friend Thór," changing his name to Thorstein.[5] Thorstein thus became the god Thór's property, but it was his father, Thórólf, who "managed" the gift. Thorstein later became a great chieftain and had two sons, Bórk (the eldest) and Grím. He gave the latter son to the god Thór, changing his name to Thorgrím, and said that he should become a chieftain and manage the temple he owned. By doing this, Thorstein was hoping to maintain his family's friendship with the god Thór and simultaneously signaling who should inherit his position as chieftain. Thorgrím married Thórdís, and after he was killed, Thórdís gave birth to a son, who was named Thorgrím after his father.[6]

The pattern we observe in this narrative seems to have been common in the pre-Christian period. The Icelandic chieftain families tried systematically to establish and maintain such relationships with the gods, especially with Thór. Lúðvík Ingvarsson lists the names of all those he believes to have been chieftains in the Free State period: all in all, this amounts to around 340 people, of whom about 110 can be dated to the period 930–1030.[7] Of these, around sixty had names associated with the heathen gods, such as Ásbjörn, Ásgrím, Thorgrím, and Thorstein, and about fifty of these had a name that began with Thór, or Thor. We do not know whether all of these people had been given to Thór, but much suggests that sons who were dedicated to Thór were preferred to their brothers (even over older brothers). It would be inappropriate to give a boy whom the donor did not intend to have a key position in society to Thór. In the Viking Age and the high Middle Ages, it was crucial that a chieftain's best son (legitimate or otherwise), rather than simply the eldest, took over his position of power. Personal names with the prefix "Thor" were among the most common in the Viking Age, and they constitute about a quarter of all names found in *Landnámabók* (book of settlement).[8] It should be noted that the figures from *Landnámabók* can be problematic: because it focuses mainly on the upper strata of the society, it is likely that Thór names are overrepresented in *Landnámabók*, and this may also be the case with the Icelandic Family Sagas.

It was the cult—the sacred rituals—which were the focus of the Old Norse religion. The cult can be divided into the *central* practice of the cult, which took place at assemblies, religious places, and the chieftains' estates—chieftains played a key role in the performance of the central cult practices—and the *local* practice, which took place at home on the farm. The cult primarily consisted of making offerings to the gods, the purpose of which was to establish friendship with them and thus ensure their support.[9] Although it is likely that other participants contributed some of the gifts, it was the chieftain who offered them to the gods on behalf of the group. Pre-Christian religion in the Norse world was not a matter of individual conviction, but of group cohesion.

But could everyone become the gods' friends? Yes, in theory, but the gods could not be everywhere at the same time and had to choose which gifts to accept, and in the end it was the size and quality of the gift that determined whether they would accept it or not. Groups could give more valuable gifts collectively, and it was more likely that the gods would accept these. As friendship was established between the giver and the receiver of a gift, then the chieftains (assuming it was they who led the offering in the central practice of the cult) would have been the only ones who became the gods' friends. However, as we learn in stanza 43 of *Hávamál*, friends should support the friends of their friends: thus the gods had a duty to support the friends of the chieftain, namely the householders. In this way, the chieftains functioned as intermediaries between their earthly and divine friends. The chieftains' dual function as secular and religious leaders contributed to their friends' subordination to them, both secularly through friendship and religiously through common worship of the gods.

Even though the chieftains used the pre-Christian religion to sanction their position in society, that is not to say that their ties toward the Old Norse gods were necessarily strong. The chieftains attempted to establish friendship with the gods through the giving of gifts, but such ties of friendship were inherently vulnerable as they depended on reciprocity. In the Icelandic power game, ties of friendship were unstable and could easily be severed; chieftains would readily exchange a weak friend for a more powerful one. This same attitude doubtless applied to their relations with the Old Norse gods. If they did not fulfill their side of the bargain—that is, protecting their friends from the chieftains and kings who were supported by the almighty Christian God—it was perfectly permissible to simply change gods. A change of religion was thus nothing more than a simple shift in allegiance from the Norse gods to the Christian God, as is depicted in the verses of Hallfred vandrædaskáld.[10] Additionally, some Icelandic chieftains came into contact with Christianity on their travels abroad, with several of them taking the new faith and receiving baptism before Christianity was introduced to Iceland.[11]

Old Norse religion appears to have been an aristocratic religion. "Communication" between the social elite and the Old Norse gods was based on a friendship that other members of society were not able to establish. What then did the common people believe in? And which gods could they ask for help? The lack of source material makes it difficult to give a clear answer to this question. In many cases, people seemed to have relied on powerful ancestors or an *ármaðr*, a guardian spirit.[12]

The role of the king in the old cult is unclear. In the *Saga of Hákon Aðalsteinfóstri*, *Heimskringla* relates that the householders forced Hákon to take part in a sacrifice at Mære.[13] According to the story, it was the local chieftains who led the cult, but as the king was in the area, both they and the householders thought it important for him to participate. Thus it seems that the king had a relatively passive role in the old cult. As the monarchy was a new institution, no clear norms had been established concerning the king's religious duties, and no locations for the cult that could be associated with the kingdom as a whole had been established. There can be little doubt that the Norwegian kings were interested in introducing the new religion in their realm. King Harald Fairhair sent his son, Hákon, to the court of Æthelstan in England and must have been well aware that he would return to Norway a Christian. Actually, Harald Fairhair is the only king of Norway who was not baptized.

In Norway, the introduction of the Christian religion had a strong political motive, with kings using the new religion to legitimize their power. The king became the leader of Christianity in his country, with all others becoming subordinate to him. The relationship between church and king was one of mutual dependency: the king protected the church, which was necessary for spreading Christianity and building up ecclesiastical institutions, while in return, the church provided the king with both ideological and administrative support. In Iceland, however, the case was quite different. The Icelandic church, which was firmly under the control of the Icelandic chieftains until 1238, did not provide the chieftains with the same ideological structure as the church in Norway had done for the kings, nor did the chieftains operate any kind of administrative system. Rather, when Christianity was introduced in Iceland the chieftains became the leaders and guardians of a new religion rather than the old.

Job: God's Best Friend

Our starting point is the Old Norse religious literature, in particular the two homily books: the *Icelandic Homily Book* and the *Old Norwegian Homily Book*. Both were originally composed in the twelfth century and are known from manuscripts dating from around 1200. The divergence between them is substantial; however, they have eleven nearly identical sermons, which draw on the tradition of sermon literature dating back to the early church and the church fathers.[14]

Of these two sources, the story of Job is only found in the *Icelandic Homily Book*. We hear about Job and his trials most notably in the homily on *Kirkjuhelgi* (the sanctity of the Church). *Kirkjuhelgi* opens with an account of Solomon the Wise, who said if we intend to do good deeds and serve God, we must be patient (*þolinmóðr*, having the ability to withstand; *patientia* in Latin) and resist temptation. We are to act this way despite the possible loss of our possessions, our health, or our family and friends. The enemy, the Devil, can exploit such losses to tempt us when we are weak: therefore, we should look to Job's example when this happens to us.[15]

Kirkjuhelgi goes on to say that the Devil met God and told him of his travels on earth and how he had tried to lure people away from the straight and narrow path. God then asked the Devil if he had met his honorable righteous friend, Job, a man who shunned evil. The Devil answered it was hardly surprising that Job was so faithful and served God in every way. The prosperity God had given him in riches, renown, health, and all kinds of happiness was not inconsiderable. Job's loyalty and love had never been put to the test—what would happen if his prosperity disappeared? God therefore gave the Devil permission to test Job's love, loyalty, and friendship by taking from him both his wealth and his children.[16]

Kirkjuhelgi emphasizes that God knew how Job would react, but nonetheless chose to test him, as he does all his friends in order to see why they perform their good deeds. Friends of God fall into three categories: first, those who are loyal to and love God out of desire for eternal salvation; second, those who wish to secure worldly possessions, renown, and good health; and finally, those who want both success in this life and eternal salvation in the next. The difference between these three groups is that those who belong to the first, like Job, will keep their loyalty to and love for God regardless of their fate, whereas those who focus on worldly goods will betray God when he tests them and they lose the possessions he has given them.[17] *Kirkjuhelgi* elaborates on Job's loss and sorrows and how he reacted. After the Devil took from Job all his children and the whole of his wealth—7,000 sheep, 3,000 camels, 500 oxen, and 500 donkeys—Job threw ashes over his head, fell to the ground, and thanked God for the trial, saying that he came into this world naked and naked he would leave it: "God gave me my wealth and it was he who took it from me." Job did not abandon his friendship with God, even when he lost everything.[18]

Shortly after this, the Devil again came to God. God said that as the Devil had now met his friend Job, he should be aware of his excellent qualities. In response, the Devil replied that as long as Job had his good health, he would not betray God. Again God gave the Devil permission to test Job, and this time he took his health from him. Job was afflicted with terrible leprosy, and no one wanted to come near him. His wife and neighbors came to visit from time to time, not to give him consolation, but to reproach him and criticize his faith. Job answered that God loved him as much as before, and that this was merely the punishment he had merited for his sins. If he accepted his situation and showed God the same love and loyalty as before, God would comfort him in the end. God saw Job's reaction, healed him, and gave him even greater riches, renown, and happiness than he had had before the Devil tested him.[19]

The *Icelandic Homily Book* instructs us to have good and holy men as our role models (a theme we discuss in more detail later). Job was given as an example of how one should resist temptation and be patient: God rewards his friends with wealth, esteem, good health, and eternal salvation, but in return they have to be loyal, humble, patient, follow his commandments, and do good deeds.[20] In the Christianization of Europe, examples, like that of Job, played an important role and were actively used by the Church to influence attitudes and behavior, and so it was vital that these examples were properly understood.[21] In modern reception theory, the focus is on receivers and how they create textual meanings through their readings of texts. Reception theory therefore assumes an active reader who "creates" literature.[22] However, unlike modern readers, who create and recreate their experiences of texts through private reading, the medieval audience, almost without exception, would have heard these stories orally. These two processes are not entirely equivalent, and thus require different theories of approach. Similarly, medieval society was of a different nature than modern society because the church had a strong position in the former, including a dominating monopoly on the interpretation of stories from the Bible and legends about holy men and women. Most people in the Middle Ages were probably not particularly critical of the church's teachings. Thus there became a certain canonization of the story of Job and how it was understood.

When Christianity became the official religion in Iceland and Norway around the year 1000, people were not familiar with the main figures of Christian literature and the moral values associated with them. In the beginning, it was necessary for the church to provide fairly detailed accounts of (among others) Job and his trials. Later, however, as such stories became an integrated part of a Christian culture, it was no longer necessary to provide such long explanations; it was enough to merely mention the name "Job." This is evident in the legends from the thirteenth and fourteenth centuries, where it is taken for granted that the audience knows the story of Job.[23]

If we compare the story of Job in the *Icelandic Homily Book* with that in the Bible, we find an important difference. In the Book of Job, the main questions are the following: Can the righteous suffer? Why does Job suffer?[24] Job accuses God of being unjust; he has not opposed God and would rather die than accept his misfortune as the consequence of his own wrongdoing. Job's friends try to make him understand that he must not complain about his misfortune and that he must put his faith in God. Job claims that he is righteous and yet God punishes him anyway. God finally reveals himself to Job, who accepts

God's omnipotence, confesses his sins, and humbles himself before God. The central message is that the righteous can also suffer.[25] Job is then rewarded with more wealth and good fortune than he had before: he has seven sons, three very beautiful daughters, and many grandchildren. The message in the Bible is one of humility and patience, whereas in the *Icelandic Homily Book* the focus is on friendship, loyalty, and patience.

The *Icelandic Homily Book* only reproduces the small section of the Book of Job that deals with Job's trials; the Bible allots significantly more space to the dialogue between Job and his friends, which the *Icelandic Homily Book* omits. This omission is not attributable to a lack of knowledge about the Book of Job in Iceland, as is made clear from legends that explicitly refer to it.[26] For the author of *Kirkjuhelgi*, it was most important to adapt the story of Job to Icelandic conditions and especially to the role of friendship and loyalty in Icelandic society, so that Icelanders could understand and relate to it.

The *Old Norwegian Homily Book* does not mention the story of Job at all. It is problematic to explain why, given the weight it has in the *Icelandic Homily Book* and the role friendship played in both Iceland and Norway. Even though the *Old Norwegian Homily Book* does not refer at all to the story of Job, it does focus strongly on patience.[27] *Konungs skuggsjá* emphasizes, however, how ready Job was to endure suffering, but its main purpose in mentioning him is to stress God's power over the Devil. It is God who allows the Devil to test Job and sets the boundaries of his power.[28]

Yet even though the *Norwegian Homily Book* does not mention Job, it does, like the Icelandic version, refer to God's friends. To become God's friend, one must serve him by following his commands, fighting his battles, and introducing others to God's friendship, much as Saint Ólaf did (d. 1030). One should give gifts, particularly to the poor, with a good and proper disposition; God appreciates such *gjafvinir* (gift friends). One can also become God's friend, or even son, by emulating the deeds of Christ. One should love God more than anything else, renounce all desire, do good work for God's sake and not for oneself or one's reputation, and love one's neighbor as oneself. God's friends (and those who wish to be his friends) should *þjóna* (serve) him with prayers and good deeds, as the saints did.[29]

As we saw in the story of Job in the *Icelandic Homily Book*, God rewards his friends: for example, when he gave his laws to Moses and other friends. He sends his angels to support his friends, and, as we saw with Job, to give them good gifts. Those who receive God's *ástgjafir*—a term that emphasizes the love behind God's gifts, as opposed to other gifts that are not always given with such love—should be dutiful to him and proclaim his name. Before Jesus was born, all of God's friends went to Hell, but after his death, Jesus saved them and led them up to Heaven. On Judgment Day, God will send the Holy Spirit to bring his friends up to Heaven so that they can experience heavenly peace and bliss.[30]

God also has enemies, such as those who oppose him and who do not have faith in him. These people incur God's wrath and must suffer punishment in Hell, and on Judgment Day they will remain there. God's enemies also fight against his earthly friends and are punished for doing so, as when God drowned the enemies of the Israelites in the Red Sea.[31] The chief enemy is, of course, the Devil: he and his followers do everything in their power to lure people away from God, thereby hoping to prevent them from going to Heaven and claiming their rightful inheritance.[32]

The two homily books refer to the twelve apostles, John the Baptist, Saint Ólaf, and other male saints explicitly as God's friends, but no women; even the Virgin Mary is not designated as such.[33] This should not be interpreted to mean that women could not be God's friends; indeed, both homily books make it clear that God's friendship is open to everyone, both men and women. The confusion stems from the fact that the word *vinr* (friend, masc.), like the word *maðr* (man, masc), was used for both men and women. In the saga about Martha and Mary Magdalen, both women are referred to as God's friends using the masculine form of the word friend.[34] If exclusively female friendship was the issue, the female form of the word *vinkona* (friend, fem.) would have been used.[35]

The Church used the notion of God's friendship to encourage people to follow his commandments. Those who did so and received his friendship would secure a place in Heaven and possibly earthly riches as well. It was widely known in Norse society that friendship was a relationship only available to a small group. By opening up the possibility of everyone being able to establish a friendship with God, friendship ceased to be exclusive and became inclusive, for in theory everyone could be a friend of God.

God's Other Friends

Both the *Old Norwegian Homily Book* and the *Icelandic Homily Book* have sermons on the martyrdom of Stephen (d. c. 35).[36] He was the first Christian martyr, who met his end while preaching about Jesus and upbraiding his audience for their wicked deeds and lack of belief. The Acts of the Apostles describes his death in the following manner:

> Now when they heard these things, they were cut to the heart, and they gnashed on him with their teeth. But he, being full of the Holy Spirit,

looked up steadfastly into heaven, and saw the glory of God, and Jesus standing on the right hand of God, and said, Behold, I see the heavens opened, and the Son of Man standing on the right hand of God. But they cried out with a loud voice, and stopped their ears, and rushed upon him with one accord; and they cast him out of the city, and stoned him: and the witnesses laid down their garments at the feet of a young man named Saul. And they stoned Stephen, calling upon the Lord, and saying, Lord Jesus, receive my spirit. And he kneeled down, and cried with a loud voice, Lord, lay not this sin to their charge. And when he had said this, he fell asleep.[37]

The homily on Stephen emphasizes that he loved and prayed for his enemies, making him a good example for those who would do as Jesus did. By loving our friends in God, and our enemies for God's sake, we can attain eternal joy. When we consider all the wrongs we ourselves have committed against God, our neighbor's misdeeds against us seem less worthy of our attention; and the more wholeheartedly we forgive our enemies for their misdeeds, the more abundantly will God forgive ours. Jesus himself says, "If you forgive people their sins, the heavenly father will forgive you. But if you do not forgive, the heavenly father will not forgive you either."[38] One should be reconciled to one's enemies and thus emulate Jesus who prayed for his enemies when he was led away to be crucified and said, "Father, forgive them their sin, for they know not what they do."[39]

The *Icelandic Homily Book* and the *Old Norwegian Homily Book* not only emphasize how one should interact with and care for one's friends, but also place equal weight on how one should deal with one's enemies: by loving them as Jesus did. Jesus did not want anyone to avenge him after he had been captured and bound by the Jews: this magnanimity is visible in his healing of the slave's ear that Peter had cut off. One's relationship with one's enemies should not be characterized by vengeance, but by good deeds. Whereas some may give gifts to powerful men to escape just condemnation, Jesus accepted a false judgment and prayed for those who wrongly sentenced him to crucifixion.[40] We can be reconciled to our enemies before we have even met them by letting our thoughts turn toward reconciliation, allowing God to see that we will forgive our enemies for their misdeeds and accepting the compensation agreed on by good men: it pleases God to see our willingness to enter into a settlement and to forgive our enemies. Through this love of our enemies, we show our respect for God's commandments. And even when our enemies reject reconciliation, we will benefit from praying to God for them. Moreover, we must not repay evil with evil, but love our enemies and be good and faithful.[41]

The *Icelandic Homily Book* sets up an opposition between the old and the new conceptions of friendship in the following: Moses had learned from God that one should love one's friends and hate one's enemies, but according to the new law of the Gospels, we should not hate our enemies, but rather love them and pray for them. Nonetheless, we should still honor the words of Moses and love our friends loyally.[42] Thus the core of Christian friendship given here is to love one's enemies as one loves one's friends.

The two homily books' views on friendship can be summed up as follows: worldly wealth will be of no use to us in the Kingdom of Heaven, and if we have not taken care of our friends and treated them well, they will not speak to us in Paradise. But neither should we let helping our friends or taking revenge on our enemies make us lose sight of what is right and just. We must be sincere in our conversation with our friends and not only tell them what they want to hear. And if our friends give us bad advice, we should still love them, just as we do our enemies. We should love genuine and honorable friends, and not hate the bad deeds of our enemies. Finally, to avoid having problems with our friends, we should not enter into friendships with wicked men.[43]

God's Friends as Models and Intermediaries

The saints are often referred to as God's friends (*guðs vinir*), and they were actively used as models by the church to inspire people to follow God's commandments.[44] The saints could also help people with their problems by working miracles. The central position of the cult of saints in medieval Christianity is indicated in the dedication of all churches to at least one saint. Also, it was these saints who were the official owners of the church's property, although donors to the church (and their families) could still administrate their gifts.[45] This gift to the church indicates a friendship was established between the church founder, his or her family, and the saint. Thus the saints constituted an important part of the local community, both as God's helpers and as landowners. The first churches in the Norse world were founded in the eleventh century. The written sources, such as *Heimskringla*, emphasize especially the king's initiative in this area. Building a church was often politically motivated and employed as a strategy to obtain or maintain a leading position in society for the church was a symbol of the founder's power.

According to *Fyrsta málfræðiritgerðin* (the *First Grammatical Treatise*) written c. 1150, Icelanders were occupied with *þýðingar helgar*: the translation of devotional writings, sermons, and legends.[46] However, not all saints' lives were translated into Old Norse: on his deathbed in 1237, Bishop Gudmund Arason (like many others) had the lives of holy men read to him in Latin.[47] Little by little, stories of the saints began to influence society and behavior. This is seen from the careers of some Icelandic bishops (many of whom would later be the subjects of sagas): there is hardly any doubt that Bishop Gudmund Arason of Hólar (1203–37) and Bishops Thorlák and Árni of Skálholt were well acquainted with the saga about saint Ambrose (he was a bishop of Milan and a doctor of the church) and saw the saint as their ideal. The authors of the sagas about Bishop Gudmund Arason draw attention to the relationship between him and Ambrose, who is mentioned as Gudmund's father, foster-father/teacher (*fóstri*), and "friend."[48] The friendship between the two is evident in *Prestssaga Guðmundar góða*: the saga reports that when Gudmund took leave of a sick old woman who was on her deathbed at the farm in Svínafell, he told her that she should go to God and give his regards to "the blessed Mary, the Archangel Michael, John the Baptist, Peter and Paul, King Ólaf the Holy and especially my friend Ambrose."[49] It is difficult to explain how this friendship between Gudmund and Ambrose first arose; it was probably due to Gudmund's decision to use him as a role model.

As bishop, Gudmund fought for the church's independence and strove to prevent secular chieftains from interfering with the management of the episcopal see of Hólar; this inevitably led to conflict with these chieftains. In the difficult struggles that followed, Gudmund used Ambrose's life as a guide, looking to see what the man of God had done in similar situations. If we compare Gudmund's conduct and viewpoint with how the saga of Ambrose reports Ambrose's own clashes with the emperors, kings, and other secular magnates, the similarities are great. One notable difference is that Ambrose succeeded in subduing the secular leaders whereas Gudmund failed. Otherwise, Gudmund was, like Ambrose, an ascetic, generous to the poor, involved in court judgments, and a collector of relics.[50]

Another important detail of this story is the order in which the saints and the archangel are mentioned. The order follows the church's hierarchy for saints based on their influence in Heaven: Mary, the archangels, patriarchs and prophets (including John the Baptist), apostles and evangelists, martyrs (such as Ólaf), popes and bishops together with true believers, the church fathers, priests and deacons, monks and hermits, virgins, and widows.[51] It would have been unthinkable for the writer of Gudmund's saga to place his "friend Ambrose" anywhere other than at the end of the list of saints.

A central motif in most of the legends is martyrdom: after their death by torture, the saints were raised up to Heaven. Eventually, the idea of martyrdom began to influence society in Norway and Iceland. In the attack on Laufás at Eyjafjörður in 1198, the sons of Arnthrúd (Thorstein and Snorri) and Hákon Thórdarson were captured:

> The two brothers, Thorstein and Snorri, prepared themselves for execution; they washed their hands and combed their hair, as if they were on the way to a feast. Then Snorri said: "I wish," he says "that I will be executed before Thorstein because I trust him, that he will forgive you even if he sees me killed." [Then they were executed.]
>
> Then Hákon was alone. He asked them to cut off a hand and a foot—and then let him travel abroad and go on a pilgrimage and atone for his sins and for those of others.
>
> Thorgrím said that they would not torture him in that way.
>
> Hákon then asked if they would run him through with a sword instead of killing him with an axe.
>
> Thorgrím refused.
>
> No one would kill Hákon. Sölvi would not do it, because he had granted Hákon a personal truce over the killing of Thórodd.
>
> The Sigurd grikkur said: "I will solve this problem and kill Hákon."
>
> Hákon replied: "I would also prefer that, because of all the men here, I deserve this least from you. When you arrived in Iceland from abroad, you were poor, and I took you into my household. I surprised you three times in bed with my wife Gudrún."[52]

The motivation behind Hákon's wish is the idea that those who suffer greatly in death will avoid purgatory and go directly to Heaven. It is also clear that Hákon, possibly inspired by the story of Saint Stephen, forgives his killer: the one among his enemies who has wronged him the most.

It is much more difficult to evaluate the influence that the legends of the saints had on women, as we are only occasionally told about women's religious faith. Nevertheless, there can be little doubt that they helped to shape the image of women in Iceland in the High Middle Ages (both women's image of themselves and men's view of women). In the power game in Iceland in the period c. 1150–1260, it was common that the chieftains had a high number of concubines. It is this situation we ought to bear in mind when discussing the vitas about female saints translated into Old Norse and the saints' motives. Most sagas of holy women share a common theme of a daughter rebelling against the official religion and patriarchy by refusing to marry; this threatened the established social order and was met with torture and death.[53] The legend of Saint Cecilia contains an important variation on this theme: she sought to preserve her virginity as a married woman. Cecilia was engaged to a man named Valerian. Because of the power of the two families who had arranged the union, she dared not refuse. On her wedding night, she prayed to God to defend her virginity and told her husband that she loved Jesus and that God's angels would protect her body. During the night, Cecilia convinced her husband to be baptized, and he in turn persuaded his brother to do the same; after this, the brothers were executed for refusing to worship the old gods. Later Cecilia was also accused of renouncing the official cult and tortured to death.

In *Maríu saga Egipzku* (the *Life of Mary the Egyptian*) and in part the legends of Martha and Mary Magdalene stand out among the legends of women on account of their applicability to Icelandic society. The sagas tells that at the age of twelve, Mary left her parents' home in Alexandria and became a prostitute: she procured the most beautiful clothes in order to attract the interest of men, and later on became an actress and singer, so that men would desire her even more. In her thirties, she traveled to Jerusalem, and she slept with all the men on board the ship during the journey. Some days after arriving, on Holy Cross Day, she found she was physically unable to enter a church—God prevented it. She saw an image of the Virgin Mary outside and called on her with bitter regret, promising that if she were allowed to go inside, she would reject her earlier life and become a hermit, to punish herself for her wickedness and failure to fear God. Her prayers were answered, and she spent the rest of her life as a hermit.[54] Concubinage was pervasive in Iceland from the middle of the twelfth century on, which the church found unsatisfactory. As is evident from the *Life of Mary the Egyptian*, the church took the view that women were weak by nature and furthermore had the ability to tempt men to fornication.[55] To remedy this, legends were translated into Old Norse to inspire women to fight against their weakness and live as virgins for Christ, which would give them eternal victory and salvation.[56]

At death, the saints come into the presence of God in the Kingdom of Heaven. They are God's friends, role models, and a tool he uses to show his power through miracles. The saints were seen as intermediaries between God and humanity, who could turn to them for help in times of need. As God's friends, their friendship was valuable. To establish and maintain a friendship with a saint, one could found a church in the saint's name or give gifts to a church already dedicated to the saint. As discussed previously, all churches in Iceland and Norway were dedicated to God and one or more saints, and it was the saint who was the legal owner of the church and its property. A large portion of the gifts given to religious institutions in the Middle Ages—through which the church obtained vast landed wealth—must be seen in light of these friendships with the saints. These relationships, based on reciprocity, were understood as similar to friendships between humans.

The gifts presented to the saints were usually given under certain conditions. We see this in King Hákon Hákonarson's confirmation of the foundation charter of the town of Stavanger and its cathedral. This document, written between 1226 and 1254, begins with King Hákon sending God's and his own greetings to Bishop Askell of Stavanger, the cathedral canons, and others.[57] Hákon then lists the obligations they, as Christians, have toward the church, especially for those persons God has "raised up with authority and the name of leader." He particularly notes they should not take from the church what good men and God's friends have given to it. The king then confirms the donation of the town of Stavanger, which his kinsman King Magnús had given to God and Saint Swithun. Hákon issued this confirmation at the request of his friend Bishop Askell, in order to "honor God, and for the glory of his noble mother, the Holy Virgin Mary, Saint Swithun and all God's saints." In return, the bishop was to have the names of the king's father (Hákon) and grandfather (Sverrir) written in the holy church of Saint Swithun (the cathedral of Stavanger) as well as in all the other churches of his diocese. The king's own name would be added after his death. And

> their souls should be prayed for every Sunday of the year and all our [souls] when God calls us to him. I hope that God and St. Swithun will give us thanks for [this], for the souls of those who have died as well as for the souls of those who are still living. I also confess that, for the sake of friendship, I have supported those who govern the Church now and will govern it in future. Now, all the kings or leaders who, as God wills, shall rule the kingdom after me and who comply with my wishes will receive thanks from God and a reward from St. Swithun and the holy men to whom the church is dedicated. But all those who violate my gift, or encourage others to violate it, be they either greater or lesser men in rank, will be subjected to excommunication from the Holy Church and to God's wrath.

Saint Swithun whom the cathedral church of Stavanger was dedicated was the official owner of the gift, and the bishop and his followers were merely responsible for administering it. Through the gift, a friendship was established between the donor and the recipient, the king and Saint Swithun, and because of this relationship, the king had the right to compensation, prayers, and support on Judgment Day.

It is unclear whether the administration of the saint's property could also establish friendship between the administrator (householder, chieftain, or priest) and the saint. We certainly cannot reject the possibility that Bishop Askell, as the manager of Saint Swithun's property, was also the saint's friend, especially as friendship was considered the best way to ensure loyalty in such a relationship. This makes the importance of the church having full control over its property all the clearer: it could not only secure its economic foundation but also consolidate its control over the saints' cults.

In *Sverris saga*'s account of King Sverrir's speech in Bergen in 1184, he thanks all "God's friends" for attending. In the period up to c. 1300, we have about fifty-five official documents where the issuer sends greetings to his own and God's friends. A good example of this phenomenon is King Hákon Sverrisson's letter of reconciliation to the bishops of his realm (probably from 1202). It opens with the king sending "greetings to Archbishop Eirík and all the other bishops, learned men, all householders, all living men, all of God's and his own friends."[58] However, it was not only kings who sent greetings to God's friends but also archbishops, bishops, canons, abbots, priests, the secular aristocracy, lawspeaker, the more influential householders, merchants, and high-ranking women.[59]

Here we must discuss some aspects of Latin charters, which so far have been absent from the discussion. When people in Norway began to use writing as their main form of record keeping, Latin models served as a template—this was particularly the case for charters, the drafting of which followed strict rules. All charters began with a protocol consisting of three sections: the *intitulatio*, naming the sender; the *inscriptio*, naming the recipient; and the *salutatio*, the greeting. In this instance, we are particularly concerned with the recipient. In Hákon's charter, it has been pointed out that the phrase "all God's and his own friends" in Old Norse is equivalent to the Latin *Christi fidelibus* (Christ's faithful):[60] when Christianity was introduced and the phrase had to be translated, a term that could reflect to the realities of life in Norway and Iceland was needed. Thus a relationship familiar to all was employed: friendship.

Who were these friends of God? The only ones who could be referred to with any certainty as God's friends in the Norwegian and Icelandic sources were the saints. Yet the king was not sending his greeting to them—had he wished to do so, the formulation would have been simply "all the saints." In Norway, there was no specific group of "God's friends"—rather this formulation refers to *all* those men and women who attempted to follow God's commands.

According to the ideology of Christian friendship, one should emulate Christ and Saint Stephen by loving one's enemies, trying to be reconciled with them and not repaying evil with evil. One should treat one's enemies as one does one's friends. The *Icelandic Homily Book* sets up a contrast between the old and new concepts of how one should treat enemies and friends, disassociating itself from what Moses had originally learned from God about loving one's friends and hating one's enemies. According to the Gospels, we should love and pray for our enemies, but also love our friends and be loyal to them just as before. In this formulation of Christian friendship, the *Icelandic Homily Book* distances itself not only from the old laws of Moses but also indirectly from *Hávamál*. Although *Hávamál* does not provide any direct advice about how to deal with one's enemies, it does emphasize that a man should avoid bad friends. We can hardly suppose that enemies should be treated better than bad friends in the eyes of the poet.

The clergy in Norway and Iceland had a good familiarity with the discourse on friendship in the learned circles of Europe. This is evident from the translation of Alcuin's (c. 753–804, often referred to as Charlemagne's "education minister") work *De virtutibus et vitiis* (On Virtues and Vices) into Old Norse in the second half of the twelfth century.[61] It also appears that learned men in Norway and Iceland knew of Cicero's *De amicitia* (On Friendship), although we know no further details.[62] Nonetheless, there is no evidence that confirms that the ideas in these works had any influence on native concepts of friendship.

At the beginning of this chapter, we defined religion as the dealings and communication that people had with deities or the supernatural. There are great similarities in the forms of communication in the Christian and pre-Christian periods: humans tried to use friendship to secure support from higher powers, both before and after the introduction of Christianity. In Iceland, Christianity became the official religion c. 1000, and about twenty years later in Norway. It was important for the church to adapt its teachings to native ideas in as many areas as possible in order to make the transition to a new faith easier for society. Thus the church actively promoted what we might call "friendship theology."

Chapter 6

Kinsmen and Friends

"Let There Be a Fjord between Kinsmen, but a Bay between Friends"

> There was an intense battle. Steinthór was foremost among his group of followers and slashed on both sides, but his ornamented sword bent when it struck the shields, so he often had to straighten it out with his foot. He resolutely sought out the chieftain Snorri. His kinsman Styr Thorgrímsson also fought fearlessly at Steinthór's side [they were related in the second or third degree],[1] and soon killed a man in Snorri's—his own son-in-law's—retinue. When the chieftain Snorri saw this, he said: "Is this how you avenge Thórodd, your grandson, who Steinthór has mortally wounded? You are no better than a traitor." [Snorri was previously married to Styrr's daughter.][2] Styrr replied: "I will soon remedy that," and with that he changed sides. He joined Snorri's following and killed one of Steinthór's men.[3]

> —Eyrbyggja saga chapter 44

The introduction to this book discussed how the notion of a strong kin group played an important part in the academic debate about Icelandic and Norwegian society in the Viking period and the high Middle Ages until about 1970. The basic assumption behind this idea was that kin should band together in conflicts. Yet the claim that the story of the struggle between the chieftains Steinthór Thorláksson and Snorri godi Thorgríms-son supports such an argument is not quite accurate. Rather, this narrative stresses the ambiguity surrounding decisions about whom to support when family ties overlapped. But what was the relationship between friends and kinsmen? And why did kinship not afford the same protection as friendship? Again Iceland provides the main model for this discussion because the sources for Norway are not as good.

The Bilateral Kinship System

The kinship system in Norway and Iceland was bilateral; that is, a person could trace his kin though both the male and female lines. This meant that only siblings of the same parents had an identical kin group. Their parents and children each had their own distinct kin group, and these groups overlapped with each other and formed a continuous network of family relations.[4] The term most often used to describe male relations in the Old Norse sources is kinsman (*frændi*); to describe female relations, it is kinswoman (*frændkona*); and kinship (*frændsemi*) is used to express the relationship between them. The term kin (*ætt*) occurs much less frequently. We can see this clearly in the Icelandic Family Sagas. In them, the term *ætt*—and here I include also the compound words which begin with "ætt-"—occurs about three hundred times, whereas the other terms—that is, "kinsman," "kinswoman," and all the other words which begin with "frænd-"—occur about twelve hundred times. Both Norwegian and Icelandic laws generally limit kinship to the third degree. In other words, the terms for kinship encompassed an individual and his son, daughter, father, mother, son's son, son's daughter, daughter's son, daughter's daughter, maternal and paternal grandparents, brother, sister, nephew, niece, male and female cousins, and aunts and uncles. In some instances, the kinship terms indicated more distantly related individuals, usually when a secular leader was one of the parties involved. The terms were also used at times to describe the relationship between men who had entered into sworn brotherhood, friends, and even one's relation with Adam himself.[5]

The Norwegian and Icelandic bilateral kinship system had clear patrilineal tendencies. Only sons could carry on the family. This is evident from the custom of using the patronymic. A child's second name was his or her father's first name, with "son" or "dóttir" added to it; for example, Thórdarson or Thórdardóttir. In some cases, where a mother's kin were more noble and more powerful than a father's, the children followed her family.[6] Nonetheless, women could not be the founding ancestor of a clan, as men could.[7] Establishing and maintaining a family was an ongoing process. If a chieftain family or householder family was to survive, it had to be able to produce sons who could protect and avenge the family's position; otherwise, they would disappear. Therefore, as a rule, no distinction was made between legitimate and illegitimate sons. If an illegitimate son inherited the position of power, he and his children became the family's focal point. Kolbein Arnórsson, from the Ásbirningar family, had two sons, the legitimate Arnór and the illegitimate Tumi.[8] Tumi became head of the family, as did his sons later, and his son's son,

Kolbein ungi. However, when Kolbein ungi died, Arnór's grandson in the male line, Brand Kolbeinsson, took over the position of power within the family. He was able to do this because he owned many chieftaincies in Skagafjörður and Húnaþing, which Kolbein had administered.[9]

Norwegian and Icelandic families were rarely named after the first name or nickname of the founder. Of the roughly two hundred alleged family names in Iceland, only about eleven were named after people; for example, the Ás-birningar or the Snorrungar. As a rule, families were named after the locality with which they had a particular association, most often a farm, more seldom a district. In the settlement and saga periods in Iceland (c. 870–1030), it was not uncommon for families to be named after districts, for example, the Álft-firðingar after the fjord Álftafjörður. The reason they were referred to as the Álftfirðingar is because the father of the man who is perceived as the founder of the family was probably the first to live in Álftafjörður.[10] The family alone kept the name for three generations. After that, it was used for all the residents in the district. Family names, names common to all members of a kin group and which they regularly used in addition to a first name, did not occur in Norway or Iceland in the period c. 800–1300.

In a bilateral kinship system, it is difficult for individuals to maintain equally close contact with all their relatives. In Iceland, one had to make choices, and what determined one's choice was a kinsman's power. It was more important to nurture a relationship with a secular leader, even though he was a distant relation, than with a brother. Therefore, the chieftain's kin group was gener-ally wider than that of other families in society.[11] It could be advantageous for householders to be both a friend and a kinsman of a chieftain. It could pro-vide them with "additional protection" in relation to the usual chieftain-friend bond. However, it should be noted that only a small percentage of people in the householder class were related to chieftains. Power and wealth also deter-mined the degree of family loyalty. This loyalty was greater in families that had much power and wealth to defend than in families who had little or noth-ing to protect. Therefore, we must recognize the different degrees of family loyalty; it was usually strong at the highest level of society and usually weak at the bottom.

The population of Iceland was probably about ten thousand in the tenth century, while barely three hundred years later it had risen to around fifty thou-sand individuals.[12] On account of this low population, we can assume that family overlapping was extensive. If we look at modern Iceland, the majority of Icelanders are related if they trace their genealogy back just five to seven generations. This phenomenon is visible in the kinship relations between me and my brother-in-law, Páll Hjalti Hjaltason, described in table 1.

Table 1   Family ties between Páll Hjalti Hjaltason and Jón Viðar Sigurðsson
Böðvar Sigurðsson (1772–1852) ~ Þuríður Bjarnadóttir (1778–1821)

Halldóra Böðvarsdóttir	(1808–79)	Guðrún Böðvarsdóttir	(1810–86)
Steinþór Þórðarson	(1840–95)	Vigdís Jónsdóttir	(1843–1914)
Halldóra Steinþórsdóttir	(1882–1956)	Guðrún Þuríður Hannesdóttir	(1881–1963)
Margrét Magnúsdóttir	(1906–71)	Hjalti Pálsson	(1922–2002)
Halldóra Edda Jónsdóttir	(1933–)	Páll Hjalti Hjaltason	(1959–)
Jón Viðar Sigurðsson	(1958–)		

In 1772, when Böðvar Sigurðsson was born, the population of Iceland was 48,207, not a significant change from the thirteenth century. By 1 January 1958, the total number of inhabitants in Iceland had increased to 166,831.[13] Thus, there were three times as many people in 1958 as at the end of the thirteenth century. This does not mean that the overlapping of family ties had been three times as great in the thirteenth century as the overlapping is today, but it supports the assumption that it was significant. The overlapping would have resulted in divided familial loyalties. This, in addition to the ambiguous norms about the assistance one needed to give to relatives, led to kinship generally having little impact during conflicts. And as a result, the position of the family was weak.

The sagas sometimes mention that the chieftains had many kinsmen, indicating that they belonged to a large family. Gissur Thorvaldsson, one of Iceland's most powerful chieftains after about 1240, had eight siblings, his father also had eight, and his mother three.[14] A large and substantial kin group not only provided support, but it also enabled the acquisition of many in-laws. Icelandic chieftains, as well as chieftains and kings in Norway, generally had great power over their families and controlled the marriages of their kinsmen and kinswomen. Thus, a large kin group provided the basis for establishing alliances with many of the other chieftains and more influential householders.

But how was loyalty between kinsmen created? To ensure the family relationship, friendship had to be used in many instances. Blood was no guarantee of support. This is evident from the phrase "they were relatives and friends." The difference between friendship and kinship was that relations of friendship were most often contracted willingly, unlike bonds of kinship that were established at birth. However, because of all the overlapping of family relationships and the limited support kin could give most people in conflicts, kinship took a back seat to friendship, except among the chieftain families. The chieftain Thorgils Böðvarsson supposedly said that he would "be a friend to those from whom he received friendship, and a kinsman to those from whom he received kinship."[15] This statement emphasizes that there was no automatic support merely from bonds of kinship. Rather, these bonds had to be built up before one could expect any consideration. In other words, reciprocity is equally important in the relationships between kin as it was in friendships. Thorgils knew all too well from his own family history that kinship was no guarantee of support; he was a member of the Sturlungar, who had fought intense battles against each other. If a conflict arose between kinsmen, or friend and kinsmen, one had to either mediate or not interfere in the dispute. This resulted in certain ambiguity between these two relationships: "I am caught in the middle, because you are my friend, but he is my brother and is dear to me."[16]

In the article "The Semantic Range of Wine and Freond in Old English," David Clark argues that we must fight the temptation to impose our contemporary hierarchies and taxonomies "of interpersonal relationships" on the "more fluid situation reflected in Old English literature."[17] In the conclusion to his article, he raises the question: "Is the fact that *freond* and *wine* can refer to a kinsman, lover, friend, or ally a sign that the terms themselves are vague, or does [it] represent rather a cultural recognition on the part of the Anglo-Saxon that friendship is multiple and central?" His answer is that we westerners regard friendship as secondary to kinship and sexual love, and that was not necessarily the case among the Anglo-Saxons. He stresses, though, that this "must remain a suggestion in the absence of explicit comment in Anglo-Saxon texts."[18] This ambiguity is not visible in the Old Norse sources; *frændi* is kinsman, *vinr* is friend. However, a *frændi* could well be a *vinr*, and there can be little doubt that friendship in most cases was considered more valuable than family ties. How the difference between Anglo-Saxon England and Norway and Iceland should be explained is an important question, although it will not be addressed here.

The overlapping of friendship and family was extensive, something that the saying "everyone has a friend among his enemies" alludes to.[19] This overlapping is visible in a reconciliation meeting between the kings Sverrir Sigurdarson and Magnús Erlingsson in 1179. In the meeting a number of men participate that had friends, kinsmen, and in-laws on the opposing side.[20] Indeed, it was favorable to have friends, relatives, and in-laws in the faction one fought against. This would guarantee security and protection if one was taken prisoner, and it is also likely that the intensity of the fighting would be reduced in such circumstances.[21] The narrative from *Sverris saga* is one of the few where we hear about friendship among householders in Norway. The reason for this is the source situation, the kings' sagas focus on the kings and their deeds, rather than the householders. There is, however, indication that there existed a friend-ship between the householders in Norway. In the Gulating's law we find a statement advising the bishop to refrain from moving a priest, if he had built a house and established friendships with the householders. This suggests householders did establish friendships with each other.[22] We do not know the extent of overlapping friendships—or family ties—in Norway, but there is no reason to believe that they were more common than in Iceland.

Hávamál makes it clear that friends were viewed as a more important sup-port group than relatives. The poem describes in detail how a friendship should be cultivated, but gives no corresponding advice about how kinship should be preserved. A possible claim is that loyalty among kin was so self-evident in the Viking period that it was unnecessary to mention it. Yet the reverse is also valid, if bonds of kinship were important, one might expect the relationship to one's kin to be mentioned. For most people, it was the protection one re-ceived from a chieftain that was of greatest importance to their everyday ex-istence. One's relatives or kin played a lesser role in most instances. Relatives often lived in other regions and therefore could not be mobilized in local con-flicts. Nevertheless, we must not forget that the transference of property through inheritance was linked to the family. But the right to inherit was no guarantee of support, and inheritance itself was a source of strife in many cases.

Kinsmen, Loyalty, Feud, and War

Before we leave the theme of kinship, we must explain the difference between the pattern of conflict in the Icelandic Family Sagas, and the sagas in Sur-lunga that cover events that occurred in Icelandic society in the thirteenth century. The Icelandic Family Sagas tell of feuds that were conflicts between two groups such as households, "expressed as a sequence of one killing and at least two subsequent killings in revenge." Honor drives the feud on, which "arises from a retaliatory killing which is not resolved, and concludes through a permanent resolution in the form of a settlement, judgment or predomi-nance on one side."[23] The feud between the Laugarmenn and the Hjarðhylt-ingar in *Laxdæla saga*, which involved twenty or thirty men, provides a good model of a typical feud. When we move forward to the thirteenth century, these feuds have more or less disappeared and have been replaced by war between regions. Without doubt, the best example is the battle at Ör-lygsstaðir in 1238, in which about twenty-seven hundred men took part. Listed in table 2 are the major battles of this later period.

Table 2   Battles in the Free State period

YEAR	NAMES OF BATTLES	ADVERSARIES	APPROXIMATE NUMBER OF PARTICIPANTS	NUMBER KILLED
1208	Víðinesbardagi	Ásbirningar, Svínfellingar vs. Bishop Gudmund	c. 700	c. 10
1222	Grímseyjarför	Sturlungar vs. Bishop Gudmund	c. 400	c. 40
1237	Bæjarbardagi	Sturlungar vs. Mýra og Garðamenn	c. 1200	c. 30
1238	Örlygsstaðabardagi	Sturlungar vs. Haukdælir, Ásbirningar	c. 2700	c. 60
1242	Skálholtsbardagi	Sturlungar vs. Haukdælir	c. 900	1
1244	Flóabardagi	Sturlungar vs. Ásbirningar	c. 700	c. 90
1255	Haugsnesfundur	Sturlungar vs. Ásbirningar	c. 1300	c. 100
1255	Þverárfundur	Sturlungar, Svínfellingar vs. Hvammverjar, Seldælir	c. 600	c. 15

The difference between feud and war is seen not only in the number of participants but also in the duty to take revenge. In *Laxdæla saga*, this duty is expressed through the goading of women; namely, Thorgerd Egilsdóttir and Gudrún Ósvífursdóttir after the killing of Kjartan Óláfsson and Bolli Thorlei-fsson.[24] We do not find a corresponding duty stated as clearly in connection with the battle of Örlygsstaðir. Here, the chieftain Gissur killed the chieftain Sturla. Sturla's father, the chieftain Sighvat, and three of Sighvat's other sons were also killed during the battle.[25] When Thórd kakali, another of Sighvat's sons, returned to Iceland from Norway in 1242, he did not seek out and try to kill Gissur. Instead, he attempted to gain control over his father's property and his area of power, which was then controlled by Kolbein ungi Arnórsson.

There was a difference between dying in a battle where several hundred or a thousand men took part and whole regions and parts of the country were involved and dying in a feud that involved twenty to thirty participants from two or three farms. In a war the participants were not engaged in the same "personal" way as when they were involved in a feud. The families of those who died in war could not take revenge against the killer. He was not the only adversary. The householders fought for their chieftains, not for their own interests. Was the family more important during the saga period than in the thirteenth century? It might seem so. Nonetheless, the few stories about feuds in the Icelandic Family Sagas cannot be taken as evidence for the existence of a clan-based society in Iceland in the saga period. As we have seen, Icelandic society was socially layered, and the conflicts reported in the Icelandic Family Sagas relate almost exclusively to the highest-ranking people in society, just like the disputes in the thirteenth century. The focus is on the household in the Family Sagas. The terms "Laugarmenn" and "Hjarðhyltingar" referred not only to the families who lived at the farms Laugar and Hjarðarholt but to everyone in the household; that is, the people who ate at the same table and slept under the same roof for the majority of the year.

The household usually included a married couple, their children, any laborers, and occasionally the couple's parents. The oldest reliable figures for the size of population in Norway or Iceland are from the Icelandic census in 1703. This recorded 50,358 individuals in the country: 22,867 men and 27,491 women, and 8,191 farms. Thus, the average farm had about six people.[26] To what extent these figures are representative of the average farm population in medieval Iceland is uncertain. However, the little information we have from the sagas about the size of households indicates that six people was not an unlikely number. As for medieval Norway, the source situation makes it problematic to argue that the average number of people on a farm in Norway would have been very different from that of Iceland. It is important to emphasize that the economic and social differences between households was great, and the feuds reported in the Icelandic Family Sagas were always linked to households that were considerably larger than the average household.

In Old Norse, there is no word for nuclear family. The term "family," in the sense of the nuclear family (from the Latin *familia*), came into use in English in the fifteenth century and in German in the sixteenth.[27] Information is inconclusive about when this term was first used in Norway and Iceland, possibly in the sixteenth century. The term *fjölskylda*, signifying "family" in modern Icelandic, meant in the High Middle Ages, "that which is imposed as a duty shall be fulfilled, a task which must not be neglected."[28]

Friendship, Kinship, and Sagas

Without the sagas, we could not have had a discussion about friendship in Norway and Iceland. The law codes in Iceland and Norway for c. 900–1300 only mention the terms "friends," "friendship," and "gifts" about twenty times. In the Icelandic Family sagas alone these words occur more than 2000 times. Without the sagas we would be looking at the medieval Icelandic and Norwegian landscape with completely different eyes. The sagas remain very problematic sources, and a long and intense discussion about their value has occurred. The sagas about the Norwegian kings and the Icelandic Family Sagas, *Sturlunga saga*, and the sagas about bishops (*biskupasögur*) are usually divided into two groups: contemporary sagas (*samtíðarsögur*) and "sagas about the distant past" (*fortíðarsögur*), most of which were written down in the thirteenth century. Where the dividing line between these two groups of sagas falls is unclear. *Sverris saga* and *Hákonar saga* are always labeled as contemporary sagas, and so are the sagas in *Heimskringla* dealing with the period after c. 1130.[29] The Icelandic Family Sagas, describing the period c. 930–1030, are always characterized as sagas dealing with the distant past, whereas the *Sturlunga saga* and *biskupasögur* dealing with the period after c. 1120, are called contemporary sagas.

Scholars generally agree that the contemporary sagas are rather reliable sources, based on the short time between the events and the recording of the sagas, normally twenty to seventy years. *Þorgils saga ok Hafliða*, which is the oldest of the contemporary sagas, was written down about 120 years after the events described took place. The main argument for this view on the reliability of these sources is that the audience would have noticed if the saga authors were slandering and not faithfully portraying the past.[30]

Until the beginning of the twentieth century, belief in the historical value of *Heimskringla* and the Icelandic Family Sagas was considerable. However, researchers, especially those who studied Icelandic history, overlooked a significant problem. How do you explain the major differences between the picture of the political situation in *Grágás* and in the Icelandic Family Sagas? As long as the Icelandic Family Sagas were seen as a good source that described society in the saga period, this problem could not be solved. In about 1910, three studies that changed this view of the *Heimskringla* and the Icelandic Family Sagas were published. In the wake of these publications, a strong skepticism of the sagas' credibility emerged. Lauritz Weibull published his lectures on the earliest history of Scandinavia in 1911, under the title *Kritiska undersökningar i Nordens historia omkring år 1000* (Critical Studies of History of Scandinavia around the Year 1000), a work that has been considered a milestone in Scandinavian historical research ever since.[31] The Norwegian Halvdan Koht published an article in 1914, "Sagaenes opfatning av vor gamle historie" (The Sagas' Conception of Our Old History), based on a lecture he had given the previous year, where he presented a radical new view on the sagas, especially *Heimskringla*, as sources.[32] The Icelandic contribution to this discussion did not come from a historian, but from the literary scholar Björn Magnússon Ólsen, who in 1911 published the book *Om Gunnlaugs Saga Ormstungu: En kritisk Undersøgelse* (On Gunnlaugs Saga Ormstunga: A Critical Examination).[33] An important background for this debate was the influence of the

"German historical school" and the source-critical discussion that stressed the difference between the laws and the sagas. The result of this debate was that the historians lost their confidence in the sagas about the distant past.[34] By perceiving the Icelandic Family Sagas and *Heimskringla* in part as literature, the tension between these sagas and the laws disappeared. The laws now became the main sources.

However, as discussed in the introduction to this book, Norwegian and Icelandic research began to be influenced by social history and social anthropological perspectives from about 1970. Not only did researchers begin to focus on new themes, but *Heimskringla* and the Icelandic Family Sagas were also reexamined, and particular attention was paid to their portrayal of society, with less emphasis placed on the historical specifics in the sagas. And now scholars are using these sagas to discuss the period from the middle of the twelfth to the end of the thirteenth century.[35] However, viewing the Icelandic Family Sagas as such evidence by no means solves the problems connected to their use as sources. Why should we prefer the Icelandic Family Sagas, or the sagas about the earliest kings of Norway in *Heimskringla*, to the contemporary sagas in discussing Icelandic and Norwegian society in the thirteenth century? The contemporary sagas, especially those describing the thirteenth century, depict a different political situation from the Icelandic Family Sagas or the sagas about the first kings in Norway.

The sagas about the distant past are historical literature,[36] something on the boundary between history and literature in the modern sense. The saga writers can be called "retellers and commentators," and there is a fundamental difference between this way of writing and the "role of the novelist."[37] The mixture of fact and fiction in the sagas about the distant past makes it difficult to connect persons to events. For example, it is possible that incidents and patterns of conflicts were known from elsewhere and were used to place narratives in new contexts. We are unlikely to be able to answer the question of whether the descriptions of people and events in sagas about the distant past are factual or fictional. Despite this, the picture the sagas give of society is not dependent on the historicity of the individual narratives. Fictional conversations or characters do not automatically imply that the social structure of these sagas is invented. The difference between history and literature is often small, sometimes consisting of no more than the fact that the writers of literature use invented names, unlike the writers of historical accounts. This is probably best demonstrated in a study of the social networks of five Icelandic Family Sagas by Pádraig Mac Carron and Ralph Kenna. They conclude that "whether the sagas are historically accurate or not, the properties of the social worlds they record are similar to those of real social networks. Although one cannot conclusively determine whether the saga societies are real, on the basis of network theory we can conclude that they are remarkably realistic."[38]

One important element in the discussion about the use of sagas about the distant past as historical sources is the question of the level of *continuity* in the way society developed. Was it high or low, did society alter little or much? If it was low between the beginning of the tenth century and the end of the twelfth, it is difficult to argue in favor of the use of the above-mentioned sagas as reliable sources. But if we assume that there was a high level of continuity, these sagas can be used as "models" of social life and how it "lasted for several centuries."[39] I think there are reasons to assume a high level of continuity and stability in these Icelandic and Norwegian societies in most areas, including the kinship systems, ways of doing business, playing the political game, and the level of generosity expected.[40] I would attribute significant social changes primarily to the consequences that the introduction of Christianity had on Icelandic and Norwegian society and to purely political developments in the thirteenth century.

The general knowledge present in the thirteenth century about the tenth and eleventh centuries would have provided a framework for the authors of the sagas to work with. If we regard the sagas about the distant past as a traditional literary genre that grew out of an ancient culture, we cannot claim that these stories merely reflect the authors' thirteenth-century Icelandic or Norwegian society. The subject matter and internal consistency of these sagas demonstrate that they must have been based on a tradition that was rooted in history. If we accept that there existed a general knowledge about the early Norwegian kings in the Old Norse society, it is hard to argue that the saga authors could significantly alter a portrayal of the rulers and make them more gracious than they actually were. The thirteenth-century audience would have reacted to this inaccurate portrayal.

In spite of similarities between the stories (e.g., in the Icelandic Family Sagas and the *Sturlunga saga*), we must be careful not to arrive at any overhasty conclusions about how much influence the author's contemporary milieu had on the Icelandic Family Sagas. Similarities may simply be due to certain social conditions existing for quite a long time. Similar social structures often lead to similar attitudes without one society necessarily having influenced the portrayal of another. However, the similarities between the Icelandic Family Sagas and the contemporary sagas could also have arisen because the literary form *created* similarities, such as in the descriptions of wounds.[41] Form was extremely important in medieval historiography. Direct speech, for example, was "regularly used as a device to give colour and drama, to enable the actors or the author to comment; no one supposed them to be stenographically accurate."[42] I think it right to assume that most people were relatively well informed about their forebears—and earlier rulers—and that there was a high level of social stability in most of these areas. It is much more difficult to argue that a group of authors in the thirteenth century agreed to invent a glorious past for the North Atlantic society and decided among themselves precisely how society, culture (e.g., the role of gift-giving, religion, and a number of important individuals and their genealogical trees) were to be described.[43]

Heimskringla and the Icelandic Family Sagas are historical literature on the border between the modern conceptions of history and literature. These sagas' mix of fact and fiction, together with an inexact chronology, make it difficult to associate people with events. Generally, there are no independent sources to confirm the veracity of these sagas. The events and the pattern of conflict in them may have been known from other sources and used to set the stories and heroic deeds in a new context. For the most part, we must accept that it is not possible to know whether *Heimskringla*'s and the Icelandic Family Sagas' portrayal of people and events is real or fictitious. Nonetheless, we can agree on the *picture* of society they provide. The accuracy of their portrayal of society is not dependent on the historicity of the individual accounts. Fictitious conversations or people do not automatically mean that the image we have from the sagas about the feuds, motives, norms, gift exchange, or society's structure is fictional. An important argument supporting the accuracy of the portrayal of society found in *Heimskringla* and the Icelandic Family Sagas is the major difference between that portrayal and the one given by the sagas describing events of the thirteenth century. The saga authors who wrote *Heimskringla* and the Icelandic Family Sagas and the contemporary sagas tried as much as possible to distinguish between their contemporary society and the old society they described. One way they accomplished this was by using different terms when they described events in *Heimskringla* and the Icelandic Family Sagas and the contemporary sagas.[44] The conscious decision to create a distinction between their distant past and present day suggests they themselves appreciated that the past was not merely a mirror of the present.

The fact is that most of the stories only appear in one saga, making it extremely difficult to link characters and events—and to distinguish between fact and fiction. This does not necessarily mean that the society depicted in these sagas is a fictional one. The stories in the sagas about the distant past only represent a selection, so historians have to decide how far they believe them to be representative of the period. They must try to create a comprehensive picture of the society that produced such accounts and of the society that the sagas depict. The sagas must be used both as source material for the society they originated in and as sources for the society they describe. We will never be able to prove that all the events happened exactly as described. The heart of the matter is that we cannot get closer to the tenth and eleventh centuries than the "sagas about the distant past" permit us to. However, by focusing on the description of society in every single saga and the picture of society that they present collectively, *we can grasp the main features* of the way society was organized in the period covered by the sagas, and how friendship shaped the society.

The saying that we started this chapter with, "Let there be a fjord between kinsmen, but a bay between friends," expresses precisely the relationship between friendship and kinship.[45] There was no strong notion that kinsmen should unite in conflicts. Blood was not a guarantee of support. The multifaceted overlapping of family relations saw to this. Friendship was generally of greater significance, especially when we focus on support and protection.

CHAPTER 7

Friendship Loses Its Power

Political Changes in the Second Half of the Thirteenth Century

The death of the last rebel in Norway, Skúli Bár-darson in 1240, and the death of the Danish king Valdimar Valdimarsson the year after caused a shift in Norwegian politics; the kings consolidated their power in Norway and also began to be more active in foreign policy toward the insular societies in the west. As early as around the year 900, the Orkneys and Shetland were subjected to the Norwegian royal power, and some 150 years later the Faroe Islands suffered the same fate. Following this, Greenland was subjected to the Norwegian throne in 1261. In the years 1262–64, Iceland became a tributary land under the Norwegian crown, and in 1271 and 1281 the Norwegian administrative system was brought into Iceland with the law books Járnsíða and Jónsbók. Friendship lost much of its significance in Iceland when the country became part of the Norwegian realm. The new administrative system turned the chieftain's role upside down. Chieftains now got their power from the king, who, in turn, got his power ostensibly from God. This meant that the chieftains no longer needed to build up their power base from below through protection, feasting, and gifts to householders. Now, as the king's officials, the chieftains were to prosecute the householders and possibly punish them, not help them in their conflicts. This transition occurred relatively quickly, and it was probably established by the end of the 1200s. In the following pages, we examine two aspects of this process in Iceland. The first is how the new political situation and the king's new administration influenced the chieftains' role. The second is the householders' reaction to these changes. Finally, we discuss how the new political situation in Norway affected the local community.

The "Norwegian" Administrative System in Iceland

The period from 1262–64 until 1271 differs little from the years before the end of the Free State. The political structure remained primarily the same. The men and families who played the most active role in the politics of the Free State after about 1240 continued to dominate politics. However, already by 1245, King Hákon had begun to put his royal officials in charge of the chieftaincies he controlled. In 1258, he gave Gissur Thorvaldsson the title of earl with authority over Borgarfjörður, the southern quarter, and the northern quarter. Gissur died in 1268 without ever having been earl over the whole country.[1] After his death, the office of earl was discontinued. The sources make no distinction between Earl Gissur's position of power before and after the end of the Free State. He probably made use of the same power apparatus he himself had built up as a chieftain, and the other chieftains in the country certainly did the same.

The break with the Free State came with the law books Járnsíða in 1271 and Jónsbók in 1281 and the introduction of a new administrative system. The system consisted of a leading official or governor. He was the leader of the king's officials in Iceland, and consequently Iceland's most powerful person. In 1271, there was one lawman who held this position over the whole of Iceland. But in 1277, this position was altered to be held by two men, and their field of action was related to assembly and judicial activities at the Althing. According to Grágás, the Law Council should make new laws, interpret the laws when there was disagreement about them, and decide on various kinds of exemption from the laws. The new law code altered the function of the Law Council. It now became the highest court in the country under the auspices of the lawmen. The lawmen led the activity and were chairmen of the court. The law-making authority now lay with the king. The country was divided into twelve sýslur (districts). The sýslumenn (district governors) who controlled several districts, were those who meted out official prosecution and executed the orders of the authorities. The district governors got their offices directly from the king. To staff these official positions, the monarchy relied on those men and their sons who had sworn an oath of allegiance to the king on behalf of the Icelanders in 1262–64. Of the twenty-one men the sources mention directly in this context of district governors in the last decades of the thirteenth century, eighteen were certainly descended from chieftains, and the other three probably were as well. In other words, continuity between the "old" and the "new" elite was great.[2]

Within the new aristocracy in Iceland, friendships continued to be established, but these were not as important as before. The political game had changed radically. The king now stood at the center, and it was only as a member of his court that one could achieve a position of power. The political friendship bonds between chieftains lost much of their significance. The chieftains no longer needed each others' support in the power struggles. These struggles had ceased. The only way to maintain a position of power was to show loyalty to the king and secure a royal office.

The crown was aware of the danger the chieftains' local network in Iceland posed for peace in the country. Therefore, it was fixed by law how much one could give as a gift to a friend. In the Norwegian Landslög (Land's law) from 1274, it states that the king did not have the right to take back the gifts he gave. The same also applied to the gifts that the householders gave to the king. Later it states that each person can give to their legitimate children or others a quarter of the property she or he had gained.[3] In the Icelandic Jónsbók from 1281, which replaced Járnsíða, it states (as in Landslög) that the king and the householders could not take back their gifts. Jónsbók then adds that each person can also give gifts of friendship; for example, a horse or a weapon, but these gifts cannot reduce the inheritance their heirs legally are entitled to.[4] In other words, the maker of these laws attempted to limit the aristocracy's ability to build up a local position of power and potentially disturb the peace that the country experienced in the second half of the thirteenth century.

The special position of the king's liege men in society, which, to a large degree, was inherited and emphasized through external symbols, separated them out from other people. They were soon perceived as their own social group. This new social reality can be found in the saga about Bishop Árni. It reports that when Jónsbók was introduced at the Althing in 1281, there were three social classes in the country: clerics, the king's liege men, and the householders.[5] In the period after the end of the Free State until 1281, an aristocratic class consciousness emerged, caused by solidarity among the king's retainers in the *hirð*. This was not the case with the chieftains during the Free State. They knew themselves to be society's most powerful men, but they saw each other as rivals, not as members of a common class.

To mark the differences between the rich and the poor, and between the king's men and the rest of society, in 1281 the law stipulated that all people should dress in relation to their wealth and position in society. The regulations in Jónsbók about this are quite detailed. The group allowed to dress in all types of clothing, were the householders who owned more than 120 hundreds and the liege men who owned *öll skyldarvopn*; that is, the weapons dictated by law for their rank as members of the *hirð*.[6] In other words, it was the king's men and the country's richest men who were not legally restricted in their dress. In most instances, the richest men *were* the king's men. The king's retainers were the only ones who could use certain symbols characteristic of their class, such as a shield and a helmet. That the *hirð* was a community with common interests is also indicated by the fact that the king's retainers were under a common Icelandic royal banner and law of the *hirð*.

The *hirð* man's duty was to the king. Therefore, officially he could not take part in the exchange of letters between the Icelanders and the king. This was the responsibility of the common people, who communicated with the king in 1302, 1306, and 1319. However, there is no doubt that the Icelandic aristocracy pulled the strings and helped to formulate the demands the Icelanders put forward to the king. We see this in one of the additional paragraphs in Gizurarsáttmáli from 1302. In this document, the common people set forth their desire for lawmen and district governors to be Icelandic and should be selected from among the descendants of the old chieftain families who had once held the chieftaincies.[7] The demand that royal officials in Iceland should be Icelandic was a protest against the king having sent Norwegian lawmen and district governors to the country. For the common people in Iceland, it must have played a relatively small role whether the royal officials were either Icelandic or Norwegian. But for the Icelandic aristocracy, it was a question of existence. They had to secure for themselves the revenue that flowed from the king's offices in Iceland. Without this revenue and without the prestige that came with the positions of power, the aristocracy probably would have disappeared.

The transition to the new Norwegian system was economically favorable for the king's retainers in Iceland. According to Gamli sáttmáli, each assembly tax-paying householder should pay a tax of twenty ells to the king. Of this, the district governors were to get half. The total number of tax-paying householders in Iceland in 1311 was 3,812. If we assume that all of these paid their tax, the amount comes to about 635 hundreds, which could buy roughly thirty average-sized farms. The district governors were to use part of the tax to pay those men who were to travel to the Althing as jury members. All the same, there can be no doubt that the district governors had the majority of the profit from the tax, especially when we consider that very often they kept the entire amount.[8]

The economic system of Iceland was characterized by the political system. On the whole, we can describe the economic system in Iceland during the period of the Free State as an amalgamation of market, reciprocal, and redistribution economies. A reciprocal economy implies movement of economic resources, like the exchange of gifts. Redistribution describes a system where the economic resources were channeled through a social and political center that then redistributed them. Reciprocal and redistribution systems quite often occur in combination with each other, and most often in such a way that the former principal becomes a part of the latter.[9] For example, it was acceptable in Iceland to earn money through trade, something that both the chieftains and householders did, and this was not seen as an inferior way to make a living. In other words, one could gain wealth through a market economy livelihood, but profits should be shared within the redistributive system in the form of gifts and feasts for friends. There was no honor in being rich but miserly.

However, after Iceland became a part of the Norwegian realm and the country was subject to a new political system, certain changes occurred in the economic system. When the bonds of friendship between chieftains and householders were, for the most part, dissolved, the chieftains no longer needed to use a large portion of their economic profits for feasting and gifts for the householders. The chieftains could now use their wealth to invest and become even richer. The system more clearly took on an identity of a market economy than it had earlier.

An important incentive in the development of society in Iceland until about 1260 was the competition between local chieftains. Among other things, they competed over who could offer the best protection, hold the biggest feasts, and give the biggest gifts. The ending of gift exchange had long-term consequences for the householders. Arguably, the chieftains' feasts and gifts had led to a certain economic cohesion and balancing out. In a series of letters to the king from around 1300, the householders complained about the country's poverty. This should not be perceived only as a tactical move from their side but also as an indication of the changes in their condition after gift exchange between them and the chieftains was reduced.

The social elite in Iceland continued to organize feasts; however, the feasts got a new profile.[10] Earlier we discussed both the entrepreneurial feast and patron-role feast and linked them to the political situation in Iceland in the Free State. After Iceland came under control of the Norwegian kings and a new political dynamic grew up, the old types of feast were redundant, and a new type of feasting among the social elite became dominant: the diacritical feast. This type of feast differs from the other two feast types in terms of its different consumption patterns. A transformation took place from quantity to "style." But more important is the shift from "commensal" bonds between different social partners to what Michael Dietler terms "a statement of exclusive and unequal commensal circles: obligations of reciprocal hospitality are no longer the basis of status claims and power."[11] After Iceland came under the control of the Norwegian king and a "new" administrative system came into effect, a group consciousness came into being among the Icelandic aristocracy. Power came from above, from the king, and not from below, from the householders, as before. These changes resulted in the aristocracy beginning to see themselves as a group with common and not competing interests. The distance between the chieftains and householders grew. Their friendship was for the most part gone. In response to this change, the horizontal ties became more important for the householders, especially the *hreppr* bounds.

The *Hreppr*

In Iceland we find a local organization, the *hreppr*.[12] It was a geographically bounded entity led by five *hreppr* administrators, who were chosen for one year at a time, with autonomy over a number of internal issues. We do not know when the *hreppr* organization originated. Scholars dispute whether it was brought to Iceland with the first settlers, or whether it was introduced in the middle of the tenth century. However, all agree the *hreppr* organization was well developed by 1096–97, when tithes were introduced. At that point, the *hreppr* gained the right of disposal of the tithe for the poor in the same manner as the householders in Norway had.

During the period of the Free State, the family was primarily responsible for looking after the welfare of its members. If they were not able to manage this, and there were no other near relations, the duty of care fell on the *hreppr*, the parish, the quarter, or the country as a whole. In practice, it was the *hreppr* that took on this task. The administrators of the *hreppr* were to distribute the poor tithe and gifts of food to the poor and organize the movement of these poor around the *hreppr*. The *hreppr*'s other main task was to arrange mutual insurance between the farmers. They should jointly pay half the compensation needed for two types of loss: if a householder lost more than a quarter of his cattle and horses or if parts of his farm, dwelling, outhouse for washing and baking, or food store burned down. This compensation was not to be paid out more than three times to the same householder and should never constitute more than 1 percent of the total wealth of each contributing householder, even if it did not cover half the damage. If the householders wished to give more, they were free to do so.

We do not know the number of *hreppr* in Iceland during the Middle Ages, although we do have figures once we reach the 1700s when there were 163 in the country. The Icelandic chieftains probably had a certain influence over the *hreppr*. As already mentioned, the householders were in a subordinate position in relation to the chieftains in the introduction to the Norwegian administrative system, and it is unlikely that the householders controlled an institution at the local level without a certain amount of intervention from the chieftains.

There is much to indicate that the *hreppr* filled the void that was created when bonds of friendship between householders and chieftains for the most part ceased when the country was subjugated to Norwegian rule. The *hreppr* was a well-integrated part of the Icelandic society in about 1260. This is evident in the Gizurarsáttmáli. In the agreement's first paragraph, we read

> that they [the Icelanders] swore an oath to their lord King Hákon and King Magnús to pay tax forever, accept his lordship over the country and be his subjects, paying twenty ells for each man who was liable to pay the assembly-tax. The *hreppr* administrators were to collect this tax, take it to the ship and hand it over to the royal official. After that, the administrators were no longer responsible for the tax.[13]

That the *hreppr* was entrusted with such an important task clearly emphasizes the *hreppr*'s position.

The law books from 1271 and 1281 did not change the *hreppr*'s position to any great extent, except for removing the paragraphs about mutual help and the *hreppadómr*, a court dealing with minor issues inside the *hreppr*. There should still be five administrators, but contrary to Grágás, the *hreppr* administrators could now remain in office as long as they wished. With the introduction of Jónsbók, new local assemblies were also established, and it can be argued that the assembly organization founded in 1281 was of greater significance for the householders than the one that existed before the 1260s. From now on, they played a more active and important part in local public life than they had done previously. In the Free State period, Grágás mentions commune meetings (*hreppsfundir*). Three regular meetings were to be held each year. Additional meetings could be held if the need arose. At these, cases were decided by a majority. In the new administrative organization, these meetings were converted into assemblies and given an important place in the assembly organization. All householders in the country thus became members of the royal administration. There can hardly be any doubt that these commune assemblies were of great importance to the local population. Indeed, for the householders, the *hreppr* assemblies were probably the most important of all the local assemblies. At the *hreppr* level, many local issues were dealt with, which meant that minor local disputes could be settled and decisions taken on how common land should be used.[14]

The chieftains had been the householders' most important social and economic security during the Icelandic Free State. After the local aristocracy was transformed into a service aristocracy and the strong bonds between the householders and the chieftains weakened, the householders were forced to cooperate with each other to a greater extent than before. Society had taken on clearer horizontal divisions. It was likely that this transition led to the *hreppr* and its officials resolving local disputes much more frequently than before.

The Kings and the Guilds

The Norwegian kings used friendship up till the middle of the thirteenth century to ensure the householders' and the chieftains' support. Paragraph one in Gulating's law about the king being "our friend and we his" was removed from Landslög (Land's law) in 1274. This was in line with a new ideology that emerged at the end of the twelfth century and in the first half of the thirteenth; the king now got his power from God above, and not below from the householder. The householders became the king's subjects, and not his friends. Friendship with its endless overlapping loyalties was unsuitable as a political foundation for the royal power. It is likely these changes started to take place in the last decades of the twelfth century and that the exclusion of the Gulating's law paragraph from the Landslög was just the final step in a long and complicated process. The king, however, continued to use friendship to secure the loyalty of the most central persons in his inner circle and to give gifts to the upper layer of the society. The day after Archbishop Einar declared the young Magnús Hákonarson king in 1257, the king gave good gifts to many men. The archbishop himself received a longship. Magnús became then *vinsæll*.[15] The growing concentration of power in Norway in the eleventh, twelfth, and thirteenth centuries resulted in the king being increasing isolated. The men and women in his innermost circle were thus in a key position with great power. They could influence who was allowed to access the king. This pattern emerges very clearly in *Konungs skuggsjá*. In this work, a father gives his son the advice that if he wants to engage the king in dialogue, he should establish friendship with those who most often brought people's cases before the king, and those whom the king likes to listen to the most.[16]

   The political developments in Norway resulted in a change of character in the aristocracy over the course of the High Middle Ages: the old aristocracy with a local power base was replaced by an aristocracy that built its position of power on participation in the royal administration, both local and central. Presumably, the local power of the chieftains began to weaken in Norway after the middle of the twelfth century, when we no longer hear of great chieftains like Erling Skjalgsson and Einar Thambarskelfir Eindridason. The struggle for power in the country led to a number of chieftain families losing their local positions of power and their property being confiscated by the crown. At the same time, not all the families were able to produce capable sons. With the king's help, some individuals managed to climb the social ladder. Yet there is little reason to assume that those who did filled the vacuum that the power struggles created. In other words, the overall number of chieftain families in Norway declined, and their local power was reduced. How then did the householders react to these changes?

During the Viking Age in Norway, there were local guilds in the whole of the country. These were social-religious groups with common interests for the men and women in the community and their families. We know of three surviving sets of regulations for the guilds. They demonstrate that the guilds had a long history of development behind them and that with the introduction of Christianity the old religious content changed such that it could be adapted to the new faith. Membership in the guilds was voluntary, but because of the support and help the guild could give, it was difficult—if not impossible—to avoid being a part of the local guild. Guild members had strong reciprocal obligations, including giving aid during sickness, in conflicts with those outside the guild and when a house, crop, or cattle were lost. The mutual obligations were so strong that if one guild brother was killed in another brother's presence, the surviving guild brother had to avenge the killing on the spot or risk being excluded from the guild. Guild members, the men and women who belonged to the guild, not only had obligations to living members of the guild but also to those who had died. These included following the coffin to the grave and having masses sung for the dead.[17]

Guild members held a number of religious feasts, and these were to strengthen the mutual social obligations between the guild members. Most Norwegian rural districts had a guild and a guild house, such as Finnesloftet at Voss or Haugenloftet at Åraksbø in Setesdal. Everyone was to bring the same amount of food and beer to guild meetings. In this way, no relationships of dependency created by an unequal gift exchange could develop. Yet not all guild members were equally rich or powerful, and it is likely the richest householders held the most central positions within the guild. However, the guild was not an arena for a political power struggle. They were common insurance organizations, and if the guilds were to function as intended, they needed to try and prevent gifts and friendship from encroaching on this purpose, otherwise it could lead to a split in loyalty between guild members.

The first guilds probably did not cooperate much among themselves, but eventually they began to work together and organize themselves into county guilds; for example, Miklagildet in Trondheim, which covered all eight counties in Trøndelag, Norway. The county guilds had a regular guild meeting every year that usually coincided with the feast day of the guild's patron saint.[18]

The guilds had extensive internal jurisdiction. Their regulations indicate that the guilds were to judge in the majority of conflicts between guild members. Thus they took on themselves a large part of society's need for conflict resolution. It was only in cases of murder and, after 1274, in cases that concerned farming and land ownership, that the guild did not have jurisdiction. If the guilds took care of most internal conflicts, then they took over some of the tasks that chieftains had previously had responsibility for and that the crown did not acquire. The crown quickly realized the necessity of the guilds for solving conflicts and helping to maintain the local peace, and therefore it ensured that their status corresponded with their importance.

The importance of the guilds appears to have increased in the twelfth and thirteenth centuries, presumably in relation to the weakening of the chieftains' power. The king could not provide the same protection that the chieftains had earlier, which caused a political vacuum that forced the householders to cooperate even more closely than before.

The main lines in the development of the Norwegian aristocracy in the period c. 900–1300 had, naturally enough, much in common with the development we saw in Iceland. Political developments in Norway reduced the chieftains' power, and, the old aristocracy with a local power base was replaced by an aristocracy whose position in society was based on taking part in the royal administration. With the aristocracy being drawn more toward the monarchy, bonds of friendship between the chieftains and the householders weakened. This led to an even closer cooperation between the latter on a local level, namely through guilds. Reciprocal bonds were replaced by more unilateral ones. The king could demand loyalty from his subjects, but he also continued to use friendship to secure the loyalty of his closest staff, and reciprocal bonds were still important in these circumstances. This also applied to the king's friendships with foreign princes, which were as popular in the Viking Age as at the end of the thirteenth century.

The weakening of friendships between the local chieftains and householders resulted in stronger horizontal ties, a development that can be traced in both Iceland and Norway. These horizontal ties had been an essential feature of both societies, but it was first in the thirteenth century, after a new political situation had occurred in both countries with the strengthening of royal power, that the *hreppr* and the local guilds now became the most important social institutions for the householders.

CHAPTER 8

Pragmatic Friendship

We have touched on many important aspects of friendship, and it is hoped that we have convinced our readers that friendship was an absolutely essential factor in Norwegian and Icelandic society and the most important social tie for a large part of the period c. 900–1300. However, there are two areas that need further clarification; namely, how friendship evolved between the parties, and how great the variations were between different types of friendships. In the introduction to this book, we quoted stanza 41 of *Hávamál*: "With weapons and clothes friends should gladden one another, / that is most obvious; / mutual givers and receivers are friends for longest, / if the friendship is going to work at all."[1] Entry into friendship was only the first step on an otherwise uncertain path. The relationship had to be cultivated, which determined its content and how important it was for the two participants. Finally, all friendships came to an end, usually because one of the friends died. In other words, any friendship included three stages: establishment, development, and conclusion.[2]

Those able to establish friendships were heads of "households": householders (farms), chieftains (chieftaincies), kings (realms), bishops (episcopal sees), abbots and abbesses (monasteries), and female and male members of the highest ranks in society. By all accounts, this group constituted fifteen to twenty percent of the population. The friendships that they established between themselves can be characterized as "political friendships." The purpose of the friendships was to secure support and protection. These political friend-ships also extended to the households, and thus nearly all of society was influ-enced by these friendships.

We can refer to friendship between most people and the saints as "holy friendship." It was such that, through gifts to the saints or by honoring them, one could gain assistance for day-to-day problems.[3] An important reason to establish friendship with the saints was because they could plead one's case, or the case of a friend's friend, before God on Judgment Day. Because this friendship remained largely linked to gifts, it was reserved primarily for the wealthier men and women of society.

Friendship with God is clearly different from the other forms of friendship. First, everyone could enter into this kind of friendship. Second, it only affected the relationship between the person concerned and the Creator; no one else was influenced by it or had influence over it.

It was generally those at the higher levels of the social hierarchy who could take the initiative to establish political friendships. It was important for secu-lar leaders to control recruitment to their group of friends, or else they risked being drawn into conflicts they would not normally engage in. The opposite was true for friendship with God. Anyone who wished to could seek out such a friendship, but here the conditions were clear: one must follow God's com-mands, and it was God who ultimately decided if one would revel in the King-dom of Heaven or endure the torments of Hell. Friendship with the saints was nearer to friendship with God; those who were subordinate could take the initiative to establish the friendship.

In political friendships, gifts generally moved down the social hierarchy (e.g., from a chieftain to a householder), and it was the leaders who organized and invited others to feasts. A strong demand for compensation or service was linked to the gifts and the feasts: a gift, after all, required a countergift.[4] In friendships with the saints, gifts moved "upwards," from ordinary mortals to God's friends. The countergift often took the form of help with acute prob-lems, such as sickness, and such miracles were often referred to as "gifts of health."[5] The saints generally were not drawn into conflicts between secular leaders. This role was usually attributed to God—he had control over all things. In friendships with God, gifts also moved upwards. However, these were not material gifts, but attempts to live according to God's commands.

The establishment of political friendship was characterized by rituals. We see this in the story of King Ólaf Haraldsson and King Önund and their meet-ing at Konghelle. They began by promising each other their friendship, and then they allegedly spoke together alone, certainly about the conditions of that friendship. When they departed, they exchanged gifts and left the meeting as friends.[6] We also find other rituals linked to the establishment of friendship; for example, a kiss was occasionally used to initiate the relationship.[7]

Friendships between people and saints and friendships between most people and God were not characterized by rituals as strong as those depicted with political friendships. This meant that these two types of friendship were not entered into on a "stage" such as within a chieftain's hall.

A claim exists that friendships were established to secure political and economic benefits for both parties in this period.[8] This type of dual benefits could arise in horizontal political friendships, but not in the vertical kind, which was the most common form. Neither the Icelandic chieftains nor the Norwegian kings gained any economic advantage from their friends. If a ruler began to impose financial burdens on his friends, he would risk losing their friendship. Concerning the vertical political relationship, both parties did appear to benefit. There was no explicit economic motive behind the establishment of friendship with saints, but it cannot be ruled out that many of those who tried to establish a friendship with God thought material wealth might come their way as a result of the relationship.

The establishment of friendship was only the first step in a relationship between two individuals. The contribution each party then made to the relationship determined its depth, importance, and content. There were different stages in this development process. Whether a friendship was young or old, or good or bad, influenced how this development played out. We also hear of *hleytivinátta*, which was friendship between kin or those with some other relation of affinity.[9]

It was not only the friendship that was characterized in different ways; the friends themselves were as well. In the Old Norse material, we know of at least twenty-five different types of friend—nowhere in medieval Europe do we find as many words about friends as in the Old Norse sources—some of which are evidenced in the following terms: *alda-* (old), *alúðar-* (dear), *ást-* (loving), *atgerða-* (business), *einka-* (private), *forn-* (old), *gjaf-* (gift), *guðs-* (God's), *göfgir-* (noble), *half-* (half), *hjarta-* (heart), *höfuð-* (main), *konungs-* (king), *leyndar-* (secret), and *trúnaðar-* (trusted).[10] These terms emphasize the different aspects of friendship. We cannot discuss here what lies behind all the different designations, but we can look more closely at two, the private friend and the gift friend. It is uncertain how the term "private friend" should be understood. A possible interpretation is that such people were the friend of only one person. The private friend's loyalty would never be divided, and that someone would willingly refrain from friendship with all others emphasizes how highly he valued his only friend. We have discussed how friendship was established and maintained through gifts. It should be unnecessary then to emphasize this reality with its own term, the "gift friend." This term presumably refers to a person who exchanged gifts with his leader, something which underlines the close relationship between the two. It also is, as we have seen, used in the discussion of God's friends, in particular those who gave gifts to the poor because gifts given to the needy were considered gifts given to God.

The key factor in friendships—regardless of who entered into them—was loyalty. In a society without institutions that could guarantee support and security, it was crucial that a bond existed that created loyalty and provided assistance, and that was friendship. This is why it was such an important aspect of society in Norway and Iceland in the greater part of the period we have considered. By all accounts, most friendships lasted a good while. In the relationship between chieftains and householders, if both parties fulfilled their obligations, the friendship would likely be lifelong. Loyalty was strong in this type of relationship. Relations between chieftains and kings, among chieftains, and among kings were frequently characterized by opportunism and therefore were usually brief. This also applies in part to relationships between people and saints. Demands were made on the saints, and if they stopped performing miracles, fewer people would attempt to establish friendships with them. In one's relationship with God, we can assume that most people tried to remain friends with God. The consequences of not doing so were dire.

Discussing friendship and loyalty and different types of friends brings us finally to the question of whether friendship is an emotion. The terms for dear or loving friends definitely points in that direction. In many cases there must have been a strong affection between friends, as with Gunnar Hámundarson and Njál Thorgeirsson or kings and their closest friends. There is, however, no reason to overestimate this aspect of friendship, especially regarding the political friendship.[11] In most cases friendship was an instrument to create support and protection. Nonetheless, the notion of a dear or loving friend should be considered a sign of a loyal friend.

In the introduction to this study, we mentioned Aristotle. He divided friendship into three types: pragmatic friendship based on utility, friendships of pleasure, and perfect or true friendship. Of these, he perceived the last to be the most noble.[12] If we were to apply one of these three terms to describe friendship in Norway and Iceland, it has to be pragmatic friendship. Friendship involved belonging to or forming networks that one could have recourse to in an economic crisis or a political conflict. A man had a duty to support his friends, but if they refused to give their support in return, there was only one thing to do: end the relationship.

Our earlier analysis of Hávamál and the poem's emphasis on reciprocity between equals showed how the poem drew a clear distinction between friends and enemies. Christian friendship, which stressed that a man should love his enemies as he loved his friends, did not fit into this political culture and therefore had little effect on traditional Old Norse ideas of friendship.

The most common reason for the discontinuation of friendship was probably the death of one of the friends. Friendship could also cease because of divorce or the death of one member of a couple. Otherwise, we are rarely told about the ending of a friendship.[13] We have already mentioned one of the few stories in which this occurs—when Brodd-Helgi dropped his friendship with Ketil when he did not carry out the task he was given. The reason for the ending of this friendship is obvious: Ketil did not carry out the task required of him. The chieftains had a hold over their friends, and the threat that they might end the friendship certainly led on some occasions to householders being forced to carry out tasks they were not always happy with. However, given the lack of sources about the ending of a friendship, it is probable that most did not end until one of the friends died—on this point *Hávamál*'s advice was followed. Although all worldly friendships ended at some point, friendship with God lasted forever. How durable friendships were between most people and the saints is not certain. It is possible they did not always last particularly long. As noted earlier, the saint had to live up to the expectation of performing miracles; otherwise, there was a danger that people would stop bestowing gifts or honor on him.

Friendship played an essential role in Icelandic, and Norwegian, society up to the second half of the thirteenth century. It was the net that held society together, having a direct and indirect bearing on people's lives. It had the greatest degree of influence in forming the societal and personal qualities that were valued in the political game; for example, generosity and loyalty. Friendship was also used to group people together, even though not everyone could create such relationships. In fact, the majority of people could not do so, and this explains why most traces of friendship disappeared so quickly after Iceland was subjugated by Norway.

How should we define the term "friendship" in Norwegian-Icelandic society in the period c. 900–1300?[14] As we have seen, the term is an ambiguous word, where the significance and obligations of the friendship depended on the social position of those who entered into it. There was a difference between the vertical friendships between chieftains and householders, kings and chieftains, God and most people, and the horizontal friendship among householders, among bishops, among chieftains, and among kings. What these relationships had in common was that gifts (objects, service, and political support) were associated with the establishment and maintenance of the bonds, and that reciprocity was an important aspect of this. Yet the loyalty and longevity of these relationships was not equal across the board. Within vertical friendship bonds, especially in the relationships between chieftains and householders, the loyalty and longevity of vertical friendship bonds was considerable. Without the householders' support, the chieftains were power-less, and without protection from a chieftain, the householders' position was precarious. In contrast, friendship among chieftains was characterized by opportunism, and they tried to exploit each other to attain their goals. The same could be said of the relationship between the chieftains and the kings; loyalty in this relationship, especially on the chieftain's side, was not always particularly great.

The term most often used about relationships of this type is "dyadic." A dyadic relationship is a direct relationship between two parties that is built on reciprocity, as distinct from the coercive relations, such as those that occur because people belong to the same family. Dyadic relations can last for a few days, weeks, whole lifetimes, or from one generation to the next.[15] Was this type of dyadic friendship a sign of crisis in the political system in Norway and Iceland?[16] No. On the contrary, in a large part of the period we have discussed, no other method existed for building up power, or attempting to secure support from the gods, the saints, or God. Its importance reveals important features of the societies in Norway and Iceland. Its prevalence tells us not only about the political situation but equally as much about how vital personal relationships were in these societies.

For the last few years, there has been a strong focus on social networks in academia. A network has been defined as a collection of *nodes* (persons) connected by *links* (ties or connections between them).[17] If we apply these con-cepts about networks to friendship between kings, chieftains, and householders, it is clear that the kings had a much higher number of "links" (or relationships) than the chieftains. According to paragraph one in Gulating's law, the kings were actually friends with all the householders in their realm; however, the chieftains were friends mostly with the householders in their own chieftaincy. What is of interest is that the sagas use the term *vinsæll* to describe the networks of both groups, despite the king's generally greater number of relationships. When it comes to the saints and God, it can be argued that many links were connected with them, but neither they nor God is ever described as *vinsælir*.

The key factor in friendships—regardless of who entered into them—was loyalty. In a society without institutions that could guarantee support and se-curity, it was crucial that a bond existed that created loyalty and provided as-sistance, and that was friendship. This is why it was such an important aspect of society in Norway and Iceland in the greater part of the period we have considered.

Service relationships have been called a humiliating form of subordination.[18] An important aspect of the term "friendship" was that it partly concealed the service relationship. After a while, however, as the monarchy became stronger and a new ideology was introduced, it was no longer necessary to attempt to conceal social inequalities; on the contrary, they were now emphasized. Yet because of all the overlapping in friendship, and because in many instances friendship was not binding enough, the monarchy needed a new way of securing the loyalty of its subordinates—a bond created by an oath of loyalty. Of all the king's *hirð* men, it was only dukes and earls who had permission to allow their followers to swear an oath of loyalty. This situation resulted in the creation of a bond between the king and the householders without the householders entering into a corresponding relationship with anyone else.

To put it simply, a transition occurred from friendship, a bilateral and personal relationship, to obedience, a one-sided and impersonal relationship. In Norway, these changes probably began in the second half of the twelfth century and were complete in the second half of the thirteenth century. In Iceland, however, this transition occurred over the course of the last decades of the thirteenth century. These changes also signaled that power was no longer built up from below, through the support of the householders, but came from above—from God. The king got his power from the Almighty and delegated it downwards in society to the aristocracy. The king was no longer the householders' friend, but their lord. This development weakened the power base of the local leaders in both Norway and Iceland. They were now the king's officials and not the householders' friends. A power vacuum created by this development imbued the householders with an even greater desire for cooperation, and this was carried out through the *hreppr* in Iceland and the guild in Norway. However, in the milieu around the bishops and kings, friendship continued to be utilized. It was now reserved for society's elite, and thus became even more exclusive than it had been earlier. In "foreign politics," which can perhaps be characterized in this period as the relationships between kings, friendship continued to play an important role.

Let us end this book with a story from *Islendzk æventyri* from the fourteenth century, which splendidly reveals the tenuousness of friendships and the worth of loyalty within such relationships. In this narrative, the master suggested to his pupil that he should test all one hundred of his friends. He should slaughter a calf and cut it up into small pieces, and then consult his friends and tell them that he had killed a man and that he needed their help to bury the body. The pupil did this, but all of his friends refused to support him. When the pupil told his tutor this, the tutor answered: "Many people are friends, as long as everything goes well, but in reality they are few."[19] Go now to my half friend (hálfvinr) and ask him for help. The half friend did not hesitate to help the pupil, and after he had dug a grave, the pupil told him the truth. The pupil went back to his master, who, when he heard the result, replied, "He is a true friend who helps you when the world fails you."[20]

NOTES

Introduction

1. This book is based on a book I published in 2010, *Den vennlige vikingen: Vennskapets makt i Norge og på Island ca. 900–1300* (The Friendly Viking: The Power of Friendship in Norway and Iceland c. 900–1300), Oslo: Pax.

2. Etymologically, *vinr* in Old Norse means a dear friend or companion; Ásgeir Blöndal Magnússon, *Íslensk orðsifjabók* (Reykjavík: Orðabók Háskólans, 1989). For a thorough discussion about the etymological and semantic development of *vinr*, see Theodor Nolte, "Der Begriff und das Motiv des Freundes in der Geschichte der deutschen Sprache und älteren Literatur," *Frühmittelalterliche Studien* 24 (1990): 126–36. Cf. David Clark, "The Semantic Range of Wine and Freond in Old English," *Neuphilologische Mitteilungen* 114, no. 1 (2013): 79–93.

3. All medieval personal names will be anglicized; Icelandic and Norwegian place names will be written in contemporary Icelandic and Norwegian.

4. Aristotle = Aristotle, *Nicomachean Ethics*, Oxford World's Classics, trans. David Ross, ed. Lesley Brown, rev. ed. (Oxford: Oxford University Press, [1980] 2009), 145; Aristoteles, *Den nikomakiske etikk*, Bokklubbens kulturbibliotek, ed. Øyvind Rabbås, Anfinn Stigen, and Trond Berg (Eriksen, Oslo: Bokklubben dagens bøker, 1999), xxxvi–xxxvii.

5. Cicero, *De senectute; De amicitia; De divinatione*, Loeb Classical Library, ed. William Armistead Falconer, vol. 154 (Cambridge, MA: Harvard University Press, 1927), 195.

6. Daniel Schwartz, *Aquinas on Friendship*, Oxford Philosophical Monographs (Oxford: Clarendon Press, 2007), 1.

7. Per Sveaas Andersen, *Samlingen av Norge og kristningen av landet 800–1130*, Handbok i Norges historie 2 (Bergen: Universitetsforlaget, 1977), 247, 336.

8. KLNM = *Kulturhistorisk leksikon for nordisk middelalder 1–22*, ed. Finn Hødnebø et al. (Oslo: Gyldendal, 1956–78 [2. oppl. 1980–82]), 11, col. 333.

9. Arne Odd Johnsen, *Fra ættesamfunn til statssamfunn* (Oslo: Aschehoug, 1948).

10. Íslenzk fornrit Eddukvæði = *Eddukvæði 1–2*, Íslenzk fornrit, ed. Jónas Kristjánsson and Vésteinn Ólason (Reykjavík: Hið Íslenzka fornritafélag, 2014), 1:329–31, 352. All translations of *Hávamál* are from Edda 2008 = *The Poetic Edda*, Oxford World's Classics, ed. Carolyne Larrington, 19–20, 35 (Oxford: Oxford University Press, 2008). I have, however, made two changes. In stanza 39 Larrington translates *fé* with "money," and in stanza 41 *váðom* as "gift," which I translated as "wealth."

11. Marcel Mauss, *The Gift: Forms and Functions of Exchange in Archaic Societies*, trans. Ian Cunnison, ed. E. E. Evans-Pritchard (1925; repr., London: Cohen and West, 1970), 1.

12. Ibid., 8–10.

13. Eddukvæði 1:330.

14. Both the Danish religious historian Vilhelm Grønbech (1873–1948) in *Vor folkeæt i oldtiden 1–2* [The culture of the Teutons], (København: Pios Boghandel, [1909–12] 1955), 2:50, 51–67, and the Norwegian philologist Johan Hovstad (1896–1959) in *Mannen og samfunnet: Studiar i norrøn etikk* [Man and society: Studies in Norse ethics] (Oslo: Samlaget, 1943), 56–67, discussed gift giving and friendship. Disappointingly, neither study inspired any further discussion.

15. Jesse L. Byock, *Feud in the Icelandic Saga* (Berkeley: University of California Press, 1982), 217.

16. Jesse L. Byock, *Medieval Iceland: Society, Sagas, and Power* (Berkeley: University of California Press, 1988), 131.

17. Ibid., 130. Cf. Byock, *Feud*, 42, 75; Byock, *Medieval Iceland*, 132; Jesse L. Byock, *Viking Age Iceland* (London: Penguin Books, 2001), 135.

18. William Ian Miller, in an article from 1983, addressed the pragmatic friendship in Iceland; Miller, "Justifying Skarphéðinn: Of Pretext and Politics in the Icelandic Bloodfeud," *Scandinavian Studies* 55 (1983): 338–42. He states that "[v]inátta is less a state of reciprocal affection than a juridical status or political state of affairs. Hence the legalism of the phrase 'mæla til vináttu' . . . with its sense of 'to stipulate, to bargain for'" (338–42). Seven years later in his book *Bloodtaking and Peacemaking*, Miller touches briefly on friendship and claims that support was "often socialized positively by being formalized as 'friendships'"; Miller, *Bloodtaking and Peacemaking: Feud, Law, and Society in Saga Iceland* (Chicago: University of Chicago Press, 1990), 107.

19. Grágás 3 = *Grágás: Stykker, som findes i det Arnamagnæanske haandskrift, nr. 351 fol. Skálholtsbók og en række andre haandskrifter*, ed. Vilhjálmur Finsen (København: Gyldendalske Boghandel, 1883), goðar, þingfararkaup, þingmaðr.

20. Walter Ysebaert, "Friendship and Networks," in *Handbok of Medieval Studies: Terms, Methods, Ttrends*, ed. Albrecht Classen (Göttingen: de Gruyter, 2010), 580–93.

21. The traditional dating of the battle is c. 872, but it is uncertain; Claus Krag, *Vikingtid og rikssamling: 800–1130*, Aschehougs Norgeshistorie 2 (Oslo: Aschehoug, 1995), 86; Claus Krag, *Norges historie fram til 1319* (Oslo: Universitetsforlaget, 2000), 44–46, 215–17. For an overview of the political development in Norway in this period, see Knut Helle, *Norge blir en stat 1130–1319*, Handbok i Norges historie 3, [2. utg.] (Bergen: Universitetsforlaget, 1974), 37–145; Knut Helle, *Under kirke og kongemakt: 1130–1350*, Aschehougs Norgeshistorie 3 (Oslo: Aschehoug, 1995), 12–77; Sveaas Andersen, *Samlingen av Norge*, 75–158; Krag, *Vikingtid og rikssamling*, 72–225; Knut Helle, ed., *The Cambridge History of Scandinavia* (Cambridge: Cambridge University Press, 2003), 184–201, 369–91; James H. Barrett, "The Pirate Fishermen: The Political Economy of a Medieval Maritime Society," in *West over Sea: Studies in Scandinavian Sea-Borne Expansion and Settlement before 1300*, The Northern World: North Europe and the Baltic, c. 400–1700 AD; Peoples, Economies and Cultures, ed. Beverly Ballin Smith, Simon Taylor, and Gareth Williams, 310–11. (Leiden: Brill, 2007); Sverre Bagge, *From Viking Stronghold to Christian Kingdom: State Formation in Norway, c. 900–1350* (Copenhagen: Museum Tusculanum Press, 2010), 21–68.

22. Narve Bjørgo, Øystein Rian, and Alf Kaartvedt, *800–1536: Makt og avmakt; Selvstendighet og union; fra middelalderen til 1905*, Norsk utenrikspolitikks historie 1 (Oslo: Universitetsforlaget, 1995), 43.

23. For an overview of the political development in Iceland in this period, see Jón Jóhannesson, *Íslendinga saga 1: Þjóðveldisöld* (Reykjavík: Almenna Bókafélagið, 1956); Jón Viðar Sigurðsson, *Chieftains and Power in the Icelandic Commonwealth*, The Viking Collection, trans. Jean Lundskær-Nielsen, vol. 12 (Odense: Odense University Press, [1993] 1999); Jón Viðar Sigurðsson, *Det norrøne samfunnet: Vikingen, kongen, erkebiskopen og bonden* (Oslo: Pax, 2008); Jón Viðar Sigurðsson, "The Making of a 'Skattland': Iceland 1247–1450," in *Rex Insularum: The King of Norway and His "Skattlands" as a Political System, c. 1260–c. 1450*, ed. Steinar Imsen (Bergen: Fagbokforlaget, 2014), 181–94; Gunnar Karlsson, *Goðamenning: Staða og áhrif goðorðsmanna í þjóðveldi Íslendinga* (Reykjavík: Heimskringla, 2004).

24. Árný E. Sveinbjörnsdóttir, Jan Heinemeier, and Gardar Gudmundsson, "14C Dating of the Settlement of Iceland," *Radiocarbor* 46 nr. 1 (2004), 387–94.

25. Jón Viðar Sigurðsson, "Noen hovedtrekk i diskusjonen om det islandske middelaldersamfunnet etter 1970," *Collegium Medievale* 18 (2005): 109–13.

26. For an overview of this development, see, e.g., Jón Viðar Sigurðsson, *Kristninga i Norden 750–1200*, Utsyn & innsikt (Oslo: Samlaget, 2003); Sigurðsson, *Det norrøne samfunnet*, 147–76; Anthony Perron, "Metropolitan Might and Papal Power on the Latin-Christian Frontier: Transforming the Danish Church around the Time of the Fourth Lateran Council," *Catholic Historical Review* 89 (2003): 182–212; Heidi Anett Øvergård Beistad, "An Almost Fanatical Devotion to the Pope? Power and Priorities in the Integration of the Nidaros Province, c.1152–1300." (Trondheim: Norwegian University of Science and Technology, 2015).

27. Diplomatarium Islandicum = *Diplomatarium Islandicum: Íslenzkt fornbréfasafn 1–16*, ed. Jón Sigurðsson et al. (København & Reykjavík: Hið íslenzka bókmenntafjelag, 1857–1972), vol. 1, no. 29.

28. Sigurðsson, *Det norrøne samfunnet*, 15; Jón Viðar Sigurðsson, "The Norse Community," in *The Norwegian Domination and the Norse World, c. 1100–c. 1400*, Trondheim Studies in History, ed. Steinar Imsen (Trondheim: Tapir Academic Press, 2010), 67–68.

29. Sigurðsson, *Det norrøne samfunnet*, 189.

30. Helgi Þorláksson, "Urbaniseringstendenser på Island i middelalderen," in *Urbaniseringsprosessen i Norden 1: Middelaldersteder; Det 17; nordiske historikermøte Trondheim 1977*, ed. Grethe A. Blom (Oslo: Universitetsforlaget, 1982), 13–20; Knut Helle et al., *Norsk byhistorie urbanisering gjennom 1300 år*, ed. Knut Helle (Oslo: Pax, 2006), 41–88; Sigurðsson, "The Norse Community," 67–68.

1. Friendship

1. Sturlunga saga = *Sturlunga saga 1–2*, ed. Jón Jóhannesson, Magnús Finnbogason, and Kristján Eldjárn, (Reykjavík: Sturlunguútgáfan, 1946), 1:190.

2. There is comprehensive research dealing with the Poetic Edda and *Hávamál*. For example, see Guðrún Nordal, Vésteinn Ólason, and Sverrir Tómasson, *Íslensk bókmenntasaga 1* (Reykjavík: Mál og menning, 1992), 75–187; Hermann Pálsson, *Hávamál í ljósi íslenskrar menningar* (Reykjavík: Háskólaútgáfan, 1999), 11–103; Óttar M. Norðfjörð, "Hugtakakerfi Hávamála," *Skírnir* 179 (2005): 33–55; John McKinnell, "The Making of Hávamál," *Journal of Viking and Medieval Scandinavia* 3 (2007): 75–113; John McKinnell,, *Essays on Eddic Poetry*, Toronto Old Norse and Icelandic Series (Toronto: University of Toronto Press, 2014); Medieval Scandinavian = *Medieval Scandinavian: An*

Encyclopedia, Garland Encyclopedias of the Middle Ages, ed. Phillip Pulsiano and Kirsten Wolf, vol. 1. (New York: Garland, 1993), 149–53; Eddukvæði 1:19–39.

3. Eddukvæði 1:331–32.

4. Ibid., 1:322 (st. 1).

5. Ibid., 1:329–31 (sts. 39, 40, 48).

6. Ibid., 1:335 (st. 67).

7. Ibid., 1:337–38, 346–47 (sts. 78, 121, 124).

8. Ibid., 1:330, 346 (sts. 41, 44, 119).

9. Ibid., 1:332 (st. 52).

10. Norðfjörð, "Hugtakakerfi Hávamála," 48.

11. Eddukvæði 1:330 (st. 42). Cf. Robert E. Bjork, "Speech as Gift in Beowulf," *Speculum* 69, no. 4 (1994): 996; Carl Lindahl, "Bakhtin's Carnival Laughter and the Cajun Country Mardi Gras," *Folklore* 107 (1996): 57–70; Michail Bachtin, *Latter og dialog: utvalgte skrifter*, trans. Audun Johannes Mørch (Oslo: Cappelen akademisk forlag, 2003), 43; Waltraud Fritsch-Rößler, "Laughter," in *Handbook of Medieval Sstudies: Terms, Methods, Trends*, ed. Albrecht Classen (Göttingen: de Gruyter, 2010), 1524–29.

12. Eddukvæði 1:326 (sts. 24, 25).

13. Ibid., 1:323 (st. 6); Guðmundur Finnbogason, "Lífsskoðun Hávamála og Aristóteles," *Skírnir* 103 (1929): 87. Friendship could also be used metaphorically to describe values such as truth, wisdom, and the law. Eddukvæði 1:323, 337–38 (sts. 6, 78); Íslenzk fornrit 17 = *Biskupa sögur 3*, Íslenzk fornrit, ed. Guðrún Ása Grímsdóttir (Reykjavík: Hið íslenzka fornritafélag, 1998), 28, 53; Íslensk hómilíubók = *Íslensk hómilíubók fornar stólræður*, ed. Guðrún Kvaran, Sigurbjörn Einarsson, and Gunnlaugur Ingólfsson (Reykjavík: Híð íslenska bókmenntafélag, 1993), 28; Gamal norsk homiliebok = *Gamal norsk homiliebok: Cod. AM 619 4o*, ed. Gustav Indrebø (Oslo: I hovudkommisjon hjaa Dybwad, 1931), 17, 21. In some cases, the kings were referred to as "friends of peace" (*tamquam amicus pacis*); Diplomatarium Norvegicum = *Diplomatarium Norvegicum 1–23*, ed. C. C. A. Lange et al. (Christiania & Oslo: 1847–2011), vol. 8, no. 9 (2 July 1266); ibid., vol. 19, no. 281 (2 July 1266).

14. Johan Fritzner, *Ordbog over Det gamle norske Sprog 1–3: Gjenopptrykt 1954–1972 med et bd. Rettelser og tillegg (4) v. Finn Hødnebø*, Omarb., forøget og forbedret Udg. ed. (Christiania: Den norske Forlagsforening, 1883–96), 1883–96. Gjenopptrykt 1954–1972 med et bd. Rettelser og tillegg (IV) v. Finn Hødnebø.

15. Other sources sometimes use the term in this way; http://onp.ku.dk/english/ (*félgi*, 21.06.2015); Islendzk æventyri = *Islendzk æventyri: Isländische Legenden, Novellen und Märchen*, ed. Hugo Gering (Halle an der Saale: Verlag der Buchhandlung des Waisenhauses, 1882), 165; Eirspennill = *Eirspennill, AM 47 fol.*, ed. Finnur Jónsson (Kristiania: 1916), 556, 571, 636; Íslenzk fornrit 34 = *Orkneyinga saga: Legenda de sancto Magno; Magnúss saga skemmri; Magnúss saga lengri; Helga þattr ok Úlfs*, Íslenzk fornrit, ed. Finnbogi Guðmundsson (Reykjavík: Hið íslenzka fornritafélag, 1965), 215. On a runic inscription from Bergen, probably from c. 1300, we can read that Þórir fagur sends God's and his greetings to his *félagi* (partner) Hafgrímur with "true comradeship and friendship" (*sannan félagskap ok vináttu*); Norges innskrifter 6 = *Norges innskrifter med de yngre runer 6: Bryggen i Bergen*, ed. Aslak Liestøl, James E. Knirk, and Ingrid Sanness Johnsen (Oslo: Kjeldskriftfondet, 1980–90), 99. Here it looks like friendship is used to create the loyalty beteween the partners. The term *fulltrúi* can also mean "friend"; Hermann Pálsson, "Forn vinátta," *Húnavaka* 40 (2000): 127. Cf. Judith Jesch, *Ships and Men in the*

Late Viking Age: The Vocabulary of Runic Inscriptions and Skaldic Verse (Woodbridge, UK: Boydell Press, 2001), 235.

16. Eddukvæði 1:328 (st. 34).

17. Ibid., 1:354 (st. 156).

18. Ibid., 1:330–32, 346 (sts. 45, 46, 51, 121).

19. Ibid., 1:330 (st. 43).

20. Finnbogason, "Lífsskoðun Hávamála," 97–98.

21. Eddukvæði 1:331.

22. For a discussion about gifts and gift giving in Iceland, see, e.g., Sigurðsson, *Frá goðorðum til ríkja*, 81–95; Sigurðsson, *Chieftains and Power*, 120–40; Jón Viðar Sigurðsson and Thomas Småberg, eds., *Friendship and Social Networks in Scandinavia, c. 1000–1800*, Early European Research, vol. 5 (Turnhout: Brepols, 2013); Helgi Þorláksson, *Gamlar götur og goðavald: Um fornar leiðir og völd Oddaverja í Rangárþingi*, Ritsafn Sagnfræðistofnunar, vol. 25 (Reykjavík: Sagnfræðistofnun Háskóla Íslands, 1989), 89–97; Helgi Þorláksson, "Fé og virðing," in *Sæmdarmenn: Um heiður á þjóðveldisöld*, ed. Helgi Þorláksson et al. (Reykjavík: Hugvísindastofnun Háskóla Íslands, 2001), 96–134; Byock, *Medieval Iceland*, 6, 11, 77, 88, 125, 129, 131, 171, 172, 215; Miller, *Bloodtaking and Peacemaking*, 77–109; William Ian Miller, *Audun and the Polar Bear: Luck, Law, and Largesse in a Medieval Tale of Risky Business*, Medieval Law and Its Practice (Leiden: Brill, 2008), index: "gifts"; Hanne Monclair, "Lederskapsideologi på Island i det trettende århundret: En analyse av gavegivning, gjestebud og lederfremtoning i islandsk sagamateriale" (PhD, Universitetet i Oslo, 2003), 134–205.

23. Jón Viðar Sigurðsson, "Forholdet mellom frender, hushold og venner på Island i fristatstiden," *Historisk tidsskrift* 74 (1995), 323–24; Þorláksson, "Fé og virðing," 91–102.

24. *Íslenzk fornrit 16 = Biskupa sögur 2*, Íslenzk fornrit, ed. Ásdís Egilsdóttir (Reykjavík: Hið íslenzka fornritafélag, 2002), 298–99.

25. Sturlunga saga 1:236.

26. Jón Viðar Sigurðsson, "The Role of Arbitration in the Settlement of Disputes in Iceland c. 1000–1300," in *Law and Disputing in the Middle Ages: Proceedings of the Ninth Carlsberg Academy Conference on Medieval Legal History 2012*, ed. Per Andersen et al.(Copenhagen: DJØF Publishing, 2013), 123–35.

27. Preben Meulengracht Sørensen, *Fortelling og ære: Studier i islændingesagaerne*, vol. 148 (Aarhus, 1993), 158–59; Sigurðsson, "Forholdet mellom frender," 323–24.

28. Sturlunga saga 1:72.

29. *Grágás 1 = Grágás: Islændernes Lovbog i Fristatens Tid*, ed. Vilhjálmur Finsen (København: Gyldendalske Boghandel, 1852a), 137.

30. Grágás 3, goðar, þingfararkaup, þingmaðr.

31. E.g., see Konrad Maurer, *Island von seiner ersten Entdeckung bis zum Untergange des Freistaats* (München: C. Kaiser, 1874), 35–68, 142–220; Vilhjálmur Finsen, *Om den oprindelige ordning af nogle af den islandske fristats institutioner* (Kjøbenhavn: s.n., 1888), 6–98; Friedrich Boden, *Die isländische Regierungsgewalt in der freistaatlichen Zeit* (Breslau: Verlag von M. & H. Marcus, 1905), 47–58, 67; Ólafur Lárusson, *Yfirlit yfir íslenska rjettarsögu* (Reykjavík: s.n., 1932), 10–106; Aage Gregersen, *L'Islande son statut a travers les ages* (Paris, 1937), 52–97; Einar Arnórsson, *Réttarsaga Alþingis: Saga Alþingis 1* (Reykjavík: Alþingssögunefnd, 1945), 35–109, 125–34; Jón Jóhannesson, *Íslendinga saga* 1:72–102; Björn Þorsteinsson, *Ný Íslandssaga* (Reykjavík: Heimskringla, 1966), 87–105; Jakob Benediktsson, "Landnám og upphaf allsherjarríkis," in *Saga Íslands 1*, ed. Sigurður Líndal

(Reykjavík: Hið íslenzka bókmenntafélag, 1974), 173–84; Kirsten Hastrup, *Culture and History in Medieval Iceland. An Anthropological Analysis of Structure and Change* (Oxford: Clarendon, 1985), 118–30; Byock, *Medieval Iceland*, 51–71; Byock, *Viking Age Iceland*, 170–83; Karlsson, *Goðamenning*, 63–365.

32. KLNM 5, col. 410–12; Medieval Scandinavian, 234–35.

33. Sigurðsson, *Chieftains and Power*, 39–83; Sigurðsson, "Noen hovedtrekk i diskusjonen," 109–13.

34. Sturlunga saga 2:43.

35. Íslenzk fornrit 4 = *Eyrbyggja saga: Brands þáttr Örva; Eiríks saga rauða; Grænlendinga saga; Grænlendinga þáttr*, Íslenzk fornrit, ed. Matthías Þórðarson and Einar Ólafur Sveinsson (Reykjavík: Hið íslenzka fornritafélag, 1935), 191.

36. Ibid., 189–91. Another comparable story about Brand is found in the episode about Bishop Ísleifur (Íslenzk fornrit 16:335–38). Cf. Hermann Pálsson, "Brands þáttur örva," *Gripla* 7 (1990): 117–30; Theodore M. Andersson, "The King of Iceland," *Speculum* 74, no. 4 (1993): 923–34.

37. Grágás 1a:246–48; ibid., 1b:180; Grágás 2 = *Grágás: Efter det Arnamagnæanske haandskrift, nr. 334 fol., Staðarhólsbók*, ed. Vilhjálmur Finsen. (København: Gyldendalske Boghandel, 1879), 83–85; Den ældre Gulathings-Lov = *Den ældre Gulathings-Lov*, Norges gamle Love 1, ed. Rudolf Keyser et al. (Christiania: Grøndahl og søn, 1846), para. 129.

38. Mauss, *The Gift*, 1–45; KLNM 5, col. 653–61; Aaron Gurevich, "Wealth and Gift-Bestowal among the Ancient Scandinavians," *Scandinavica* 7 (1968) 127–34; Marshall Sahlins, *Stone Age Economics* (London: Routledge, [1972] 1978), 168–72.

39. For an overview of the chieftains' economic resources, see Sigurðsson, *Chieftains and Power*, 101–19.

40. Sigurðsson, *Frá goðorðum til ríkja*, 89. Cf. Lucy Mair, *An Introduction to Social Anthropology* (London: Clarendon Press, 1965), 182–85; Mauss, *The Gift*, 10–12; Sahlins, *Stone Age Economics*, 133.

41. Sturlunga saga 2:27.

42. Björn Lárusson, *The Old Icelandic Land Registers* (Lund: CWK Gleerup Lund, 1967), 65, 192, 202. Cf. Hans Jacob Orning, "Statsutvikling i Norge og på Island i høymiddelalderen belyst ut fra en analyse av Þórðr kakali Sighvatsson og Sverre Sigurdssons vei til makten," *Historisk tidsskrift* 76 (1997): 469–86.

43. Thomas Charles-Edwards, "The Distinction between Land and Moveable Wealth in Anglo-Saxon England," in *Medieval Settlement: Continuity and Change*, ed. Peter H. Sawyer (London: Edward Arnold, 1976), 183.

44. Sturlunga saga 2:70.

45. Ibid., 1:235. Cf. Jenny Jochens, "Old Norse Motherhood," in *Medieval Mothering*, Garland Reference Library of the Humanities, ed. John Carmi Parsons and Bonnie Wheeler (New York: Garland, 1996), 212–13.

46. Sigurðsson, *Frá goðorðum til ríkja*, 58–59.

47. Auður Magnúsdóttir, *Frillor och fruar: Politik och samlevnad på Island 1120–1400* (Göteborg: Historiska Institutionen, 2001), 47–97.

48. For example, see Eirspennill, 257, 282, 296, 302, 314, 347–348, 366, 440, 441, 649; Codex Frisianus = *Codex Frisianus: En Samling af norske Kongesagaer*, ed. Carl Richard Unger (Christiania: Malling, 1871), 523, 552; Íslenzk fornrit 26 = *Heimskringla 1*, Íslenzk fornrit, ed. Bjarni Aðalbjarnarson (Reykjavík: Hið íslenzka fornritafélag, 1941), 148,

166, 176, 205, 251, 372; Íslenzk fornrit 27 = *Heimskringla 2*, Íslenzk fornrit, ed. Bjarni Aðalbjarnarson (Reykjavík: Hið íslenzka fornritafélag, 1945), 288; Íslenzk fornrit 30 = *Sverris saga*, Íslenzk fornrit, ed. Þorleifur Hauksson (Reykjavík: Hið íslenska fornritafélag, 2007), 6, 93, 151. *Vinsæll* was also used to describe bishops, couples, writers, and priests (Íslenzk fornrit 16, 48; Biskupa sögur = *Biskupa sögur 1–2*, ed. Guðbrandur Vigfússon and Jón Sigurðsson (Kaupmannahöfn: Hið íslenska bókmenntafélag, 1858–78), 1:175. The word *vinsæll* could also be used to describe the relationship between God and one who was dear to him; e.g., Bishop Jón of Hólar (ibid., 1:247). Cf. Jón Viðar Sigurðsson, *Norsk historie 800–1300: Frå høvdingmakt til konge- og kyrkjemakt* (Oslo: Det norske samlaget, 1999), 27–34, 80–90, 156–157; Sigurðsson, *Chieftains and Power*, 93–95; Jón Viðar Sigurðsson, "The Appearance and Personal Abilities of *goðar*, *jarlar*, and *konungar*: Iceland, Orkney and Norway," in *West over Sea: Studies in Scandinavian Sea-Borne Expansion and Settlement before 1300*, The Northern World: North Europe and the Baltic c. 400–1700 AD; Peoples, Economies and Cultures, ed. Beverly Ballin Smith, Simon Taylor, and Gareth Williams (Leiden: Brill, 2007), 100; Sverre Bagge, *Society and Politics in Snorri Sturluson's Heimskringla* (Berkeley: University of California Press, 1991), 93, 97–99, 127–40, 149–52, 158–62.

49. Sturlunga saga 2:196, "Þótti þeim nú Kolbeinn aftr kominn ok endrborinn, ok þá langaði æ eftir."

50. Ibid., 2:207.

51. Ibid., 2:40.

52. Ibid., 2:70.

53. Íslenzk fornrit 1 = *Íslendingabók, Landnámabók*, Íslenzk fornrit, ed. Jakob Benediktsson (Reykjavík: Hið íslenzka fornritafélag, 1968), 238.

54. Christianity became the official religion in Iceland about the year 1000 and twenty years later in Norway.

55. Sturlunga saga 1:68.

56. Katrinka Reinhart, "Ritual Feasting and Empowerment at Yanshi Shangcheng," *Journal of Anthropological Archaeology* 39 (2015), 77. Cf. Gavin Lucas, ed., *Hofstaðir: Excavations of a Viking Age Feasting Hall in North-Eastern Iceland*, vol.1, Institute of Archaeology Monograph Series (Reykjavík: Fornleifastofnun Íslands, 2009); Lars Kjær and A. J. Watson, "Feasts and Gifts: Sharing Food in the Middle Ages," *Journal of Medieval History* 37, no. 1 (2011): 1–5.

57. Michael Dietler, "Feasts and Commensal Politics in the Politicial Economy," in *Food and the Status Quest: An Interdisciplinary Perspective*, ed. Polly Wiessner and Wulf Schiefenhövel (Providence: Berghahn Books, 1996), 92. Cf. Michael Dietler, "Feasting and Fasting," in *The Oxford Handbook on the Archaeology of Ritual and Religion*, ed. Timothy Ingersoll (Oxford: Oxford University Press, 2011), 184–86.

58. Dietler, "Feasts and Commensal Politics," 96–97.

59. Jón Viðar Sigurðsson, "The Wedding at Flugumýri in 1253: Icelandic Feasts between the Free State Period and Norwegian Hegemony," in *Rituals, Performatives, and Political Order in Northern Europe, c. 650–1350*, ed. Wojtek Jezierski et al. (Turnhout: Brepols, 2015), 209–35.

60. Sturlunga saga 1:50.

61. Íslenzk fornrit 11 = *Austfirðinga sögur*, Íslenzk fornrit, ed. Jón Jóhannesson (Reykjavík: Hið islenzka fornritafélag, 1950), 33–35.

62. Íslenzk fornrit 8 =Vatnsdæla saga; Hallfreðar saga; Kormáks saga; Hrómundar þáttr halta; Hrafns þáttr Guðrúnarsonar, Íslenzk fornrit, ed. Einar Ólafur Sveinsson (Reykjavík: Hið íslenzka fornritafélag, 1939), 63–64; Hovstad, Mannen og samfunnet, 58.

63. Loyalty can be defined as "perseverance in an association to which a person has become intrinsically committed as a matter of his or her identity." (John Kleinig, "Loyalty," The Stanford Encyclopedia of Philosophy, ed. Edward N. Zalta, Fall 2013 ed. (Stanford: Stanford University, 2013), 1; http://plato.stanford.edu/archives/fall2013/entries/loyalty.

64. Jón Viðar Sigurðsson, "The Role of Arbitration," 125–28. In Ljósvetninga saga, we hear of a fight between Eyjólfur Gudmundarson and Thorvald Höskuldsson. In the fight, a man took part who was a friend of both of them; Íslenzk fornrit 10 =Ljósvetninga saga með þáttum; Reykdæla saga ok Víga-Skútu; Hreiðars þáttr, Íslenzk fornrit, ed. Björn Sigfússon (Reykjavík: Hið íslenzka fornritafélag, 1940), 79. This is one of the few stories where a person fights against his friend.

65. Lárusson, Old Icelandic Land Registers, 33; these figures are from c. 1700.

66. Sturlunga saga 1:402.

67. Ibid., 1:470–71; Sigurðsson, Chieftains and Power, 131–32.

68. Sveaas Andersen, Samlingen av Norge, 251–62.

69. Grágás 1a:136–41; Grágás 2:272–78; Grágás 3:427.

70. Grágás 1a:44, 63, 106–7, 124–25, 128, 159–60, 172, 178, 182–3; Grágás 2:263–64, 320–21, 337–38, 359; Grágás 3:173, 431.

71. Sturlunga saga 1:268.

72. Íslenzk fornrit 4:156–57. For an overview of the discussion about the Free State constitution, see Jón Viðar Sigurðsson, "Fristatens forfatning: Et symbol foran sitt fall?" in Holmgang: Om det førmoderne samfunn; Festskrift til Kåre Lunden; Tid og tanke 4, ed. Anne Eidsfeldt et al. (Oslo: Historisk Institutt, Universitetet i Oslo, 2000), 188–204; Sigurðsson, "Noen hovedtrekk i diskusjonen," 107–109.

73. Sturlunga saga 1:14. Cf. ibid., 1:13, 14, 67, 97, 102, 235, 383, 390.

74. Ibid., 1:240.

75. Cf. Íslenzk fornrit 4:15; Íslenzk fornrit 6 =Vestfirðinga sögur, Íslenzk fornrit, ed. Guðni Jónsson and Björn K. Þórólfsson (Reykjavík: Hið Íslenzka fornritafélag, 1943), 133–34, 137, 347; Íslenzk fornrit 8:131; Íslenzk fornrit 10:3, 120; Sturlunga saga 1:13, 14, 67, 97, 102, 235, 383, 390.

76. Sturlunga saga 1:102. Cf. Karlsson, Goðamenning, 189.

77. Íslenzk fornrit 5 =Laxdæla saga; Halldórs þættir Snorrasonar; Stúfs þáttr, Íslenzk fornrit, ed. Einar Ólafur Sveinsson (Reykjavík: Hið íslenzka fornritafélag, 1934), 14.

78. E.g., see Biskupa sögur 1:21, 505; Íslenzk fornrit 3 =Borgfirðinga sögur, Íslenzk fornrit, ed. Guðni Jónsson and Sigurður Nordal (Reykjavík: Hið Íslenzka fornritafélag, 1956), 38, 81, 245, 314; Íslenzk fornrit 4:15, 54–55; Íslenzk fornrit 5:74, 207. Íslenzk fornrit 6:347, 348; Íslenzk fornrit 8:92; Íslenzk fornrit 9 =Eyfirðinga sögur, Íslenzk fornrit, ed. Jónas Kristjánsson (Reykjavík: Hið íslenzka fornritafélag, 1956), 33; Íslenzk fornrit 10:15, 303; Íslenzk fornrit 11:302; Íslenzk fornrit 14 =Kjalnesinga saga; Jökuls þáttr Búasonar; Víglundar saga; Króka-Refs saga; Þórðar saga hreðu; Finnboga saga; Gunnars saga keldugnúpsfífls, Íslenzk fornrit, ed. Jóhannes Halldórsson (Reykavik: Hið islenzka fornritafélag, 1959), 6; Sturlunga saga 1:68, 259, 283, 419, 423, 524; Sturlunga saga 2:6, 71, 77, 120, 121.

79. Íslenzk fornrit 4:15; Íslenzk fornrit 6:347.

80. Íslenzk fornrit 12 =Brennu-Njáls saga, Íslenzk fornrit, ed. Einar Ólafur Sveins-son (Reykjavík: Hið íslenzka fornritafélag, 1954), 53, 58–59, 75, 84, 86–87.

81. Ibid., 92, 118.

82. Ibid., 122.

83. Ibid., 240–42, 242n2.

84. Sigurðsson, *Chieftains and Power*, 139–40; Íslenzk fornrit 3:81, 209, 273, 314; Íslenzk fornrit 5:12, 120, 126; Íslenzk fornrit 6:302; Íslenzk fornrit 8:37, 291; Íslenzk forn-rit 9:188, 236; Íslenzk fornrit 10:76, 162, 166; Íslenzk fornrit 12:58–59, 82, 90, 132, 166, 168, 422; Sturlunga saga 1:264, 380, 384, 402; Sturlunga saga 2:125, 249.

85. Íslenzk fornrit 14:302–3, 306.

86. Cf. Íslenzk fornrit 3:67, 96, 306; Íslenzk fornrit 10:191–93; Íslenzk fornrit 13 =Harðar saga; Bárðar saga; Þorskfirðinga saga; Flóamanna saga; Þórarins þáttr Nefjólfs-sonar; Þorsteins þáttr Úxafóts; Egils þáttr Síðu-Hallssonar; Orms þáttr Stórólfssonar; Þorsteins þáttr Tjaldstöðings; Þorsteins þáttr Forvitna; Bergbúa þáttr; Kumlbúa þáttr; Stjörnu-Odda dra-umr, Íslenzk fornrit, ed. Bjarni Vilhjálmsson and Þórhallur Vilmundarson (Reykjavík: Hið íslenzka fornritafélag, 1991), 145; Íslenzk fornrit 14:50–57, 355–63, 374. Women's friendship is mentioned in few episodes. The *Icelandic Homily Book* mentions that Job has an unknown female friend (*vinkona*), and that Mary Magdalen was Jesus's friend (Íslensk hómilíubók, 238; Heilagra manna sögur =Heilagra manna sögur; Fortællinger og Legender om hellige Mænd og Kvinder efter gamle Haands[k]rifter 1–2, ed. Carl Richard Un-ger (Christiania: B. M. Bentzen, 1877), 1:537, 541, 543.

87. Sturlunga saga 1:103–5. And as we saw in the discussion about friendship be-tween chieftains and kings, women also negotiated the terms of their friendships; Íslenzk fornrit 12:32.

88. Sturlunga saga 1:105. Cf. Jón Viðar Sigurðsson, "Konur og kvennarán á Íslandi á 12. og 13. öld," *Ný saga* 9 (1997): 71–80.

89. Íslenzk fornrit 5:161. Cf. Natalie M. van Deusen, "Sworn Sisterhood?: On the (Near-) Absence of Female Friendship from the Íslendingasǫgur," *Scandinavian Studies* 86, no. 1 (2014): 52–71; Biskupa sögur 1:629, 587; Tristram =Saga af Tristram ok Ísönd, samt Möttuls saga, ed. Gísli Brynjúlfsson (Kjøbenhavn: Det kongelige Nordiske Oldskrift-Selskab, 1878), 99, 103, 112, 182–84.

90. Íslenzk fornrit 15 =Biskupa sögur 1, Íslenzk fornrit, ed. Sigurgeir Steingrímsson, Ólafur Halldórsson, and Peter Foote (Reykjavík: Hið íslenzka fornritafélag, 2003), 52–54; Íslenzk fornrit 16:55; Íslenzk fornrit 17:350; Biskupa sögur 1:601, 611, 620; Stur-lunga saga 1:268.

91. Alexandra Sanmark, "Women at the Thing," in *Kvinner i vikingtid*, ed. Nanna Løkka and Nancy L. Coleman (Oslo: Scandinavian Academic Press, 2014), 94–101. For the social postion of widows in the Free State society, see Philadelphia Ricketts, *High-ranking Widows in Medieval Iceland and Yorkshire: Property, Power, Marriage and Identity in the Twelfth and Thirteenth Centuries*, The Northern World: North Europe and the Baltic c. 400–1700 AD: Peoples, Economies and Cultures (Leiden: Brill, 2010), 51–296.

92. E. Paul Durrenberger, and Gísli Pálsson, "The Importance of Friendship in the Absence of States, according to the Icelandic Sagas," in *The Anthropology of Friendship*, ed. Sandra Bell and Simon Coleman (Oxford: Berg, 1999), 73.

93. Bjørn Qviller, "Patron-klient-forhold," in *Holmgang: Om førmoderne samfunn; Fest-skrift til Kåre Lunden*, Tid og Tanke 4, ed. Anne Eidsfelt et al. (Oslo: 2000), 136–137. Cf. Einar Hreinsson and Tomas Nilson, introduktion to *Nätverk som social resurs: Historiska*

exempel, Stundetlitteratur, ed. Einar Hreinsson and Tomas Nilson (Lund: 2003), 7–32; Martin Kilduff and Wenpin Tsai, *Social Networks and Organizations* (London: Sage, 2003), 1–33.

94. Bjørn Qviller, *Romersk politisk kultur og sosiologisk historie* (Oslo: Cappelen akademisk forlag, 1999), 35.

95. Ibid., 37.

96. Ibid., 34–43. Cf. Koenraad Verboven, *The Economy of Friends: Economic Aspects of Amicitia and Patronage in the Late Republic,* Collection Latomus 269 (Bruxelles: Latomus, 2002), 35–48. Verboven argues that there was a difference between *amici* (friends), who received offers of resources and help, and clients, who received offers of protection— in return for *gratia* and deference. The difference between a friend and a client was that the latter was not in a position to reciprocate with the same type of favor that had been given by the patron. Friends were. Therefore, Roman friendship can be described as "lop-sided" friendship (62). However, Qviller places friends and clients on equal footing; Qviller, *Romersk politisk kultur,* 40–41.

2. Friendship between Chieftains

1. For an overview of Snorri as a politician, see, e.g., Jón Jóhannesson, *Íslendinga saga* 1:283–291; Magnús Stefánsson, "Kirkjuvald eflist," in *Saga Íslands 2,* ed. Sigurður Líndal (Reykjavík: Hið íslenzka bókmenntafélag, 1975), 112–13; Gunnar Karlsson, "Stjórnmálamaðurinn Snorri," in *Snorri: Átta alda minning,* ed. Gunnar Karlsson and Helgi Þorláksson (Reykjavík: Sögufélag, 1979), 30–35; Sigurðsson, *Frá goðorðum til ríkja,* 63–64; Viðar Pálsson, "'Var engi höfðingi slíkr sem Snorri': Auður og virðing í valdabaráttu Snorra Sturlusonar," *Saga* 41 (2003): 55–96; Óskar Guðmundsson, *Snorri: Ævisaga Snorra Sturlusonar 1179–1241* (Reykjavík: JPV, 2009), 77–460.

2. Sturlunga saga 1:277–78.

3. Hakonar saga =*Hakonar saga, and a Fragment of Magnus saga,* Rerum Britannicarum Medii Ævi Scriptores, Icelandic Sagas 1, ed. Guðbrandur Vigfusson (London: 1887), 52; Skálholtsbók =*Skálholtsbók: Det Arnamagnæanske Haandskrift 81a Fol. Skálholtsbók yngsta,* ed. A. Kjær and Ludvig Holm-Olsen (Kristiania: 1910–86), 348; Eirspennill, 503; Codex Frisianus, 419–20; Islandske Annaler =*Islandske Annaler indtil 1578,* Det Norske historiske Kildeskriftfonds skrifter 21, ed. Gustav Storm (Christiania: Grøndahl, 1888), 125; Sturlunga saga 1:277–78.

4. Sturlunga saga 1:319; Sigurðsson, *Frá goðorðum til ríkja,* 71.

5. Sturlunga saga 1:302, "skyldr þess at gera hvat, er Snorri legði fyrir hann, hverigir sem í mót væri." Cf. ibid., 1:387.

6. Ibid., 1:300–4, 309, 310, 320–23, 334, 344, 348, 359, 471, 477, 501.

7. Íslenzk fornrit 3:191.

8. Ibid., 3:180.

9. Ibid., 3:187.

10. Ibid., 3:179–90.

11. Pierre Bourdieu, *Outline of a Theory of Practice,* Cambridge Studies in Social and Cultural Anthropology (Cambridge: Cambridge University Press, 1977), 5–6; Pierre Bourdieu and Richard Nice, *The Logic of Practice* (Oxford: Polity Press, 1990), 81, 105; Paul J. Burton, "Amicitia in Plautus: A Study of Roman Friendship Processes," *American Journal of Philology* 125, no. 2 (2004): 210.

12. Sturlunga saga 1:300, 302, 303, 304.

13. Ibid., 1:303.

14. Ibid., 1:271, 304, 319.

15. Ibid., 1:320–23.

16. Ibid., 1:345–47.

17. Ibid., 1:359.

18. Ibid., 1:359.

19. Ibid., 1:374.

20. Ibid., 1:387.

21. Hirdloven =Hirdloven til Norges konge og hans håndgangne menn: Etter AM 322 fol., ed. Steinar Imsen (Oslo: Riksarkivet, 2000), 90–92.

22. Sigurðsson, Det norrøne samfunnet, 110–12, 199–200.

23. Sturlunga saga 1:444.

24. Sigurðsson, Chieftains and Power, 139.

25. Íslenzk fornrit 12:52.

26. Following discussion based on Sigurðsson, Chieftains and Power, 165–70; Sigurðsson, "The Role of Arbitration," 124–32; Grágás 3, gerð, sátt.

27. Grágás 1a =Grágás: Konungsbók, ed. Vilhjálmur Finsen (Odense: Universitetsforlag, 1974), 108–11, 121–22; Grágás 1b, 189–92; Grágás 2:192–93, 284–86.

28. Grágás 3, fjörbaugsgarðr, skóggangr, sekr, sekt; Ólafur Lárusson, Yfirlit yfir íslenska rjettarsögu, 47, 94, 155–66; Lúðvík Ingvarsson, Refsingar á Íslandi á þjóðveldistímanum (Reykjavík: Menningarsjóður, 1970), 96–122, 140–41.

29. Sturlunga saga 1:50.

30. Sigurðsson, Chieftains and Power, 180–85.

3. Kings and Their Friends

1. Hans Jacob Orning, Unpredictability and Presence: Norwegian Kingship in the High Middle Ages, The Northern World: North Europe and the Baltic c. 400–1700 AD; Peoples, Economies and Cultures (Leiden: Brill, 2008), 51–56, 311–43.

2. Helle, Norge blir en stat, 30–34.

3. Gulatingslova =Den eldre Gulatingslova, Norrøne tekster 6, ed. Tor Ulset, Bjørn Eithun, and Magnus Rindal (Oslo: Riksarkivet, 1994), para. 1. G1 has not recived much scholarly attention, which can be seen in that Knut Helle, in his important book about Gulating and Gulating's law, only discusses the social groups represented; Knut Helle, Gulatinget og gulatingslova (Leikanger, Skald, 2001), 8. This lack of interest is obvious; G1 is not statutory provision, but a prayer.

4. Íslenzk fornrit 28 =Heimskringla 3, Íslenzk fornrit, ed. Bjarni Aðalbjarnarson (Reykjavík: Hið íslenzka fornritafélag, 1951), 210–11. In the sagas we find a series of stories about Christmas gifts. E.g., see Íslenzk fornrit 2 =Egils saga Skalla-Grímssonar, Íslenzk fornrit, ed. Sigurður Nordal (Reykjavík: Hið íslenzka fornritafélag, 1933), 213; Íslenzk fornrit 3:77, 117; Sturlunga saga 2:40, 216–17; Árni Björnsson, Jól á Íslandi (Reykjavík: Ísafoldarprentsmiðja, 1963), 83–85.

5. Íslenzk fornrit 28:212.

6. From 1277, the royal vassals were also called barons and outranked all in the king's hirð, except the members of the royal family, earls, and dukes; the title was abolished in 1308; Steinar Imsen, ed., Rex Insularum: The King of Norway and His "Skatt-

lands" as a Political System c. 1260–c. 1450 (Bergen: Fagbokforlaget Vigmostad & Bjørke, 2014), 421.

7. Íslenzk fornrit 30:152.

8. Ibid., 30:154.

9. Sverre Bagge, "Borgerkrig og statsutvikling i Norge i middelalderen," *Historisk tidsskrift* 65 (1986): 148–54; Bagge, *Society and Politics*, 64–129; Íslenzk fornrit 27:194–98.

10. Íslenzk fornrit 27:294.

11. Eirspennill, 257. Cf. ibid., 282, 302, 314, 333, 347–48, 366.

12. Ibid., 304; Íslenzk fornrit 30:81. Cf. Eirspennill, 257, 282, 296, 302, 314, 333, 347–48, 366, 440, 441.

13. Codex Frisianus, 436.

14. Íslenzk fornrit 30:280.

15. Íslenzk fornrit 28:95–96.

16. Ibid., 28:98.

17. Ibid., 28:98–101.

18. Íslenzk fornrit 28:99, 101.

19. Eirspennill, 350, 613. Cf. Codex Frisianus, 523; Íslenzk fornrit 9:40–49; Íslenzk fornrit 10:17; Íslenzk fornrit 30:155; Sturlunga saga 1:186, 442.

20. Flateyjarbók =*Flateyjarbók 1–4,* ed. Sigurður Nordal (Reykjavík: Flateyjarútgáfan, 1944), 4:221.

21. Íslenzk fornrit 27:216.

22. Íslenzk fornrit 14:142–43.

23. Bagge, *Society and Politics*, 149.

24. Íslenzk fornrit 7 =*Grettis saga Ásmundarsonar; Bandamanna saga; Odds þáttr Ófeigssonar,* Íslenzk fornrit, ed. Guðni Jónsson (Reykjavík: Hið íslenzka fornritafélag, 1936), 128.

25. Íslenzk fornrit 27:82. Cf. Codex Frisianus, 394; Íslenzk fornrit 30:39.

26. Íslenzk fornrit 28:199.

27. Ibid., 28:400–402.

28. Eirspennill, 568; Codex Frisianus, 435, 562.

29. Íslenzk fornrit 28:125; Codex Frisianus, 218. Cf. Íslenzk fornrit 26:141–42.

30. Eirspennill, 553; Codex Frisianus, 401.

31. Bagge, "Borgerkrig og statsutvikling," 159–65. For a discussion of the aristocracy's dependence on the king, see Hans Jacob Orning, "Borgerkrig og statsutvikling i Norge i middelalderen - en revurdering," *Historisk tidsskrift* (2014): 193–216; Hans Jacob Orning, "Hvorfor vant kongene?," *Historisk tidsskrift* 93 (2015): 285–92; Sverre Bagge, "Borgerkrig og statsutvikling - svar til Hans Jacob Orning," *Historisk tidsskrift* 93, no. 1 (2015): 91–110.

32. Helle, *Norge blir en stat*, 78–90; Bagge, "Borgerkrig og statsutvikling," 169–70.

33. Íslenzk fornrit 5:118.

34. Íslenzk fornrit 28:184. Cf. Konungs skuggsiá =*Konungs skuggsiá*, Norrøne tekster 1, ed. Ludvig Holm-Olsen (Oslo: Kjeldeskriftfondet, 1983), 43.

35. Jón Viðar Sigurðsson, "Kings, Earls and Chieftains: Rulers in Norway, Orkney and Iceland c. 900–1300," in *Ideology and Power in the Viking and Middle Ages: Scandinavia, Iceland, Ireland, Orkney and the Faeroes,* ed. Gro Steinsland et al. (Leiden: Brill, 2011), 69–88.

36. KLNM 10, col. 432–59; Geir Atle Ersland and Terje H. Holm, *Krigsmakt og kongemakt 900–1814* (Oslo: Eide, 2000), 42–63.

37. Íslenzk fornrit 27:82.

38. Sveaas Andersen, *Samlingen av Norge*, 295. However, it was not until after the middle of the thirteenth century that the boundary between the king's private possessions (*patrimonium*) and the royal lands (*bona regalia*) became quite clear. The king could give away his private possessions, but he could only grant royal lands for the length of his reign or lease them out; KLNM 9, col. 26–28.

39. Charles-Edwards, "Distinction between Land and Moveable Weath," 183.

40. Íslenzk fornrit 27:79–80; Sveaas Andersen, *Samlingen av Norge*, 279–82.

41. Hirdloven, 35, 147.

42. The discussion about the *hirð*'s structure builds on KLNM 6, col. 568–77; Helle, *Norge blir en stat*, 200–214; Sveaas Andersen, *Samlingen av Norge*, 134–35, 289–94; Sverre Bagge, *Mennesket i middelalderens Norge: Tanker, tro og holdninger 1000–1300* (Oslo: Aschehoug, 1998), 182–90; Ersland and Holm, *Krigsmakt og kongemakt*, 31–63.

43. Dietler, "Feasts and Commensal Politics," 92, 97.

44. Bagge, *Mennesket i middelalderens Norge*, 186.

45. KLNM 3, col. 510. Cf. F. L. Ganshof, *Feudalism*, trans. P. Grierson, 3rd ed. (London: Longman, 1977), 28; Marc Bloch, *Feudal Society*, trans. L. A. Manyon (London: Routledge and Kegan Paul, 1978), 145–48; Hartmut Bleumer, "Das Vertrauen und die Vertraute," *Frühmittelalterliche Studien* 39 (2005): 253–70; Claudia Garnier, "Wie vertraut man seinem Feind?," *Frühmittelalterliche Studien* 39 (2005): 271–92.

46. Hirdloven, 64.

47. Ibid., 70, 72. Cf. ibid., 70, 72, 92, 94, 120, 154, 156, 166, 168, 174; Eirspennill, 485.

48. Codex Frisianus, 397. Cf. ibid., 485.

49. Norges gamle love =*Norges gamle Love 1–5*, ed. Rudolf Keyser et al. (Christiania: Grøndahl og søn, 1846–95), 3:32. Cf. Eirspennill, 312, 339, 437, 440, 441, 482, 487, 508, 521, 553, 564, 565, 566, 589, 590, 609, 610, 644, 650, 651, 660; Íslenzk fornrit 26:127–28; Íslenzk fornrit 28:373; Codex Frisianus, 426, 548, 565; Knut Helle, *Konge og gode menn i norsk riksstyring ca. 1150–1319* (Bergen: Universitetsforlaget, 1972), 339, 345–47, 373–75, 498, 527.

50. Hirdloven, 106.

51. Konungs skuggsiá, 73. Sverre Bagge, *The Political Thought of The King's Mirror*, Mediaeval Scandinavia suppl. 3 (Odense: Odense University Press, 1987), 52–112.

52. The terms are taken from Naomi Standen, *Unbounded Loyalty: Frontier Crossings in Liao China* (Honolulu: University of Hawaii Press, 2007), 41–63. Cf. Orning, *Unpredictability*, 57–108.

53. Íslenzk fornrit 27:227.

54. Ibid., 27:234–35. Cf. Eirspennill, 654.

55. Íslenzk fornrit 26:144.

56. Ibid., 26:145.

57. Sverre Bagge and Knut Mykland, *Norge i dansketiden 1380–1814* (Oslo: Cappelen, 1987), 12.

58. Eirspennill, 501–2; Codex Frisianus, 418.

59. Íslenzk fornrit 28:331–32.

60. Ibid., 28:5. Cf. Íslenzk fornrit 7:265, 270.

61. Íslenzk fornrit 28:411; Eirspennill, 657; Tristram, 18, 64, 80, 81, 96, 107, 119, 124, 126, 146, 153, 166, 182, 195; Íslenzk fornrit 7:276, 277.

62. Íslenzk fornrit 28:257–58.

63. For example, see Diplomatarium Norvegicum 6, no. 97 (22 July 1318); ibid. 11, no. 5 (22 October 1295).

64. Eirspennill, 556; Codex Frisianus, 476, 542.

65. Diplomatarium Norvegicum 19, no. 101 (10 July 1213).

66. Eirspennill, 571, 636. Cf. Bjørgo, Rian, and Kaartvedt, 800–1536: Makt og avmakt, 19–95; Helle, Under kirke og kongemakt, 180–205.

67. For example, the Spanish king was Hákon's astvin (dear friend), and they had never met each other; Eirspennill, 551, 658, 647.

68. Ibid., 637; Codex Frisianus, 543; Diplomatarium Norvegicum 5, no. 2 (Summer 1248).

69. Codex Frisianus, 537.

70. Ibid., 539.

71. Ibid., 558–59; Bjørgo, Rian, and Kaartvedt, 800–1536: Makt og avmakt, 65–68.

72. Codex Frisianus, 556. Cf. Eirspennill, 649.

73. Íslenzk fornrit 28:255–56. Cf. Íslenzk fornrit 27:215–19; Íslenzk fornrit 28:91, 385.

74. Jón Viðar Sigurðsson, "Becoming a Scat land: The Skattgjafir Process between the Kings of Norway and the Icelanders c. 1250–1300," in Taxes, Tributes and Tributary Lands in the Making of the Scandinavian Kingdoms in the Middle Ages, ed. Steinar Imsen (Trondheim: Tapir, 2011), 115–31.

75. Sturlunga saga 1:269–71, 277–79; Hakonar saga, 49, 51–52; Eirspennill, 502–3; Skálholtsbók, 345, 347–48; Codex Frisianus, 418–20.

76. Sturlunga saga 1:439.

77. Berlin, Knud, Islands statsretlige stilling efter fristatstidens ophør (København: Salmonsens Boghandel, 1909), 30; Sigurðsson, Chieftains and Power, 76.

78. Codex Frisianus, 533. Cf. Flateyjarbók 3:527; HsH Sth =Hákonar saga Hákonarsonar etter Sth. 8 fol., AM 325 (8), 4:o og AM 304, 4:o, Norrøne tekster 2, ed. Marina Mundt (Oslo: Kjeldeskriftfondet, 1977), 144.

79. Sturlunga saga 1:524.

80. Skálholtsbók, 677; Eirspennill, 349.

81. HsH Sth, 190.

82. Patricia Pires Boulhosa, Icelanders and the Kings of Norway: Mediaeval Sagas and Legal Texts, The Northern World: North Europe and the Baltic c. 400–1700 AD; Peoples, Economies and Cultures (Leiden: Brill, 2005), 111. Cf. Randi Bjørshol Wærdahl, To Serve a King, as All Other Lands in the World: The Incorporation and Integration of the King's Tributary Lands into the Norwegian Realm c. 1195–1397, The Northern World: North Europe and the Baltic c. 400–1700 AD: Peoples, Economies and Cultures (Leiden: Brill, 2011), 103–5.

83. Björn Þorsteinsson and Sigurður Líndal, "Lögfesting konungsvalds," in Saga Íslands 3, ed. Sigurður Líndal (Reykjavík: Hið íslenzka bókmenntafélag, 1978), 34–35, 82–84; Boulhosa, Icelanders and the Kings, 110.

84. Boulhosa, Icelanders and the Kings, 143–44. Cf. Patricia Pires Boulhosa, Gamli sáttmáli: Tilurð og tilgangur, trans. Már Jónsson (Reykjavík: Sögufélag, 2006), 11–100.

85. Wærdahl, To Serve a King, 103–12.

86. Ibid., 111. Cf. ibid., 104–5, and references therein, esp. Björn M. Ólsen, "Um upphaf konungsvalds á Íslandi," Andvari 33 (1908): 59–76; and Jón Jóhannesson, Íslendinga saga 2: Fyrirlestrar og ritgerðir um tímabilið 1262–1550 (Reykjavík: Almenna Bókafélagið, 1958), 61–76, 226–301. For a critical response to Boulhosa's ideas, see Helgi Þorláksson, "Er gamli sáttmáli tómur tilbúningur?," in Þriðja íslenska söguþingið 18.–21.

maí 2006, ed. Benedikt Eyþórsson and Hrafnkell Lárusson (Reykjavík: Sagnfræðinga-félag Íslands, 2006), 392–98; Helgi Þorláksson, Review of *Icelanders and the Kings of Norway*, by Patricia Pires Boulhosa, *Historisk Tidsskrift* 86 (2007), 142–47; Helgi Þorláksson, "Ríkisvald gegn þingvaldi: Fulltrúar vaxandi ríkisvalds takast á við fulltrúa þingvalds," in *Nordens plass i middelalderens nye Europa: Samfunnsordning, sentralmkt og periferier*, ed. Lars Ivar Hansen, Richard Holt, and Steinar Imsen (Stamsund: Orkana akademisk, 2011), 105–7; Helgi Skúli Kjartansson, "Gamli sáttmáli – hvað næst?," *Saga* 49, no. 1 (2011): 133–53; Wærdahl, *To Serve a King*, 103–12; Sigurðsson, "Becoming a Scat Land," 122–28. For a reply from Boulhosa, see Patricia Pires Boulhosa, "A Response to 'Gamli sáttmáli - hvað næst?,'" *Saga* 49, no. 2 (2011): 137–51.

87. The agreement between King Magnús Eriksson and the Icelanders states that the king should send six ships to the country as a countergift to acknowledge the Icelanders' "skattgiofum"; Diplomatarium Islandicum 2, no. 343 (1319); Björn Þorsteinsson and Sigurður Líndal, "Lögfesting konungsvalds," 88–90; Diplomatarium Islandicum 1, no. 152; Diplomatarium Islandicum 9, no. 1.

88. Boulhosa, *Icelanders and the Kings*, 110–53.

89. Diplomatarium Islandicum 1, no. 152. Cf. ibid. 9, no. 1.

90. http://www.oed.com ("tribute," n; "scat," n. 3a), accessed 4 January 2015. The OED lists *scat* as an archaic word.

91. Jón Jóhannesson, *Íslendinga saga* 1:334–35.

92. Ibid., 1:334.

93. Codex Frisianus, 533.

94. Bjørgo, Rian, and Kaartvedt, *800–1536: Makt og avmakt*, 54.

4. Clerics and Friendship

1. Íslenzk fornrit 27:22.

2. Sigurðsson, *Kristninga í Norden*, 50–51, 72–74; Sigurðsson, *Det norrøne samfunnet*, 158–60.

3. Íslenzk fornrit 28:391, "Tóku Þrœndir vel við honum, því at flest stórmenni í Þrændalǫgum var bundit í frændsemi eða í nǫkkurum tengðum við erkibyskup, en allir fullkomnir í vináttu."

4. Ibid. For an overview of Eystein's life and deeds, see Erik Gunnes, *Erkebiskop Øystein: Statsmann og kirkebygger* (Oslo: Aschehoug, 1996).

5. Eirspennill, 257; Íslenzk fornrit 30:7. Cf. Eirspennill, 293.

6. Helle, *Norge blir en stat*, 57–68; Helle, *Under kirke og kongemakt*, 34–40; Bagge, *From Viking Stronghold*, 42–53, 166–67.

7. E.g., see Helle, *Norge blir en stat*, 105–17; Helle, Knut, "Tiden fram til 1536," in *Grunntrekk i norsk historie: Fra vikingtid til våre dager*, ed. Rolf Danielsen et al. (Oslo: Universitetsforlaget, 1991), 64; Helle, *Under kirke og kongemakt*, 180–85.

8. Eirspennill, 510–11; Codex Frisianus, 411, 429.

9. Eirspennill, 456–57, 522, 537.

10. Ibid., 595; Helle, *Konge og gode menn*, 373; Helle, *Norge blir en stat*, 112.

11. Eirspennill, 644; Codex Frisianus, 548.

12. Eirspennill, 653.

13. Helle, *Norge blir en stat*, 136–40; Norges gamle love 2:463–66. Sverre Bagge has argued that the conflict was primarily concerned with the validity of secret marriage;

Sverre Bagge, "'Salvo semper regio iure': Kampen om Sættargjerden 1277–1290," *Historisk tidsskrift* 87 (2008): 210–24.

14. Norges gamle love 2:466, 469.

15. Helle, *Norge blir en stat*, 249–53.

16. Diplomatarium Norvegicum 17, no. 1233 (29 July 1200).

17. Anthony Perron, "'*Jus metropoliticum*' on the Norwegian Periphery from Nicholas Breakspear to William of Sabina," in *Frontiers in the Middle Ages: Proceedings of the Third European Congress of Medieval Studies (Jyväskylä, 10–14 June 2003)*, ed. O. Merisalo (Louvain la Neuve: Brepols, 2006), 237–58.

18. Carl F. Wisløff, *Norsk kirkehistorie 1* (Oslo, 1966), 114.

19. Íslenzk fornrit 17:13. Cf. ibid. 17: 238, 371, 423; Sturlunga saga 1:400; Codex Frisianus, 401; Biskupa sögur 1:143.

20. Stefánsson, "Kirkjuvald eflist," 72–81; Magnús Stefánsson, "Frá goðakirkju til biskupskirkju," in *Saga Íslands 3*, ed. Sigurður Líndal (Reykjavík: Hið íslenzka bókmenntafélag, 1978), 210–26; Magnús Stefánsson, *Staðir og staðamál: Studier i islandske egenkirkelige og beneficialrettslige forhold i middelalderen*, 1, Skrifter, Historisk institutt, Universitetet i Bergen, 4 (Bergen: Historisk institutt Universitetet i Bergen, 2000), 191–216; Sigurðsson, *Chieftains and Power*, 101–20; Orri Vésteinsson, "The Formative Phase of the Icelandic Church ca. 990–1240 AD," in *Church Centres: Church Centres in Iceland from the 11th to the 13th Century and Their Parallels in Other Countries*, Snorrastofa, Rit 2, ed. Helgi Þorláksson (Reykholt: Snorrastofa, 2005), 73–75.

21. Jóhannesson, *Íslendinga saga* 1:178; Stefánsson, "Kirkjuvald eflist," 61, 77–78.

22. Stefánsson, "Kirkjuvald eflist," 111–12.

23. Susan Wood, *The Proprietary Church in the Medieval West* (Oxford: Oxford University Press, 2006), 9–726.

24. Rolf Danielsen et al., *Norway: A History from the Vikings to Our Own Times* (Oslo: Scandinavian University Press, 1995), 68.

25. Stefánsson, "Kirkjuvald eflist," 92–108.

26. Arne Odd Johnsen, *Studier vedrørende kardinal Nicolaus Brekespears legasjon til Norden* (Oslo: Fabritius, 1945), 189–200; Stefánsson, "Frá goðakirkju til biskupskirkju," 223–26.

27. Íslenzk fornrit 17:53, 62, 75, 131. Cf. Íslenzk fornrit 16:29, 65; Íslenzk fornrit 17:28, 77, 173, 178, 182, 191, 234; Jón Viðar Sigurðsson, "Island og Nidaros," in *Ecclesia Nidrosiensis 1153–1537: Søkelys på Nidaroskirkens og Nidarosprovinsens historie*, ed. Steinar Imsen (Trondheim: Tapir akademisk forlag, 2003), 131; Heidi Anett Øvregård Beistad, "Kirkens frihet: Biskop Arne Torlaksson som Islands reformator" (MA-oppgave, Norges teknisk-naturvitenskapelige universitet, 2008), 68–84.

28. Íslenzk fornrit 17:84.

29. Ibid., 17:98.

30. Norsk biografisk leksikon =*Norsk biografisk leksikon 1–10*, ed. Knut Helle and Jon Gunnar Arntzen (Oslo: Kunnskapsforlaget, 1999–2005), 6, 502; Helle, *Norge blir en stat*, 87–101; Helle, *Under kirke og kongemakt*, 72, 77.

31. Eirspennill, 440.

32. Ibid., 440, 473, 504, 521, 625; Codex Frisianus, 420; Sturlunga saga 1:400; Diplomatarium Norvegicum 1, no. 50 (1226–54), no. 51 (1226–54), no. 80 (12 May 1292), no. 82 (1 June 1300); Diplomatarium Norvegicum 2, no. 12 (before 16 December 1265); Norges gamle love 3:32; Helle, *Konge og gode menn*, 373.

33. Íf Íslenzk fornrit 16:156.

34. Codex Frisianus, 401.

35. Ibid., 533, 544.

36. Bonnie Effros, *Creating Community with Food and Drink in Merovingian Gaul*, The New Middle Ages (New York: Palgrave Macmillan, 2002), 9–24.

37. E.g., see Íslenzk fornrit 16:35–36, 80, 303; Dietler, "Feasts and Commensal Politics," 92, 96–97.

38. Biskupa sögur 1:130–31.

39. Ibid. 1:589–90.

40. Íslenzk fornrit 17:22.

41. Ibid., 17:22–23. Cf. ibid., 17:173.

42. Ibid., 17:23.

43. Sturlunga saga 1:140. Cf. ibid. 1:141, 210, 479; Biskupa sögur 1:436–39, 450; Íslenzk fornrit 17:200–201.

44. Íslenzk fornrit 16:167–68. Jóhannesson, *Íslendinga saga* 1:218–20; Stefánsson, "Kirkjuvald eflist," 98–104.

45. Íslenzk fornrit 17:235, 285, 329, 343–44, 364, 382, 394, 395–96, 408, 438, 440; Íslenzk fornrit 16:66, 157; Biskupa sögur 1:136.

46. Biskupa sögur 1:143.

47. Íslenzk fornrit 17:77.

48. Ibid., 17:106. Cf. ibid., 17:111, 173.

49. Kristoffer Mathias Vadum, "Bruk av kanonistisk litteratur i Nidarosprovinsen ca 1250–1340" (PhD thesis, Universitetet i Oslo, 2015), 164–225.

50. Íslenzk fornrit 17:232, 284.

51. Ibid., 17:422.

52. Ibid., 17:52, 86, 153, 158, 162–63.

53. Ibid., 17:56. Cf. ibid., 17:329.

54. Janus Jónsson, "Um klaustrin á Íslandi," *Tímarit Hins íslenska bókmenntafélags* 8 (1887): 174–265; Oluf Kolsrud, *Noregs kyrkjesoga* (Oslo: Aschehoug, 1958), 183–85, 206–7, 234; Helle, *Norge blir en stat*, 238–40; Erik Gunnes, "Ordener og klostre i norsk samfunnsliv," *Collegium Medievale* 8 (1995): 131–46; Jóhannesson, *Íslendinga saga* 1:227–36; Stefánsson, "Kirkjuvald eflist," 81–85; Gunnar F. Guðmundsson, *Íslenskt samfélag og Rómakirkja*, Kristni á Íslandi 2, ed. Hjalti Hugason (Reykjavík: Alþingi, 2000), 212–18.

55. Diplomatarium Norvegicum 2, no. 36 (10 August 1295); Postola Sögur = *Postola Sögur: Legendariske Fortællinger om Apostlernes Liv, deres Kamp for Kristendommens Udbredelse samt deres Martyrdød; Efter gamle Haandskrifter*, ed. Carl Richard Unger (Christiania: Trykt hos B. M. Bentzen, 1874), 849.

56. Íslenzk fornrit 17:338.

57. Rule of Saint Benedict = *The Rule of Saint Benedict*, Dumbarton Oaks Medieval Library, ed. Bruce L. Venarde (Cambridge, MA: Harvard University Press, 2011), 176–77. Cf. Klosterliv = *Klosterliv i Vesten: Augustins regel, Benedikts regel*, Thorleif Dahls kulturbibliotek, ed. Erik Gunnes (Oslo: Aschehougi samarbeid med Fondet for Thorleif Dahls kulturbibliotek og Det norske akademi for sprog og litteratur, 1986), 90.

58. Klosterliv, 48.

59. Brian Patrick McGuire, *Friendship and Community: The Monastic Experience 350–1250*, Cistercian Studies Series 95 (Kalamazoo: Cistercian Publications, 1988), xv, xviii,

xx, xxiii; Julian Haseldine, "Friendship and Rivalry: The Role of Amicitia in Twelfth-Century Monastic Relations," *Journal of Ecclesiastical History* 44 (1993): 390–414; Julian Haseldine, "Understanding the Language of Amicitia: The Friendship Circle of Peter of Celle (c. 1115–1183)," *Journal of Medieval History* 20, no. 3 (1994): 237–60; Julian Haseldine, "Friends, Friendship and Networks in the Letters of Bernard of Clairvaux," *Cîteaux: Commentarii Cistercienses* 57 (2006): 243–80; Helge Svare, *Vennskap* (Oslo: Pax, 2004), 53–57.

5. Friends of the Gods

1. Íslensk hómilíubók, 70.

2. Ingvild Sælid Gilhus and Lisbeth Mikaelsson, *Hva er religion*, Hva er (Oslo: Universitetsforlaget, 2007), 10–12.

3. Snorra Edda =*Edda Snorra Sturlusonar*, ed. Heimir Pálsson (Reykjavík: Mál og menning, 1996), 34.

4. Ibid., 34.

5. Íslenzk fornrit 4:12–13.

6. Ibid., 4:19–20.

7. Lúðvík Ingvarsson, *Goðorð og goðorðsmenn 1–3* (Egilsstaðir: Höfundur, 1986–87), 3: index.

8. Kristian Hald, *Personnavne i Danmark I: Oldtiden*, Dansk historisk fællesforenings håndbøger (København: Dansk historisk fællesforening, 1971), 42.

9. Gro Steinsland, *Norrøn religion: Myter, riter, samfunn* (Oslo: Pax, 2005), 274–303.

10. John Lindow, "Akkerisfrakki: Traditions concerning Olafr Tryggvason and Hallfredr Ottarsson vandraedaskald and the Problem of the Conversion (Iceland's Conversion to Christianity)," *Journal of English and Germanic Philology* 106, no. 1 (2007): 64–80; Erin Goeres, "The Many Conversions of Hallfreðr Vandræðaskáld," *Viking and Medieval Scandinavia* 7 (2011): 45–62.

11. Gísli Gíslason, *Íslenzkt stjórnarfar síðustu öld þjóðveldisins* (Reykjavík: Sigríður Þórarinsdóttir, 1944), 53.

12. Íslenzk fornrit 15:7–8; Jón Hnefill Aðalsteinsson, *Under the Cloak: The Acceptance of Christianity in Iceland with Particular Reference to the Religious Attitudes Prevailing at the Time*, Studia ethnologica Upsalensia 4 (Uppsala: Almqvist & Wiksel, 1978), 15–54; Terry Gunnell, "Hof, Halls, Goðar and Dwarves: An Examination of the Ritual Space in the Pagan Icelandic Hall," *Cosmos* 17 (2001): 14.

13. Íslenzk fornrit 26:167–68.

14. Gamal norsk homiliebok, 5–62; Gammelnorsk homiliebok =*Gammelnorsk homiliebok*, ed. Erik Gunnes and Astrid Salvesen (Oslo: Universitetsforlaget, 1971), 9–17; Íslensk hómilíubók, 3–19; Icelandic Homily Book =*The Icelandic Homily Book: Perg. 15 4 to in The Royal Library, Stockholm*, Íslensk handrit, Icelandic manuscripts, series in quarto, ed. Andrea de Leeuw van Weenen, vol. 3 (Reykjavík: Stofnun Árna Magnússonar á Íslandi, 1993), vii–xxi; Oddmund Hjelde, *Kirkens budskap i sagatiden* (Oslo, Solum, 1995), 29–33; Aud-Jorunn Sandal, "Synd i Gamalnorsk homiliebok og Islandsk homiliebok" (Hovedfagsoppgave, Universitetet i Bergen, 1996), 4–21.

15. Íslensk hómilíubók, 140. Cf. ibid., 221.

16. Ibid., 140–41. The Old Norse term *trú* can mean both "faith" and "assurance"; in this context, it is probably best to interpret the word as "loyalty"; Fritzner, *Ordbog over*.

17. Íslensk hómilíubók, 142–43, 220, 263–64. Cf. Gamal norsk homiliebok, 51, 52; Íslenzk fornrit 15:137; Geisli =Einarr Skúlason's Geisli: A Critical Edition, Toronto Old Norse and Icelandic Studies, ed. Martin Chase (Toronto: University of Toronto Press, 2005), 113, (st. 63).

18. Íslensk hómilíubók, 143–44.

19. Ibid., 144–46. Cf. ibid., 219–21, adds that Job had seven sons.

20. Ibid., 238, 299–300.

21. Larry Scanlon, Narrative, Authority, and Power: The Medieval Exemplum and the Chaucerian Tradition, Cambridge Studies in Medieval Literature 20 (Cambridge: Cambridge University Press, 1994), 3–134.

22. See, e.g., Lois Tyson, Critical Theory Today: A User-Friendly Guide, 2nd ed. (New York: Routledge, 2006), 169–203.

23. Heilagra manna sögur 1:71, 80, 196, 198, 330, 624; Postola Sögur, 270, 484. Cf. Ian J. Kirby, Bible Translation in Old Norse, Université de Lausanne, Publications de la Faculté des lettres 27 (Genève, 1986), 101, 107.

24. Terje Stordalen and Reidar Hvalvik, Den store fortellingen: Om Bibelens tilblivelse, innhold, bruk og betydning (Oslo: Det Norske bibelselskap, 1999), 132. Cf. Arvid S. Kapelrud, Job og hans problem: I fortid og i dag (Oslo: Land og kirke, 1976); Svein Granerud, Egil Sjaastad, and Asbjørn Kvalbein, eds., Lundes bibelleksikon (Oslo: Lunde, 1996).

25. Stordalen and Hvalvik, Den store fortellingen, 133.

26. Heilagra manna sögur 1:386, 534.

27. Gamal norsk homiliebok, 7–8, 15, 23, 27, 29, 30, 35, 45–47, 50, 51, 73, 75, 77–78.

28. Konungs skuggsiá, 20. Stjorn, which is a collection of Old Norse translations of Old Testament material from the fourteenth century, probably partly translated in the thirteenth century, refers to the Book of Job, but not to the story about him; Stjorn =Stjórn: Tekst etter håndskriftene 1–2, Norrøne tekster, ed. Reidar Astås (Oslo: Riksarkivet, 2009), 133, 191; ibid., xviii–xxxiii.

29. Íslensk hómilíubók, 5, 35, 36, 59, 111, 133, 136, 139, 172, 187, 288, 290; Gamal norsk homiliebok, 47, 51, 52, 89, 93, 103, 108, 114, 116, 125.

30. Íslensk hómilíubók, 22, 23, 27, 30, 31, 35, 53, 62–63, 70, 71, 78, 103, 106, 135, 163, 236, 264, 274, 290; Gamal norsk homiliebok, 32, 35, 52, 89, 104, 107, 170.

31. Íslensk hómilíubók, 33, 35, 36, 57, 62–63, 70, 90, 224, 236; Gamal norsk homiliebok, 144; Íslenzk fornrit 17:132, 137; Diplomatarium Islandicum 2, no. 167 (2 May 1297).

32. Íslensk hómilíubók, 27, 109, 147, 208; Gamal norsk homiliebok, 95, 125, 170.

33. Gamal norsk homiliebok, 108, 114, 115, 116, 125. Cf. Íslensk hómilíubók, 21, 27; Íslenzk fornrit 16:42; Biskupa sögur 1:215, 259, 323, 559, 610; Geisli, st. 9. The priest Jón was also God's dearest friend; later he became a bishop and a saint; Biskupa sögur 1:226. God's ástvinr (genuine friend) was also used in reference to Óláf the Holy's friends; Gamal norsk homiliebok, 111.

34. Heilagra manna sögur 1:531, 532. In the Eddic poem Hyndluljóð, it seems that the term vinr is only used about women; Eddukvæði 1:460 (st. 1).

35. Heilagra manna sögur 1:537, 541; Íslensk hómilíubók, 238.

36. Gamal norsk homiliebok, 43–47; Íslensk hómilíubók, 253–57.

37. Acts 7:54–60 (World English Bible, hereafter WEB).

38. Íslensk hómilíubók, 257; Gamal norsk homiliebok, 46. Cf. Matthew 6:14–15 (WEB).

39. Íslensk hómilíubók, 257; Gamal norsk homiliebok, 47. Cf. Luke 23:34 (WEB); Íslensk hómilíubók, 53, 273, 274; Gamal norsk homiliebok, 78–79.

40. Íslensk hómilíubók, 96–97, 171, 176; Gamal norsk homiliebok, 17, 45–47, 78, 104, 142, 170.

41. Íslensk hómilíubók, 140, 170, 178–79, 202, 206, 240; Gamal norsk homiliebok, 45–47.

42. Íslensk hómilíubók, 233–34. Cf. ibid., 292.

43. Gamal norsk homiliebok, 149–50; Íslensk hómilíubók, 154, 178–79, 202, 206, 240.

44. In the European discussion, this topic has been addressed by a number of scholars, e.g., see Patrick J. Geary, *Living with the Dead in the Middle Ages* (Ithaca, NY: Cornell University Press, 1994), 77–92; Robert Bartlett, *Why Can the Dead Do Such Great Things? Saints and Worshippers from the Martyrs to the Reformation* (Princeton, NJ: Princeton University Press, 2013), 103–12.

45. E.g., see Diplomatarium Norvegicum 3, no. 1 (c. 1220); Íslenzk fornrit 15:301–2; Íslenzk fornrit 17:271; Íslensk hómilíubók, 264; Gamal norsk homiliebok, 32, 35, 170; Biskupa sögur 1:470; Birte Carlé, *Jomfru-fortællingen: Et bidrag til genrehistorien*, Odense University Studies in Scandinavian Languages and Literatures (Odense: Odense Universitetsforlag, 1985), 76; Margaret Cormack, *The Saints in Iceland: Their Veneration from the Conversion to 1400*, Subsidia hagiographica 78 (Bruxelles: Société des Bollandistes, 1994), 71–165; Magnús Stefánsson, "Islandsk egenkirkevesen," in *Møtet mellom hedendom og kristendom i Norge*, ed. Hans-Emil Lidén (Oslo: Universitetsforlaget, 1995), 234–54. In *Konungs skuggsjá*, the father gives advice to his son the merchant that he should always have God, Mary, and especially the saint he most frequently venerates as partners, and look carefully after their wealth; Konungs skuggsiá, 6.

46. First Grammatical Treatise =*First Grammatical Treatise: Introduction, Text, Notes, Translation, Vocabulary, Facsimiles*, Publications in Linguistics, University of Iceland 1, ed. Hreinn Benediktsson (Reykjavík: Institute of Nordic Linguistics, 1972), 208.

47. Sturlunga saga 1:399.

48. Biskupa sögur 1:440, 470, 473; Sturlunga saga 1:123. Cf. Íslenzk fornrit 16: 87–88, 196.

49. Sturlunga saga 1:149.

50. Sigurðsson, "Om legender og samfunnspåvirkning," in *Norm og praksis i middelaldersamfunnet*, Kulturstudier 14, ed. Else Mundal and Ingvild Øye (Bergen: Senter for europeiske kulturstudier, 1999), 188–89.

51. Pernille H. Fredriksen, "Helgener og kirkededikasjoner i Norge i middelalderen" (MA-oppgave: Universitetet i Oslo, 2004), 53.

52. Sturlunga saga 1:198–99.

53. Carlé, *Jomfru-fortællingen*, 80–81; Birte Carlé, "Men and Women in the Saints' Sagas of Stock. 2, fol," in *Structure and Meaning in Old Norse Literature: New Approaches to Textual Analysis and Literary Criticism*, The Viking Collection 3, ed. John Lindow, Lars Lönnroth, and Gerd Wolfgang Weber (Odense: Odense University Press, 1986), 344.

54. Heilagra manna sögur 1:486–89. Cf. Sigurðsson, "Konur og kvennarán á Íslandi á 12. og 13. öld," 71–80.

55. Heilagra manna sögur 1:404.

56. Biskupa sögur 1:254–55; Heilagra manna sögur 1:21–22.

57. Diplomatarium Norvegicum 1, no. 51 (1226–54).

58. Ibid., 8, no. 5 (1202). Cf. ibid., 1, no. 50 (1226–54), no. 51 (1226–54), no. 92 (22 July 1300); ibid., 2 (before 16 December 1265), no. 16a (19 April 1276).

59. E.g., ibid. 1, no. 7 (12 March 1225), no. 81 (13 June 1292), no. 83 (11 June 1294), no. 141 (20 March 1314), no. 151 (16 July 1317), no. 160 (7 March 1320); ibid. 2, no. 4 (1202–20), no. 11 (6 February 1288), no. 13 (n.d., 1290), no. 13 (n.d., 1266), no. 16a (19 April 1276), no. 17 (30 April 1277), no. 19 (24 March 1279), no. 36 (10 August 1295), no. 49 (22 April 1299); Sturlunga saga 2:72; Norges innskrifter 6:99; Norges gamle love 3:32, 45, 74.

60. Johan Agerholt, *Gamal brevskipnad: Etterrøkjingar og utgreidingar i norsk diplomatikk.*, vol. 1, *Formelverket i kongebrev på norsk 1280–1387* (Oslo: s.n., 1929), 451–52.

61. This is found in both Norwegian and Icelandic manuscripts; *Þrjár þýðingar lærðar* = *Þrjár þýðingar lærðar frá miðöldum: Elucidarius, Um kostu og löstu, Um festarfé sálarinnar*, ed. Gunnar Ágúst Harðarson (Reykjavík: Hið íslenska bókmenntafélag, 1989), 30.

62. Historia Norwegie = *Historia Norwegie*, ed. Inger Ekrem and Lars Boje Mortensen (København: Museum Tusculanum Press, 2003), 50. One of the sagas about Bishop Gudmund refers to "Eronimus: Obsequium amicos, justitia odium pariet: eptirmæli aflar þér vina, en réttyrði rógbera"; Biskupa sögur 1:579. In an article from 1929, Guðmundur Finnbogason claims that the values that *Hávamál* conveys are mainly Norse or Germanic; Guðmundur Finnbogason, "Lífsskoðun Hávamála," 99.

6. Kinsmen and Friends

1. Íslenzk fornrit 4:3b pedigree, 5 pedigree.

2. Íslenzk fornrit 3:222; Íslenzk fornrit 4:75.

3. Íslenzk fornrit 4:122–23.

4. Robert T. Merrill, "Notes on Icelandic Kinship Terminology," *American Anthropologist* 66 (1964): 868–71; Hastrup, *Culture and History in Medieval Iceland*, 72–104; David Gaunt, *Familjeliv i Norden* (Malmö: Gidlund, 1983), 186–210; George W. Rich, "Problems and Prospects in the Study of Icelandic Kinship," in *The Anthropology of Iceland*, ed. Paul E. Durrenberger and Gísli Pálsson (Iowa City: University of Iowa Press, 1989), 53–79; Preben Meulengracht Sørensen, *Saga og samfund* (København: Berlingske forlag, 1977), 30–36; Torben Anders Vestergaard, "The system of kinship in early Norwegian law," *Mediaeval Scandinavia* 12 (1988): 160–93; Lars Ivar Hansen, "Slektskap, ekteskap og sosiale strategier i nordisk middelalder," *Collegium Medievale* 7 (1994): 103–54; Lars Ivar Hansen, " 'Ætten' i de eldste landskapslovene—realitet, konstruksjon og strategi," in *Norm og praksis i middelaldersamfunnet*, ed. Else Mundal and Ingvild Øye (Bergen: Senter for europeiske kulturstudier, 1999), 23–55; Lars Ivar Hansen, "Slektskap," in *Holmgang: Om førmoderne samfunn; Festskrift til Kåre Lunden*, Tid og Tanke 4, ed. Anne Eidsfelt et al. (Oslo: 2000), 104–32; Grete Høgset, "Frendskap og vennskap: Betydningen av sosiale relasjoner og nettverk på Island og i Norge ca 900-1264, " (MA thesis, Universitetet i Bergen, 1995), 1–98; Else Mundal, "Kvinnesynet og forståinga av biologisk arv i den norrøne kulturen," in *Atlantisk dåd og drøm: 17 essays om Island/Norge*, ed. Asbjørn Aarnes (Oslo: Aschehoug, 1998), 153–70.

5. Grágás 2:59–60; Grágás 3, *frændsemi*; Íslenzk fornrit 30:152; KLNM 20:587–93.

6. Diplomatarium Islandicum 1, no. 127 (1230).

7. Mundal, "Kvinnesynet og forståinga av biologisk arv i den norrøne kulturen," 153–70.

8. Sturlunga saga 1:53.

9. Ibid., 1:347, 455.

10. Sigurðsson, "Forholdet mellom frender," 317.

11. Miller, *Bloodtaking and Peacemaking*, 155; Sigurðsson, *Chieftains and Power*, 143–44.

12. Sigurðsson, *Frá goðorðum til ríkja*, 126–31.

13. Hagskinna =*Hagskinna: Sögulegar hagtölur um Ísland*, ed. Guðmundur Jónsson and Magnús S. Magnússon (Reykjavík: Hagstofa Íslands, 1997), 49; http://www .hagstofa.is/Hagtolur/Mannfjoldi/Yfirlit, accessed 7 August 2015.

14. Sturlunga saga 1:402; Sturlunga saga 2:7 pedigree.

15. Sturlunga saga 2:127.

16. Íslenzk fornrit 9:7.

17. Clark, "The Semantic Range of Wine," 79.

18. Ibid., 92.

19. Íslenzk fornrit 8:171.

20. Eirspennill, 313. Cf. Codex Frisianus, 518; Íslenzk fornrit 30:94.

21. Eirspennill, 343, 412; Íslenzk fornrit 30:144, 245.

22. Den ældre Gulathings-Lov, para. 15.

23. Elise M. Hansen, "En undersøkelse av drap, hevndrap og feide i Heimskringla og seks islendingesagaer" (MA-thesis, Universitetet i Oslo, 1999), 24.

24. Íslenzk fornrit 5:147–50, 161–62, 164–65.

25. Sturlunga saga 1:434–36, 438.

26. Hagskinna, 49, 264.

27. David Herlihy, "Family," *American Historical Review* 96 (1991): 2–4.

28. Fritzner, *Ordbog over*.

29. Helle, *Norge blir en stat*, 15–16.

30. Ibid., 15–16; Byock, *Medieval Iceland*, 34; Sturlunga saga 2:xxvii–li. Cf. Úlfar Bragason, *Ætt og saga: Um frásagnarfræði Sturlungu eða Íslendinga sögu hinnar miklu* (Reykjavík: Háskólaútgáfan, 2010), 13–39.

31. Lauritz Weibull, *Kritiska undersökningar i Nordens historia omkring år 1000* (Lund, 1911).

32. Halvdan Koht, "Sagaens oppfatning av vår gamle historie," *Historisk tidsskrift* 5, no. 2 (1914): 379–96.

33. Björn M. Ólsen, *Om Gunnlaugs Saga Ormstungu: En kritisk Undersøgelse* (København: s.n., 1911).

34. Weibull, *Kritiska undersökningar i Nordens historia omkring år 1000*; Björn M. Ólsen, *Om Gunnlaugs Saga*; Koht, "Sagaens oppfatning av vår gamle historie." There has been an extensive discussion about the source values of the sagas; e.g., see Miller, *Bloodtaking and Peacemaking*, 43–76; Sigurðsson, *Chieftains and Power*, 17–38; Sigurðsson, "Tendencies in the Historiography on the Medieval Nordic States (to 1350)," in *Public Power in Europe: Studies in Historical Transformation*, ed. James S. Amelang and Sigfried Beer (Pisa: PLUS-Pisa University Pres, 2006), 1–15; Knut Helle, "Den primitivistiske vendingen i norsk historisk middelalderforskning," *Historisk tidskift* 88 (2009), 571–609; Knut Helle, "Hvor står den historiske sagakritikken i dag?" *Collegium Medievale* 24 (2011): 50–86; Shami Ghosh, *Kings' Sagas and Norwegian History: Problems and Perspectives*, The Northern World: North Europe and the Baltic c. 400–1700 AD: Peoples, Economies and Cultures (Leiden: Brill, 2011).

35. Miller, *Bloodtaking and Peacemaking*, 44–45.

36. Siegfried Beyschlag, "Snorri Sturluson," *Saeculum* 7 (1956): 316.

37. Anthony Colin Spearing, *Textual Subjectivity: The Encoding of Subjectivity in Medieval Narratives and Lyrics* (Oxford: Oxford University Press, 2005), 22.

38. Pádraig Mac Carron and Ralph Kenna, "Viking Sagas: Six Degrees of Icelandic Separation Social Networks from the Viking Era," *Significance* 10, no. 6 (2013), 17. Cf. Pádraig Mac Carron and Ralph Kenna, "Network Analysis of the Íslendinga sögur—the Sagas of Icelanders," *European Physical Journal B* 86, no. 10 (2013), 1–9; Richard Gaskins, "Political Development in Early Iceland: Applying Network Theory to the Sagas," in *Applications of Network Theories (Skandinavistik: Sprache, Literatur, Kultur)*, ed. Susanne Kramarz-Bein and Birge Hilsmann (Berlin: LIT Verlag, 2014), 10–33.

39. Victor W. Turner, "An Anthropological Approach to the Icelandic Saga," in *The Translation of Culture: Essays to E. E. Evans-Pitchard*, ed. T. O. Beidelman (London: Tavistock, 1971), 358.

40. Helgi Þorláksson, *Gamlar götur og goðavald*, 25, 12.

41. Guðrún Ása Grímsdóttir, "Um sárafar í Íslendinga sögu Sturlu Þórðarsonar," in *Sturlustefna*, Stofnun Árna Magnússonar á Íslandi, Rit 32, ed. Guðrún Ása Grímsdóttir and Jónas Kristjánsson (Reykjavík: 1988), 184–203.

42. Christopher Brooke, *The Saxon and Norman Kings*, British Monarchy Series (Glasgow: Fontana/Collins, [1963] 1967), 45.

43. The skaldic poetry stresses the importance of the rulers' generosity. There has for some time been a discussion about the dating of skaldic poetry; however, most scholars today accept that their dating is reliable and that they are not thirteenth-century constructions; http://skaldic.arts.usyd.edu.au/db.php. See also Vésteinn Ólason, "Norrøn litteratur som historisk kildemateriale," in *Kilderne til den tidlige middelalders historie: Rapporter til den XX nordiske historikerkongres, Reykjavík 1987*, Ritsafn Sagnfræðistofnunar 18, ed. Gunnar Karlsson (Reykjavík: Sagnfræðistofnum Háskóla Íslands, 1987), 38.

44. We see an example of this dual vocabulary in the use of the term "oath of loyalty" (*trúnaðareiðr*). *Sturlunga saga* refers to a number of examples of this in the period 1228–62; see Sturlunga saga 1:321, 471–73, 527; Sturlunga saga 2:1–3, 11–13, 38, 94, 105, 136, 270, 280–82. Among all the Icelandic Family Sagas, it is only *Grettis saga*, written in the first quarter of the fourteenth century, which mentions this oath; Íslenzk fornrit 7:263.

45. Bjarni Vilhjálmsson and Óskar Halldórsson, *Íslenzkir málshættir*, Íslenzk þjóðfræði (Reykjavík: Almenna bókafélagið, 1991), 98.

7. Friendship Loses Its Power

1. For an overview of this devlopment, see Sigurðsson, "The Making of a 'Skatland,'" 181–94.

2. Þorsteinsson and Líndal, "Lögfesting konungsvalds," 34–75; Jón Viðar Sigurðsson, "The Icelandic Aristocracy after the Fall of the Free State," *Scandinavian Journal of History* 20 (1995): 157; Sigríður Beck, "Att vinna vänner: Vänskap som politiskt redskap på Island ca. 1250–1400," in *Vänner, patroner och klienter i Norden, Rapport till 26:e Nordiska historikermötet i Reykjavík den 8–12 augusti 2007*, Ritsafn Sagnfræðistofnunar 39, ed. Lars Hermanson et al. (Reykjavík: Háskólaútgáfan, 2007), 102–3.

3. Norges gamle love 2:90.

4. Jónsbók =Jónsbók: Kong Magnus Hakonssons lovbog for Island vedtaget paa Altinget 1281 og réttarbætr de for Island givne retterbøder af 1294, 1305 og 1314, ed. Ólafur Halldórsson (København: S. L. Møllers Bogtrykkeri, 1904), 99–100.

5. Íslenzk fornrit 17:86.

6. Jónsbók, 284.

7. Diplomatarium Islandicum 1, no. 156 (1264).

8. Þorsteinsson and Líndal, "Lögfesting konungsvalds," 93.

9. Kåre Lunden, Økonomi og samfunn (Oslo: Universitetsforlaget, 1972), 38–44.

10. Monclair, "Lederskapsideologi," 143–206.

11. Dietler, "Feasts and Commensal Politics," 98.

12. The following discussion builds on Jóhannesson, Íslendinga saga 1:103–9; Lýður Björnsson, Saga sveitarstjórnar á Íslandi I (Reykjavík: Almenna Bókafélagið, 1972), 9–64; Gunnar F. Guðmundsson, Eignarhald á afréttum og almenningum: Sögulegt yfirlit, Ritsafn Sagnfræðistofnunar 4 (Reykjavík: Sagnfræðistofnun Háskóla Íslands, 1981), 63–68; Frederik Pedersen, "A Medieval Welfare State? Welfare Provision in a Twelfth Century Icelandic Law Code," Northern Studies 34 (1999): 89–111; Jón Viðar Sigurðsson, "Hugleiðingar um hreppa, bændagildi og goðorð," in Heimtur: Ritgerðir til heiðurs Gunnari Karlssyni sjötugum, ed. Guðmundur Jónsson, Helgi Skúli Kjartansson, and Vésteinn Ólason (Reykjavík: Mál og menning, 2009), 243–55.

13. Diplomatarium Islandicum 1, no. 152–56 (1262–64); Björnsson, Saga sveitarstjórnar, 62.

14. Sigurðsson, "The Making of a 'Skattland,'" 207–9.

15. Codex Frisianus, 555.

16. Konungs skuggsiá, 45.

17. The following discussion about guilds in Norway is based on Alexander Bugge, "Tingsteder, gilder og andre gamle midtpunkter i de norske bygder," Historisk tidsskrift 4 (1920): 97–152, 195–252; Oscar Albert Johnsen, "Gildevæsenet i Norge i middelalderen," Historisk Tidsskrift 5, rekke, 5. bind (1920): 73–101; Johannes Heggland, Tysnes: det gamle Njardarlog (Tysnes: Tysnes sogelag, 1964), 102–7, 170–213; Knut Ellefsrud, "Gilder og konfliktløsning i norsk høymiddelalder" (Hovedfagsoppgave, Universitetet i Oslo, 1996), 15–90; Christoph Anz, Gilden im mittelalterlichen Skandinavien, Veröffentlichungen des Max-Planck-Instituts für Geschichte 139 (Göttingen: Vandenhoeck & Ruprecht, 1998), 83–292; Christoph Anz, "Gildernes form og funksjon i middelalderens Skandinavia," in Gilder, lav og broderskaber i middelalderens Danmark, University of Southern Denmark Studies in History and Social Sciences, vol. 247, ed. Lars Bisgaard and Leif Søndergaard (Odense: Syddansk Universitetsforlag, 2002), 21–40; Onarheim eldre =Skraa for et Olafsgilde i Gulathingslagen, Norges gamle Love 5, ed. Rudolf Keyser et al. (Christiania: Grøndahl og søn, 1846), 25–31.

18. Onarheim eldre, 17.

8. Pragmatic Friendship

1. Eddukvæði 1:330.

2. It has been claimed that friendship is a process in four stages. The first deals with the establishment; the second, the development of loyalty (fides); the third, the mutual exchange of benefits; and the fourth, the concluding of the friendship; Burton,

"Amicitia in Plautus: A Study of Roman Friendship Processes," 211. The disadvantage of this model is that there does not appear to be an overlap between stages two and three. In reality, they usually occurred in parallel.

3. The saints should be honored with prayers, a point underlined very clearly by *Mariu saga*, with a story of a young man who scorned his fiancée. Although rich in land, he prayed every day to the Blessed Mary, and thus became her beloved. With her support, he gathered all the virtues—including celibacy—in his heart, and through these he hoped to achieve Mary's friendship. His family and friends wanted him to marry, but in the middle of the wedding feast, he left in despair and went to the nearest church. There Mary appeared to him, and he begged to be her servant. Mary heard his prayers and took him to a monastery where he lived the rest of his life in celibacy in her service. Mariu saga 2 =*Mariu saga: Legende om Jomfru Maria og hendes Jertegner; Efter gamle Haandskrifter*, Det norske Oldskriftselskabs Samlinger, ed. Carl Richard Unger (Christiania: Det norske Oldskriftselskab, 1871), 764–67. Cf. ibid., 761, 848, 849, 1041, 1145.

4. We find the saying a gift requires a countergift in different cultures the whole world over; Jürgen Hannig, "Ars donandi: Sur Ökonomie des Schenkens im früheren Mittelalter," in *Armut, Liebe, Ehre: Studien zur historischen Kulturforschung*, ed. R.v. Dülmen (Frankfurt am Main: Fischer, 1988), 21.

5. Heilagra manna sögur 1:544.

6. Cf. Arne Bugge Amundsen, "Kulturhistoriske ritualstudier," in *Ritualer: Kulturhistoriske studier*, ed. Arne Bugge Amundsen, Bjarne Hodne, and Ane Ohrvik (Oslo: Universitetsforlaget, 2006), 15–20.

7. Sturlunga saga 2:214. Fostering (Íslenzk fornrit 3:7) and oaths (Íslenzk fornrit 9:65) were also used to initiate friendships.

8. Byock, *Feud*, 217.

9. Íslenzk fornrit 3:188, 222; Íslenzk fornrit 4:22; Íslenzk fornrit 5:203; Íslenzk fornrit 6:126, 133, 348, 350; Íslenzk fornrit 8:55, 127; Íslenzk fornrit 9:165, 206; Sturlunga saga 1:367, 373, 397, 439; Sturlunga saga 2:223.

10. E.g., see Sigurðsson, *Chieftains and Power*, 124; Biskupa sögur 1:217, 504, 587; Codex Frisianus, 395; Grágás 1a, 247; Íslenzk fornrit 2:213; Íslenzk fornrit 4:64; Íslenzk fornrit 6:56; Íslenzk fornrit 8:45; Íslenzk fornrit 10:31; Íslenzk fornrit 15:243; Íslenzk fornrit 16:71, 299; Íslenzk fornrit 29 =*Ágrip af Nóregskonunga sǫgum; Fagrskinna; Nóregs konunga tal*. Íslenzk fornrit, ed. Bjarni Einarsson (Reykjavík: Hið Íslenzka fornritafélag, 1985), 80, 93; Íslenzk fornrit 30:281; Postola Sögur, 2, 25, 35, 60, 150, 410, 414, 495, 516, 532, 586, 587, 646, 651, 716, 738, 764, 842; Sturlunga saga 1:97.

11. Cf. C. Stephen Jaeger, *Ennobling Love: In Search of a Lost Sensibility*, The Middle Ages Series (Philadelphia: University of Pennsylvania Press, 1999), 48–50; Auður Magnúsdóttir, "'Þeir Kjartan ok Bolli unnusk mest': Om kärlek och svek i Laxdæla saga," in *"Vi ska alla vara välkomna!": Nordiska studier tillägnade Kristinn Jóhannesson*, ed. Auður Magnúsdóttir et al. (Göteborg: Meijerbergs institut för svensk etymologisk forskning, Göteborgs universitet, 2008), 65–81; Maurice Aymard, "A History of Friendship—among Other Sentiments," *Medieval History Journal* 18, no. 1 (2015): 1–24.

12. Aristotle, Nicomachean Ethics, 145.

13. Eirspennill, 573.

14. Many other definitions of friendship exist along with those of Cicero and Aristotle. See David Konstan, *Friendship in the Classical World*, Key Themes in Ancient

History (Cambridge: Cambridge Univeristy Press, 1997), 1; Jan Brøgger, *Kulturforstå-else: En nøkkel til vår internasjonale samtid* (Oslo: Damm, [1993] 1999), 55.

15. C. H. Landé, "Introduction: The Dyadic Basis of Clientelism," in *Friends, Followers, and Factions: A Reader in Political Clientelism*, ed. Steffen W. Schmidt et al. (Berkeley: University of California Press, 1977), xiii–xiv, xviii, xxiii.

16. Cf. Pierre Bauduin, "Chefs normands et élites franques, fin IXe-début Xe siècle," in *Les fondations scandinaves en Occident et les débuts du duché de Normandie*, ed. Pierre Bauduin (Caen: CRAM, 2005), 181–94.

17. Mac Carron and Kenna, "Viking Sagas," 13.

18. Tore Iversen, *Trelldommen: Norsk slaveri i middelalderen*, Historisk institutt, Universitetet i Bergen, Skrifter 1 (Bergen: Historisk institutt, Universitetet i Bergen, 1997), 149–53.

19. Islendzk æventyri, 165.

20. Ibid., 165.

BIBLIOGRAPHY

Aðalsteinsson, Jón Hnefill. *Under the Cloak: The Acceptance of Christianity in Iceland with Particular Reference to the Religious Attitudes Prevailing at the time.* Studia ethnologica Upsalensia 4. Uppsala: Almqvist & Wiksel, 1978.

Agerholt, Johan. *Gamal brevskipnad: Etterrøkjingar og utgreidingar i norsk diplomatikk.* Vol. 1, *Formelverket i kongebrev på norsk 1280–1387.* Oslo: s.n., 1929.

Althoff, Gerd. *Verwandte, Freunde und Getreue: Zum politischen Stellenwert der Gruppenbindungen im frühen Mittelalter.* Darmstadt: Wissenschaftliche Buchgesellschaft, 1990.

Amundsen, Arne Bugge. "Kulturhistoriske ritualstudier." In *Ritualer: Kulturhistoriske studier,* edited by Arne Bugge Amundsen, Bjarne Hodne, and Ane Ohrvik, 7–28. Oslo: Universitetsforlaget, 2006.

Andersson, Theodore M. "The King of Iceland." *Speculum* 74, no. 4 (1993): 923–34.

Anz, Christoph. *Gilden im mittelalterlichen Skandinavien.* Veröffentlichungen des Max-Planck-Instituts für Geschichte 139. Göttingen: Vandenhoeck & Ruprecht, 1998.

——. "Gildernes form og funksjon i middelalderens Skandinavia." In *Gilder, lav og broderskaber i middelalderens Danmark,* University of Southern Denmark Studies in History and Social Sciences, edited by Lars Bisgaard and Leif Søndergaard, vol. 247, 21–40. Odense: Syddansk Universitetsforlag, 2002.

Aristoteles: Den nikomakiske etikk. Bokklubbens kulturbibliotek. Edited by Øyvind Rabbås, Anfinn Stigen, and Trond Berg Eriksen. Oslo: Bokklubben dagens bøker, 1999.

Aristotle =*Aristotle: Nicomachean Ethics.* Oxford World's Classics. Translated by David Ross. Edited by Lesley Brown, rev. ed. Oxford: Oxford University Press, (1980) 2009.

Arnórsson, Einar. *Réttarsaga Alþingis: Saga Alþingis 1.* Reykjavík: Alþingissögunefnd, 1945.

Aymard, Maurice. "A History of Friendship—among Other Sentiments." *Medieval History Journal* 18, no. 1 (2015): 1–24.

Bachtin, Michail. *Latter og dialog: Utvalgte skrifter.* Translated by Audun Johannes Mørch. Oslo: Cappelen akademisk forlag, 2003.

Bagge, Sverre. "Borgerkrig og statsutvikling i Norge i middelalderen." *Historisk tidsskrift* 65 (1986): 145–97.

——. "Borgerkrig og statsutvikling—svar til Hans Jacob Orning." *Historisk tidsskrift* 93, no. 1 (2015): 91–110.

——. *From Viking Stronghold to Christian Kingdom: State Formation in Norway, c. 900–1350.* Copenhagen: Museum Tusculanum Press, 2010.

———. *Mennesket i middelalderens Norge: Tanker, tro og holdninger 1000–1300*. Oslo: Aschehoug, 1998.

———. *The Political Thought of The King's Mirror*. Mediaeval Scandinavia Suppl. 3. Odense: Odense University Press, 1987.

———. "'Salvo semper regio iure': Kampen om Sættargjerden 1277–1290." *Historisk tidsskrift* 87 (2008): 201–24.

———. *Society and Politics in Snorri Sturluson's Heimskringla*. Berkeley: University of California Press, 1991.

Bagge, Sverre, and Knut Mykland. *Norge i dansketiden 1380–1814*. Oslo: Cappelen, 1987.

Barrett, James H. "The Pirate Fishermen: The Political Economy of a Medieval Maritime Society." In *Studies in Scandinavian Sea-Borne Expansion and Settlement before 1300*, The Northern World: North Europe and the Baltic c. 400–1700 AD; Peoples, Economies and Cultures, edited by Beverly Ballin Smith, Simon Taylor, and Gareth Williams, 299–340. Leiden: Brill, 2007.

Bartlett, Robert. *Why Can the Dead Do Such Great Things? Saints and Worshippers from the Martyrs to the Reformation*. Princeton, NJ: Princeton University Press, 2013.

Bauduin, Pierre. "Chefs normands et élites franques, fin IXe–début Xe siècle." In *Les fondations scandinaves en Occident et les débuts du duché de Normandie*, edited by Pierre Bauduin, 181–94. Caen: Caisse Régionale d'Assurance Maladie de Normandie, 2005.

Beck, Sigríður. "Att vinna vänner: Vänskap som politiskt redskap på Island ca. 1250–1400." In *Vänner, patroner och klienter i Norden, Rapport till 26:e Nordiska historikermötet i Reykjavík den 8–12 augusti 2007*, Ritsafn Sagnfræðistofnunar 39, edited by Lars Hermanson, Thomas Småberg, Jón Viðar Sigurðsson, and Jakob Danneskiold-Samsø, 101–22. Reykjavík: Háskólaútgáfan, 2007.

Beistad, Heidi Anett Øvergård. "An Almost Fanatical Devotion to the Pope? Power and Priorities in the Integration of the Nidaros Province, c. 1152–1300." Trondheim, Norwegian University of Science and Technology, 2015.

———. "Kirkens frihet: Biskop Arne Torlaksson som Islands reformator." Trondheim: MA-oppgave, Norges teknisk-naturvitenskapelige universitet, 2008.

Benediktsson, Jakob. "Landnám og upphaf allsherjarríkis." In *Saga Íslands 1*, edited by Sigurður Líndal, 153–96. Reykjavík: Hið íslenzka bókmenntafélag, 1974.

Berlin, Knud. *Islands statsretlige stilling efter fristatstidens ophør*. Copenhagen: Salmonsens Boghandel, 1909.

Beyschlag, Siegfried. "Snorri Sturluson." *Saeculum* 7 (1956): 310–20.

Biskupa sögur = *Biskupa sögur 1–2*. Edited by Guðbrandur Vigfússon and Jón Sigurðsson. Copenhagen: Hið íslenska bókmenntafélag, 1858–78.

Bjørgo, Narve, Øystein Rian, and Alf Kaartvedt. *800–1536: Makt og avmakt; Selvstendighet og union; fra middelalderen til 1905*. Norsk utenrikspolitikks historie 1. Oslo: Universitetsforlaget, 1995.

Bjork, Robert E. "Speech as Gift in Beowulf." *Speculum* 69, no. 4 (1994): 993–1022.

Björnsson, Árni. *Jól á Íslandi*. Reykjavík: Ísafoldarprentsmiðja, 1963.

Björnsson, Lýður. *Saga sveitarstjórnar á Íslandi 1*. Reykjavík: Almenna Bókafélagið, 1972.

Bleumer, Hartmut. "Das Vertrauen und die Vertraute." *Frühmittelalterliche Studien* 39 (2005): 253–70.

Bloch, Marc. *Feudal Society*. Translated by L. A. Manyon. London: Routledge and Kegan Paul, 1978.

Boden, Friedrich. *Die isländische Regierungsgewalt in der freistaatlichen Zeit*. Breslau: Verlag von M. & H. Marcus, 1905.

Boulhosa, Patricia Pires. *Gamli sáttmáli: tilurð og tilgangur*. Translated by Már Jónsson. Reykjavík: Sögufélag, 2006.

———. *Icelanders and the Kings of Norway: Mediaeval Sagas and Legal Texts*. The Northern World: North Europe and the Baltic c. 400–1700 AD; Peoples, Economies and Cultures. Leiden: Brill, 2005.

———. "A Response to 'Gamli sáttmáli—hvað næst?'" *Saga* 49, no. 2 (2011): 137–51.

Bourdieu, Pierre. *Outline of a Theory of Practice*. Cambridge Studies in Social and Cultural Anthropology. Cambridge: Cambridge University Press, 1977.

Bourdieu, Pierre, and Richard Nice. *The Logic of Practice*. Oxford: Polity Press, 1990.

Bragason, Úlfar. *Ætt og saga: Um frásagnarfræði Sturlungu eða Íslendinga sögu hinnar miklu*. [Summary in English]. Reykjavík: Háskólaútgáfan, 2010.

Brooke, Christopher. *The Saxon and Norman Kings*. British Monarchy Series. Glasgow: Fontana/Collins, (1963) 1967.

Brøgger, Jan. *Kulturforståelse: En nøkkel til vår internasjonale samtid*. Oslo: Damm, (1993) 1999.

Bugge, Alexander. "Tingsteder, gilder og andre gamle midtpunkter i de norske bygder." *Historisk tidsskrift* 4 (1920): 97–152, 95–252.

Burton, Paul J. "Amicitia in Plautus: A Study of Roman Friendship Processes." *American Journal of Philology* 125, no. 2 (2004): 209–43.

Byock, Jesse L. *Feud in the Icelandic Saga*. Berkeley: University of California Press, 1982.

———. *Medieval Iceland: Society, Sagas, and Power*. Berkeley: University of California Press, 1988.

———. *Viking Age Iceland*. London: Penguin Books, 2001.

Caine, Barbara, ed. *Friendship: A History*. Critical Histories of Subjectivity and Culture. London: Equinox, 2009.

Carlé, Birte. *Jomfru-fortællingen: Et bidrag til genrehistorien*. Odense University Studies in Scandinavian Languages and Literatures. Odense: Odense Universitetsforlag, 1985.

———. "Men and Women in the Saints' Sagas of Stock. 2, fol." In *Structure and Meaning in Old Norse Literature: New Approaches to Textual Analysis and Literary Criticism*, The Viking Collection 3, edited by John Lindow, Lars Lönnroth, and Gerd Wolfgang Weber, 317–46. Odense: Odense University Press, 1986.

Charles-Edwards, Thomas. "The Distinction between Land and Moveable Wealth in Anglo-Saxon England." In *Medieval Settlement: Continuity and Change*, edited by Peter H. Sawyer, 180–87. London: Edward Arnold, 1976.

Cicero: De senectute; De amicitia; De divinatione. The Loeb Classical Library 154. Edited by William Armistead Falconer. Cambridge, MA: Harvard University Press, 1927.

Clark, David. "The Semantic Range of Wine and Freond in Old English." [In English]. *Neuphilologische Mitteilungen* 114, no. 1 (2013): 79–93.

Codex Frisianus =*Codex Frisianus: En Samling af norske Kongesagaer*. Edited by Carl Richard Unger. Christiania: Malling, 1871.

Cormack, Margaret. *The Saints in Iceland: Their Veneration from the Conversion to 1400.* Subsidia hagiographica 78. Brussels: Société des Bollandistes, 1994.

Danielsen, Rolf, Ståle Dyrvik, Tore Grønlie, Knut Helle, and Edgar Hovland. *Norway: A History from the Vikings to Our Own Times.* Oslo: Scandinavian University Press, 1995.

Den ældre Gulathings-Lov =*Den ældre Gulathings-Lov.* Norges gamle Love 1. Edited by Rudolf Keyser et al. Christiania: Grøndahl og søn, 1846.

Devere, Heather. "The Academic Debate on Friendship and Politics." *AMITY: The Journal of Friendship Studies* 1, no. 1 (2013): 5–33.

Dietler, Michael. "Feasting and Fasting." In *The Oxford Handbook on the Archaeology of Ritual and Religion*, edited by Timothy Ingersoll, 179–94. Oxford: Oxford University Press, 2011.

———. "Feasts and Commensal Politics in the Politicial Economy." In *Food and the Status Quest: An Interdisciplinary Perspective*, edited by Polly Wiessner and Wulf Schiefenhövel, 87–125. Providence: Berghahn Books, 1996.

Diplomatarium Islandicum =*Diplomatarium Islandicum: Íslenzkt fornbréfasafn 1–16.* Edited by Jón Sigurðsson, Jón Þorkelsson, Páll Eggert Ólason, and Björn Þorsteinsson. Reykjavík: Hið íslenzka bókmenntafjelag, 1857–1972.

Diplomatarium Norvegicum =*Diplomatarium Norvegicum 1–23.* Edited by C. C. A. Lange et al. Christiania / Oslo: 1847–2011.

Durrenberger, E. Paul, and Gísli Pálsson. "The Importance of Friendship in the Absence of States, according to the Icelandic Sagas." In *The Anthropology of Friendship*, edited by Sandra Bell and Simon Coleman, 59–77. Oxford: Berg, 1999.

Edda =*The Poetic Edda.* Oxford world's classics. Edited by Carolyne Larrington. Oxford: Oxford University Press, 2008.

Effros, Bonnie. *Creating Community with Food and Drink in Merovingian Gaul.* The New Middle Ages. New York: Palgrave Macmillan, 2002.

Eirspennill =*Eirspennill: AM 47 fol.* Edited by Finnur Jónsson. Christiania: 1916.

Ellefsrud, Knut. "Gilder og konfliktløsning i norsk høymiddelalder." Hovedfagsoppgave, Universitetet i Oslo, 1996.

Ersland, Geir Atle, and Terje H. Holm. *Krigsmakt og kongemakt 900–1814.* Oslo: Eide, 2000.

Finnbogason, Guðmundur. "Lífsskoðun Hávamála og Aristóteles." *Skírnir* 103 (1929): 84–102.

Finsen, Vilhjálmur. *Om den oprindelige ordning af nogle af den islandske fristats institutioner.* Kjøbenhavn: s.n., 1888.

First Grammatical Treatise =*First Grammatical Treatise: Introduction, Text, Notes, Translation, Vocabulary, Facsimiles.* Publications in Linguistics, University of Iceland 1. Edited by Hreinn Benediktsson. Reykjavík: Institute of Nordic Linguistics, 1972.

Flateyjarbók =*Flateyjarbók 1–4.* Edited by Sigurður Nordal. Reykjavík: Flateyjarútgáfan, 1944.

Foote, Peter, and David M. Wilson. *The Viking Achievement. A Survey of the Society and Culture of Early Medieval Scandinavia.* Great Civilizations Series. New York: Praeger, 1970.

Fredriksen, Pernille H. "Helgener og kirkededikasjoner i Norge i middelalderen." MA-oppgave, Universitetet i Oslo, 2004.

Fritsch-Rößler, Waltraud. "Laughter." In *Handbook of Medieval Studies: Terms, Methods, Trends*, edited by Albrecht Classen, 1524–29. Göttingen: de Gruyter, 2010.

Fritzner, Johan. *Ordbog over Det gamle norske Sprog 1–3: Rev. ed. 1954–1972 Finn Hødnebø*. Omarb., forøget og forbedret Udg. ed. Christiania: Den norske Forlagsforening, 1883–96.

Gamal norsk homiliebok =*Gamal norsk homiliebok: Cod. AM 619 4o*. Edited by Gustav Indrebø. Oslo: I hovudkommisjon hjaa Dybwad, 1931.

Gammelnorsk homiliebok =*Gammelnorsk homiliebok*. Edited by Erik Gunnes and Astrid Salvesen. Oslo: Universitetsforlaget, 1971.

Ganshof, F. L. *Feudalism*. Translated by P. Grierson. 3rd ed. London: Longman, 1977.

Garnier, Claudia. *Amicus amicis, inimicus inimicis: Politische Freundschaft und fürstliche Netzwerke im 13. Jahrhundert*. Monographien zur Geschichte des Mittelalters Bd. 46. Stuttgart: Hiersemann, 2000.

——. "Wie vertraut man seinem Feind?" *Frühmittelalterliche Studien* 39 (2005): 271–91.

Gaskins, Richard. "Political Development in Early Iceland: Applying Network Theory to the Sagas." In *Applications of Network Theories*, Skandinavistik: Sprache, Literatur, Kultur, edited by Susanne Kramarz-Bein and Birge Hilsmann, 10–33. Berlin: LIT Verlag, 2014.

Gaunt, David. *Familjeliv i Norden*. Malmö: Gidlund, 1983.

Geary, Patrick J. *Living with the Dead in the Middle Ages*. Ithaca, NY: Cornell University Press, 1994.

Geisli =*Einarr Skúlason's Geisli: A Critical Edition*. Toronto Old Norse and Icelandic Studies. Edited by Martin Chase. Toronto: University of Toronto Press, 2005.

Ghosh, Shami. *Kings' Sagas and Norwegian History: Problems and Perspectives*. The Northern World: North Europe and the Baltic c. 400–1700 AD; Peoples, Economies and Cultures. Leiden: Brill, 2011.

Gilhus, Ingvild Sælid, and Lisbeth Mikaelsson. *Hva er religion*. Hva er. Oslo: Universitetsforlaget, 2007.

Gilsdorf, Sean. *The Favor of Friends: Intercession and Aristocratic Politics in Carolingian and Ottonian Europe*. Brill's Series on the Early Middle Ages, vol. 23. Leiden: Brill, 2014.

Gíslason, Gísli. *Íslenzkt stjórnarfar síðustu öld þjóðveldisins*. Reykjavík: Sigríður Þórarinsdóttir, 1944.

Goeres, Erin. "The Many Conversions of Hallfreðr Vandræðaskáld." *Viking and Medieval Scandinavia* 7 (2011): 45–62.

Grágás 1a =*Grágás: Islændernes Lovbog i Fristatens Tid*. Edited by Vilhjálmur Finsen. Copenhagen: Gyldendalske Boghandel, 1852.

Grágás 1b =*Grágás: Konungsbók*. Edited by Vilhjálmur Finsen. Odense: Universitetsforlag, 1974.

Grágás 2 =*Grágás: Efter det Arnamagnæanske haandskrift, nr. 334 fol., Staðarhólsbók*. Edited by Vilhjálmur Finsen. Copenhagen: Gyldendalske Boghandel, 1879.

Grágás 3 =*Grágás: Stykker, som findes i det Arnamagnæanske haandskrift, nr. 351 fol. Skálholtsbók og en række andre haandskrifter*. Edited by Vilhjálmur Finsen. Copenhagen: Gyldendalske Boghandel, 1883.

Granerud, Svein, Egil Sjaastad, and Asbjørn Kvalbein, eds. *Lundes bibelleksikon*. Oslo: Lunde, 1996.

Gregersen, Aage. *L'Islande son statut a travers les ages*. Paris, 1937.

Grímsdóttir, Guðrún Ása. "Um sárafar í Íslendinga sögu Sturlu Þórðarsonar." In *Sturlustefna*. Stofnun Árna Magnússonar á Íslandi, Rit 32. Edited by Guðrún Ása Grímsdóttir and Jónas Kristjánsson, 184–203. Reykjavík: Stofnun Árna Magnússonar á Íslandi, 1988.

Grønbech, Vilhelm. *Vor folkeæt i oldtiden 1–2*. Copenhagen: Pios Boghandel, (1909–12) 1955.

Guðmundsson, Gunnar F. *Eignarhald á afréttum og almenningum: Sögulegt yfirlit*. Ritsafn Sagnfræðistofnunar 4. Reykjavík: Sagnfræðistofnun Háskóla Íslands, 1981.

———. *Íslenskt samfélag og Rómakirkja*. Kristni á Íslandi 2. Edited by Hjalti Hugason. Reykjavík: Alþingi, 2000.

Guðmundsson, Óskar. *Snorri: Ævisaga Snorra Sturlusonar 1179–1241*. Reykjavík: JPV, 2009.

Gulatingslova =*Den eldre Gulatingslova*. Norrøne tekster 6. Edited by Tor Ulset, Bjørn Eithun, and Magnus Rindal. Oslo: Riksarkivet, 1994.

Gunnell, Terry. "Hof, Halls, Goðar and Dwarves: An Examination of the Ritual Space in the Pagan Icelandic Hall." *Cosmos* 17 (2001): 3–36.

Gunnes, Erik. *Erkebiskop Øystein: Statsmann og kirkebygger*. Oslo: Aschehoug, 1996.

———. "Ordener og klostre i norsk samfunnsliv." *Collegium Medievale* 8 (1995): 131–46.

Gurevich, Aaron. "Saga and History: The 'Historical Conception' of Snorri Sturluson." *Mediaeval Scandinavia* 4 (1971): 42–53.

———. "Space and Time in the Weltmodell of the Old Scandinavian Peoples." *Mediaeval Scandinavia* 2 (1969): 42–53.

———. "Wealth and Gift-Bestowal among the Ancient Scandinavians." *Scandinavica* 7 (1968): 126–38.

Hagskinna =*Hagskinna: Sögulegar hagtölur um Ísland*. Edited by Guðmundur Jónsson and Magnús S. Magnússon. Reykjavík: Hagstofa Íslands, 1997.

Hakonar saga =*Hakonar saga, and a Fragment of Magnus saga*. Rerum Britannicarum Medii Ævi Scriptores. Icelandic Sagas 2. Edited by Guðbrandur Vigfusson. London: 1887.

Hald, Kristian. *Personnavne i Danmark 1: Oldtiden*. Dansk historisk fællesforenings håndbøger. Copenhagen: Dansk historisk fællesforening, 1971.

Hannig, Jürgen. "Ars donandi: Sur Ökonomie des Schenkens im früheren Mittelalter." In *Armut, Liebe, Ehre: Studien zur historischen Kulturforschung*, edited by R. van Dülmen, 11–37. Frankfurt am Main: Fischer, 1988.

Hansen, Elise M. "En undersøkelse av drap, hevndrap og feide i Heimskringla og seks islendingesagaer." Oslo: Hovedfagsoppgave, Universitetet i Oslo, 1999.

Hansen, Lars Ivar. "Slektskap." In *Holmgang: Om førmoderne samfunn; Festskrift til Kåre Lunden*, Tid og Tanke 4, edited by Anne Eidsfelt, Knut Kjeldstadli, Hanne Monclair, Per G. Norseng, Hans Jakob Orning, and Gunnar I. Pettersen, 104–32. Oslo: Historisk institutt, Universitetet i Oslo, 2000.

———. "Slektskap, ekteskap og sosiale strategier i nordisk middelalder." *Collegium Medievale* 7 (1994): 103–54.

———. "'Ætten' i de eldste landskapslovene: Realitet, konstruksjon og strategi." In *Norm og praksis i middelaldersamfunnet*, edited by Else Mundal and Ingvild Øye, 23–55. Bergen: Senter for europeiske kulturstudier, 1999.

Haseldine, Julian. "Friends, Friendship and Networks in the Letters of Bernard of Clairvaux." Cîteaux: Commentarii Cistercienses 57 (2006): 243–80.

——. "Friendship and Rivalry: The Role of Amicitia in Twelfth-Century Monastic Relations." Journal of Ecclesiastical History 44 (1993): 390–414.

——, ed. Friendship in Medieval Europe. Stroud, UK: Sutton, 1999.

——. "Friendship Networks in Medieval Europe: New Models of a Political Relationship." AMITY: The Journal of Friendship Studies 1 (2013): 69–88.

——. "Understanding the Language of Amicitia: The Friendship Circle of Peter of Celle (c. 1115–1183)." Journal of Medieval History 20, no. 3 (1994): 237–60.

Hastrup, Kirsten. Culture and History in Medieval Iceland: An Anthropological Analysis of Structure and Change. Oxford: Clarendon, 1985.

Heggland, Johannes. Tysnes: Det gamle Njardarlog. Tysnes, NO: Tysnes sogelag, 1964.

Heilagra manna sögur =Heilagra manna sögur; Fortællinger og Legender om hellige Mænd og Kvinder efter gamle Haands[k]rifter 1–2. Edited by Carl Richard Unger. Christiania: B. M. Bentzen, 1877.

Helle, Knut, ed. The Cambridge History of Scandinavia. Cambridge: Cambridge University Press, 2003.

——. "Den primitivistiske vendingen i norsk historisk middelalderforskning." Historisk tidsskift 88 (2009): 571–609.

——. Gulatinget og gulatingslova. Leikanger, NO: Skald, 2001.

——. "Hvor står den historiske sagakritikken i dag?" Collegium Medievale 24 (2011): 50–86.

——. Konge og gode menn i norsk riksstyring ca. 1150–1319. Bergen: Universitetsforlaget, 1972.

——. Norge blir en stat 1130–1319. Handbok i Norges historie 3. [2nd ed.] Bergen: Universitetsforlaget, 1974.

——. "Tiden fram til 1536." In Grunntrekk i norsk historie: Fra vikingtid til våre dager, edited by Rolf Danielsen, Ståle Dyrvik, Tore Grønlie, Knut Helle, and Edgar Hovland, 13–106. Oslo: Universitetsforlaget, 1991.

——. Under kirke og kongemakt: 1130–1350. Aschehougs Norgeshistorie 3. Oslo: Aschehoug, 1995.

Helle, Knut, Finn-Einar Eliassen, Jan Eivind Myhre, and Ola Svein Stugu. Norsk byhistorie urbanisering gjennom 1300 år. Edited by Knut Helle. Oslo: Pax, 2006.

Herlihy, David. "Family." American Historical Review 96 (1991): 1–16.

Hermanson, Lars. Släkt, vänner och makt: En studie av elitens politiska kultur i 1100-talets Danmark. Avhandlingar från Historiska institutionen i Göteborg 24. Gothenburg: [Historiska institutionen], 2000.

Hirdloven =Hirdloven til Norges konge og hans håndgangne menn: Etter AM 322 fol. Edited by Steinar Imsen. Oslo: Riksarkivet, 2000.

Historia Norwegie =Historia Norwegie. Edited by Inger Ekrem and Lars Boje Mortensen, Copenhagen: Museum Tusculanum Press, 2003.

Hjelde, Oddmund. Kirkens budskap i sagatiden. Oslo: Solum, 1995.

Hovstad, Johan. Mannen og samfunnet: Studiar i norrøn etikk. Oslo: Samlaget, 1943.

Høgset, Grete. "Frendskap og vennskap: Betydningen av sosiale relasjoner og nettverk på Island og i Norge ca 900–1264." Hovedfagsoppgave, Universitetet i Bergen, 1995.

Hreinsson, Einar, and Tomas Nilson. Introduction to *Nätverk som social resurs: Historiska exempel*. Stundetlitteratur. Edited by Einar Hreinsson and Tomas Nilson, 7–32. Lund, SE: Studentlitteratur, 2003.

HsH Sth =*Hákonar saga Hákonarsonar etter Sth. 8 fol., AM 325 (8), 4:o og AM 304, 4:o*. Norrøne tekster 2. Edited by Marina Mundt. Oslo: Kjeldeskriftfondet, 1977.

Hyatte, Reginald. *The Arts of Friendship: The Idealization of Friendship in Medieval and Early Renaissance Literature*. Brill's Studies in Intellectual History, vol. 50. Leiden: Brill, 1994.

Icelandic Homily Book =*The Icelandic Homily Book: Perg. 15 4to in The Royal Library, Stockholm*. Íslensk handrit. Icelandic manuscripts. Series in quarto. Edited by Andrea de Leeuw van Weenen, vol. 3. Reykjavík: Stofnun Árna Magnússonar á Íslandi, 1993.

Imsen, Steinar, ed. *Rex Insularum: The King of Norway and His "Skattlands" as a Political System c. 1260–c. 1450*. Bergen: Fagbokforlaget Vigmostad & Bjørke, 2014.

Ingvarsson, Lúðvík. *Goðorð og goðorðsmenn 1–3*. Egilsstaðir: Höfundur, 1986–87.

———. *Refsingar á Íslandi á þjóðveldistímanum*. Reykjavík: Menningarsjóður, 1970.

Islandske Annaler =*Islandske Annaler indtil 1578*. Det Norske historiske Kildeskrift-fonds skrifter 21. Edited by Gustav Storm. Christiania: Grøndahl, 1888.

Islendzk æventyri =*Islendzk æventyri: Isländische Legenden, Novellen und Märchen*. Edited by Hugo Gering. Halle an der Saale: Verlag der Buchhandlung des Waisenhauses, 1882.

Íslensk hómilíubók =*Íslensk hómilíubók fornar stólræður*. Edited by Guðrún Kvaran, Sigurbjörn Einarsson, and Gunnlaugur Ingólfsson. Reykjavík: Híð íslenska bókmenntafélag, 1993.

Íslenzk fornrit Eddukvæði =*Eddukvæði 1–2*. Íslenzk fornrit. Edited by Jónas Kristjáns-son and Vésteinn Ólason. Reykjavík: Hið Íslenzka fornritafélag, 2014.

Íslenzk fornrit 1 =*Íslendingabók, Landnámabók*. Íslenzk fornrit. Edited by Jakob Benediktsson. Reykjavík: Hið íslenzka fornritafélag, 1968.

Íslenzk fornrit 2 =*Egils saga Skalla-Grímssonar*. Íslenzk fornrit. Edited by Sigurður Nordal. Reykjavík: Hið íslenzka fornritafélag, 1933.

Íslenzk fornrit 3 =*Borgfirðinga sögur*. Íslenzk fornrit. Edited by Guðni Jónsson and Sigurður Nordal. Reykjavík: Hið Íslenzka fornritafélag, 1956.

Íslenzk fornrit 4 =*Eyrbyggja saga; Brands þáttr Örva; Eiríks saga rauða; Grænlendinga saga; Grænlendinga þáttr*. Íslenzk fornrit. Edited by Matthías Þórðarson and Einar Ólafur Sveinsson. Reykjavík: Hið íslenzka fornritafélag, 1935.

Íslenzk fornrit 5 =*Laxdæla saga; Halldórs þættir Snorrasonar; Stúfs þáttr*. Íslenzk fornrit. Edited by Einar Ólafur Sveinsson. Reykjavík: Hið íslenzka fornritafé-lag, 1934.

Íslenzk fornrit 6 =*Vestfirðinga sögur*. Íslenzk fornrit. Edited by Guðni Jónsson and Björn K. Þórólfsson. Reykjavík: Hið Íslenzka fornritafélag, 1943.

Íslenzk fornrit 7 =*Grettis saga Ásmundarsonar; Bandamanna saga; Odds þáttr Ófeigsso-nar*. Íslenzk fornrit. Edited by Guðni Jónsson. Reykjavík: Hið íslenzka fornritafélag, 1936.

Íslenzk fornrit 8 =*Vatnsdæla saga; Hallfreðar saga; Kormáks saga; Hrómundar þáttr halta; Hrafns þáttr Guðrúnarsonar*. Íslenzk fornrit. Edited by Einar Ólafur Sveinsson. Reykjavík: Hið íslenzka fornritafélag, 1939.

Íslenzk fornrit 9 =Eyfirðinga sögur. Íslenzk fornrit. Edited by Jónas Kristjánsson. Reykjavík: Hið íslenzka fornritafélag, 1956.

Íslenzk fornrit 10 =Ljósvetninga saga með þáttum; Reykdæla saga ok Víga-Skútu; Hreiðars þáttr. Íslenzk fornrit. Edited by Björn Sigfússon. Reykjavík: Hið íslenzka fornritafélag, 1940.

Íslenzk fornrit 11 =Austfirðinga sögur. Íslenzk fornrit. Edited by Jón Jóhannesson. Reykjavík: Hið islenzka fornritafélag, 1950.

Íslenzk fornrit 12 =Brennu-Njáls saga. Íslenzk fornrit. Edited by Einar Ólafur Sveinsson. Reykjavík: Hið íslenzka fornritafélag, 1954.

Íslenzk fornrit 13 =Harðar saga; Bárðar saga; Þorskfirðinga saga; Flóamanna saga; Þórarins þáttr Nefjólfssonar; Þorsteins þáttr Úxafóts; Egils þáttr Síðu-Hallssonar; Orms þáttr Stórólfssonar; Þorsteins þáttr Tjaldstöðings; Þorsteins þáttr Forvitna; Bergbúa þáttr; Kumlbúa þáttr; Stjörnu-Odda draumr. Íslenzk fornrit. Edited by Bjarni Vilhjálmsson and Þórhallur Vilmundarson. Reykjavík: Hið íslenzka fornritafélag, 1991.

Íslenzk fornrit 14 =Kjalnesinga saga; Jökuls þáttr Búasonar; Víglundar saga; Króka-Refs saga; Þórðar saga hreðu; Finnboga saga; Gunnars saga keldugnúpsfífls. Íslenzk fornrit. Edited by Jóhannes Halldórsson. Reykavik: Hið islenzka fornritafélag, 1959.

Íslenzk fornrit 15 =Biskupa sögur 1. Íslenzk fornrit. Edited by Sigurgeir Steingríms-son, Ólafur Halldórsson, and Peter Foote. Reykjavík: Hið íslenzka fornritafélag, 2003.

Íslenzk fornrit 16 =Biskupa sögur 2. Íslenzk fornrit. Edited by Ásdís Egilsdóttir. Reykjavík: Hið íslenzka fornritafélag, 2002.

Íslenzk fornrit 17 =Biskupa sögur 3. Íslenzk fornrit. Edited by Guðrún Ása Grímsdót-tir. Reykjavík: Hið íslenzka fornritafélag, 1998.

Íslenzk fornrit 26 =Heimskringla 1. Íslenzk fornrit. Edited by Bjarni Aðalbjarnarson. Reykjavík: Hið íslenzka fornritafélag, 1941.

Íslenzk fornrit 27 =Heimskringla 2. Íslenzk fornrit. Edited by Bjarni Aðalbjarnarson. Reykjavík: Hið íslenzka fornritafélag, 1945.

Íslenzk fornrit 28 =Heimskringla 3. Íslenzk fornrit. Edited by Bjarni Aðalbjarnarson. Reykjavík: Hið íslenzka fornritafélag, 1951.

Íslenzk fornrit 29 =Ágrip af Nóregskonunga sǫgum; Fagrskinna; Nóregs konunga tal. Íslenzk fornrit. Edited by Bjarni Einarsson. Reykjavík: Hið Íslenzka fornritafé-lag, 1985.

Íslenzk fornrit 30 =Sverris saga. Íslenzk fornrit. Edited by Þorleifur Hauksson. Reykjavík: Hið íslenska fornritafélag, 2007.

Íslenzk fornrit 34 =Orkneyinga saga; Legenda de sancto Magno; Magnúss saga skemmri; Magnúss saga lengri; Helga þáttr ok Úlfs. Íslenzk fornrit. Edited by Finnbogi Guðmundsson. Reykjavík: Hið íslenzka fornritafélag, 1965.

Iversen, Tore. Trelldommen: Norsk slaveri i middelalderen. Historisk institutt, Univer-sitetet i Bergen skrifter 1. Bergen: Historisk institutt, Universitetet i Bergen, 1997.

Jaeger, C. Stephen. Ennobling Love: In Search of a Lost Sensibility. The Middle Ages Series. Philadelphia: University of Pennsylvania Press, 1999.

Jesch, Judith. Ships and Men in the Late Viking Age: The Vocabulary of Runic Inscriptions and Skaldic Verse. Woodbridge, UK: Boydell Press, 2001.

Jochens, Jenny. "Old Norse Motherhood." In *Medieval Mothering.* Garland Reference Library of the Humanities, edited by John Carmi Parsons and Bonnie Wheeler, 201–22. New York: Garland, 1996.

Johnsen, Arne Odd. *Fra ættesamfunn til statssamfunn.* Oslo: Aschehoug, 1948.

——. *Studier vedrørende kardinal Nicolaus Brekespears legasjon til Norden.* Oslo: Fabritius, 1945.

Johnsen, Oscar Albert. "Gildevæsenet i Norge i middelalderen." *Historisk Tidsskrift,* 5 (1920): 73–101.

Jóhannesson, Jón. *Íslendinga saga 1:* Þjóðveldisöld. Reykjavík: Almenna Bókafélagið, 1956.

——. *Íslendinga saga 2: Fyrirlestrar og ritgerðir um tímabilið 1262–1550.* Reykjavík: Almenna Bókafélagið, 1958.

Jónsbók =*Jónsbók: Kong Magnus Hakonssons lovbog for Island vedtaget paa Altinget 1281 og réttarbætr de for Island givne retterbøder af 1294, 1305 og 1314.* Edited by Ólafur Halldórsson. Copenhagen: S. L. Møllers Bogtrykkeri, 1904.

Jónsson, Janus. "Um klaustrin á Íslandi." *Tímarit Hins íslenska bókmenntafélags* 8 (1887): 174–265.

Kapelrud, Arvid S. *Job og hans problem: I fortid og i dag.* Oslo: Land og kirke, 1976.

Karlsson, Gunnar. *Goðamenning: Staða og áhrif goðorðsmanna í þjóðveldi Íslendinga.* Reykjavík: Heimskringla, 2004.

——. "Stjórnmálamaðurinn Snorri." In *Snorri: Átta alda minning,* edited by Gunnar Karlsson and Helgi Þorláksson, 23–51. Reykjavík: Sögufélag, 1979.

Kilduff, Martin, and Wenpin Tsai. *Social Networks and Organizations.* London: Sage, 2003.

Kirby, Ian J. *Bible Translation in Old Norse.* Publications de la Faculté des lettres 27. Geneva: University of Lausanne, 1986.

Kjartansson, Helgi Skúli. "Gamli sáttmáli—hvað næst?" *Saga* 49, no. 1 (2011): 133–53.

Kjær, Lars, and A. J. Watson. "Feasts and Gifts: Sharing Food in the Middle Ages." *Journal of Medieval History* 37, no. 1 (2011): 1–5.

Kleinig, John. "Loyalty." In *The Stanford Encyclopedia of Philosophy,* edited by Edward N. Zalta. Stanford, CA: Stanford University, 2013. http://plato .stanford.edu/archives/fall2013/entries/loyalty.

KLNM =*Kulturhistorisk leksikon for nordisk middelalder 1–22.* Edited by Finn Hødnebø et al. Oslo: Gyldendal, 1956–78.

Klosterliv =*Klosterliv i Vesten: Augustins regel, Benedikts regel.* Thorleif Dahls kulturbibliotek. Edited by Erik Gunnes. Oslo: Aschehoug, 1986.

Koht, Halvdan. "Sagaenes opfatning av vår gamle historie." *Historisk tidsskrift* 5, no. 2 (1914): 379–96.

Kolsrud, Oluf. *Noregs kyrkjesoga.* Oslo: Aschehoug, 1958.

Konstan, David. *Friendship in the Classical World.* Key Themes in Ancient History. Cambridge: Cambridge University Press, 1997.

Konungs skuggsiá =*Konungs skuggsiá.* Norrøne tekster 1. Edited by Ludvig Holm-Olsen. Oslo: Kjeldeskriftfondet, 1983.

Krag, Claus. *Norges historie fram til 1319.* Oslo: Universitetsforlaget, 2000.

——. *Vikingtid og rikssamling: 800–1130.* Aschehougs Norgeshistorie 2. Oslo: Aschehoug, 1995.

Landé, C. H. "Introduction: The Dyadic Basis of Clientelism." In *Friends, Followers, and Factions. A Reader in Political Clientelism*, edited by Steffen W. Schmidt, James C. Scott, Carl Lande, and Laura Guasti, xiii–xxxvii. Berkeley: University of California Press, 1977.

Lárusson, Björn. *The Old Icelandic Land Registers*. Lund, SE: CWK Gleerup Lund, 1967.

Lárusson, Ólafur. *Yfirlit yfir íslenska rjettarsögu*. Reykjavík: s.n., 1932.

Lindahl, Carl. "Bakhtin's Carnival Laughter and the Cajun Country Mardi Gras." *Folklore* 107 (1996): 57–70.

Lindow, John. "Akkerisfrakki: Traditions concerning Olafr Tryggvason and Hallfredr Ottarsson vandraedaskald and the Problem of the Conversion (Iceland's Conversion to Christianity)." *Journal of English and Germanic Philology* 106, no. 1 (2007): 64–80.

Lucas, Gavin, ed. *Hofstaðir: Excavations of a Viking Age Feasting Hall in North-Eastern Iceland*. Institute of Archaeology Monograph Series 1. Reykjavík: Fornleifastofnun Íslands, 2009.

Lunden, Kåre. *Økonomi og samfunn*. Oslo: Universitetsforlaget, 1972.

Mac Carron, Pádraig, and Ralph Kenna. "Network analysis of the Íslendinga sögur: The Sagas of Icelanders." [In English]. *European Physical Journal B* 86, no. 10 (October 2013): 1–9.

——. "Viking Sagas: Six Degrees of Icelandic Separation Social Networks from the Viking Era." *Significance* 10, no. 6 (2013): 12–17.

Magnúsdóttir, Auður. *Frillor och fruar: Politik och samlevnad på Island 1120–1400*. Göteborg: Historiska Institutionen, 2001.

——. "'Þeir Kjartan ok Bolli unnusk mest': Om kärlek och svek i *Laxdæla saga*." In *"Vi ska alla vara välkomna!" Nordiska studier tillägnade Kristinn Jóhannesson*, edited by Auður Magnúsdóttir, Henrik Janson, Karl. G Johansson, Mats Malm, and Lena Rogström, 65–81. Gothenburg: Meijerbergs institut för svensk etymologisk forskning, Göteborgs universitet, 2008.

Magnússon, Ásgeir Blöndal. *Íslensk orðsifjabók*. Reykjavík: Orðabók Háskólans, 1989.

Mair, Lucy. *An Introduction to Social Anthropology*. London: Clarendon Press, 1965.

Mariu saga 2 =Mariu saga; *Legende om Jomfru Maria og hendes Jertegner; Efter gamle Haandskrifter*. Det norske Oldskriftselskabs Samlinger. Edited by Carl Richard Unger. Christiania: Det norske Oldskriftselskab, 1871.

Maurer, Konrad. *Island von seiner ersten Entdeckung bis zum Untergange des Freistaats*. Munich: C. Kaiser, 1874.

Mauss, Marcel. *The Gift: Forms and Functions of Exchange in Archaic Societies*. Translated by Ian Cunnison. Edited by E. E. Evans-Pritchard, rev. ed. London: Cohen and West, (1925) 1970.

McEvoy, James. "The Theory of Friendship in the Latin Middle Ages: Hermeneutics, Contextualization and the Transmission and Reception of Ancient Texts and Ideas, from *c*. AD 350 to *c*. 1500." In *Friendship in Medieval Europe*, edited by Julian Haseldine, 3–44. Stroud, UK: Sutton, 1999.

McGuire, Brian Patrick. *Friendship and Community: The Monastic Experience 350–1250*. Cistercian Studies Series 95. Kalamazoo, MI: Cistercian Publications, 1988.

McKinnell, John. *Essays on Eddic Poetry*. Toronto Old Norse and Icelandic Series. Toronto: University of Toronto Press, 2014.

——. "The Making of Hávamál." *Journal of Viking and Medieval Scandinavia* 3 (2007): 75–115.

Medieval Scandinavian =*Medieval Scandinavian: An Encyclopedia*. Garland Encyclopedias of the Middle Ages. Edited by Phillip Pulsiano and Kirsten Wolf, vol. 1. New York: Garland, 1993.

Merrill, Robert T. "Notes on Icelandic Kinship Terminology." *American Anthropologist* 66 (1964): 867–72.

Meulengracht Sørensen, Preben. *Fortælling og ære: Studier i islændingesagaerne*. Aarhus: Aarhus Universitetsforlag, 1993.

——. *Saga og samfund*. København: Berllingske forlag, 1977.

Miller, William Ian. *Audun and the Polar Bear: Luck, Law, and Largesse in a Medieval Tale of Risky Business*. Medieval Law and Its Practice. Leiden: Brill, 2008.

——. *Bloodtaking and Peacemaking. Feud, Law, and Society in Saga Iceland*. Chicago: University of Chicago Press, 1990.

——. "Justifying Skarphéðinn: Of Pretext and Politics in the Icelandic Bloodfeud." *Scandinavian Studies* 55 (1983): 316–44.

Mitterauer, Michael. "Familie und Arbeitsorganisation in städtischen Gesellschaften des späten Mittelalters und der frühen Neuzeit." In *Haus und Familie in der spätmittelalterlichen Stadt*, edited by Alfred Haverkamp, 1–12. Cologne: Böhlau 1984.

Monclair, Hanne. "Lederskapsideologi på Island i det trettende århundret. En analyse av gavegivning, gjestebud og lederfremtoning i islandsk sagamateriale." PhD diss., Universitetet i Oslo, 2003.

Mullett, Margaret E. "Byzantium: A Friendly Society?" *Past and Present* 118 (1988): 3–24.

Mundal, Else. "Kvinnesynet og forståinga av biologisk arv i den norrøne kulturen." In *Atlantisk dåd og drøm: 17 essays om Island/Norge*, edited by Asbjørn Aarnes, 153–70. Oslo: Aschehoug, 1998.

Mustakallio, Katariina, and Christian Krötzl. *De Amicitia: Friendship and Social Networks in Antiquity and the Middle Ages*. Vol. 36. Rome: Institutum, 2009.

Nolte, Theodor. "Der Begriff und das Motiv des Freundes in der Geschichte der deutschen Sprache und älteren Literatur." *Frühmittelalterliche Studien* 24 (1990): 126–44.

Nordal, Guðrún, Vésteinn Ólason, and Sverrir Tómasson. *Íslensk bókmenntasaga 1*. Reykjavík: Mál og menning, 1992.

Norðfjörð, Óttar M. "Hugtakakerfi Hávamála." *Skírnir* 179 (2005): 33–56.

Norges gamle love =*Norges gamle Love 1–5*. Edited by Rudolf Keyser et al. Christiania: Grøndahl og søn, 1846–95.

Norges innskrifter 6 =*Norges innskrifter med de yngre runer 6: Bryggen i Bergen*. Edited by Aslak Liestøl, James E. Knirk, and Ingrid Sanness Johnsen. Oslo: Kjeldskriftfondet, 1980–90.

Norsk biografisk leksikon =*Norsk biografisk leksikon 1–10*. Edited by Knut Helle and Jon Gunnar Arntzen. Oslo: Kunnskapsforlaget, 1999–2005.

Ólsen, Björn M. *Om Gunnlaugs Saga Ormstungu: En kritisk Undersøgelse*. Copenhagen: s.n., 1911.

——. "Um upphaf konungsvalds á Íslandi." *Andvari* 33 (1908): 18–88.

Onarheim eldre =*Skraa for et Olafsgilde i Gulathingslagen.* Norges gamle Love 5. Edited by Rudolf Keyser et al. Christiania: Grøndahl og søn, 1846.

Orning, Hans Jacob. "Borgerkrig og statsutvikling i Norge i middelalderen: En revurdering." *Historisk tidsskrift* (2014): 193–216.

——. "Hvorfor vant kongene?" *Historisk tidsskrift* 93 (2015): 285–92.

——. "Statsutvikling i Norge og på Island i høymiddelalderen belyst ut fra en analyse av Þórðr kakali Sighvatsson og Sverre Sigurdssons vei til makten." *Historisk tidsskrift* 76 (1997): 469–86.

——. *Unpredictability and Presence: Norwegian Kingship in the High Middle Ages.* The Northern World: North Europe and the Baltic c. 400–1700 AD; Peoples, Economies and Cultures. Leiden: Brill, 2008.

Pálsson, Hermann. "Brands þáttur örva." *Gripla* 7 (1990): 117–30.

——. "Forn vinátta." *Húnavaka* 40 (2000): 123–38.

——. *Hávamál í ljósi íslenskrar menningar.* Reykjavík: Háskólaútgáfan, 1999.

Pálsson, Viðar. "'Var engi höfðingi slíkr sem Snorri': Auður og virðing í valdabaráttu Snorra Sturlusonar." *Saga* 41 (2003): 55–96.

Pedersen, Frederik. "A Medieval Welfare State? Welfare Provision in a Twelfth Century Icelandic Law Code." *Northern Studies* 34 (1999): 89–111.

Perron, Anthony. "'Jus metropoliticum' on the Norwegian Periphery from Nicholas Breakspear to William of Sabina." In *Frontiers in the Middle Ages: Proceedings of the Third European Congress of Medieval Studies (Jyväskylä, 10–14 June 2003),* edited by O. Merisalo, 237–58. Louvain-la-Neuve, BE: Brepols, 2006.

——. "Metropolitan Might and Papal Power on the Latin-Christian Frontier: Transforming the Danish Church around the Time of the Fourth Lateran Council." *Catholic Historical Review* 89 (2003): 182–212.

Postola Sögur =*Postola Sögur: Legendariske Fortællinger om Apostlernes Liv, deres Kamp for Kristendommens Udbredelse samt deres Martyrdød; efter gamle Haandskrifter.* Edited by Carl Richard Unger. Christiania: Trykt hos B. M. Bentzen, 1874.

Qviller, Bjørn. "Patron-klient-forhold." In *Holmgang: Om førmoderne samfunn; Festskrift til Kåre Lunden,* Tid og Tanke 4, edited by Anne Eidsfelt, Knut Kjeldstadli, Hanne Monclair, Per G. Norseng, Hans Jakob Orning, and Gunnar I. Pettersen, 133–43. Oslo: Historisk institutt, 2000.

——. *Romersk politisk kultur og sosiologisk historie.* Oslo: Cappelen akademisk forlag, 1999.

Reinhart, Katrinka. "Ritual Feasting and Empowerment at Yanshi Shangcheng." *Journal of Anthropological Archaeology* 39 (2015): 76–109.

Rich, George W. "Problems and Prospects in the Study of Icelandic Kinship." In *The Anthropology of Iceland,* edited by Paul E. Durrenberger and Gísli Pálsson, 53–79. Iowa City: University of Iowa Press, 1989.

Ricketts, Philadelphia. *High-ranking Widows in Medieval Iceland and Yorkshire: Property, Power, Marriage and Identity in the Twelfth and Thirteenth Centuries.* The Northern World: North Europe and the Baltic c. 400–1700 AD; Peoples, Economies and Cultures. Leiden: Brill, 2010.

Rule of Saint Benedict =*The Rule of Saint Benedict.* Dumbarton Oaks Medieval Library. Edited by Bruce L. Venarde. Cambridge, MA: Harvard University Press, 2011.

Sahlins, Marshall. *Stone Age Economics.* London: Routledge, (1972) 1978.

Sandal, Aud-Jorunn. "Synd i Gamalnorsk homiliebok og Islandsk homiliebok."
Hovedfagsoppgave, Universitetet i Bergen, 1996.

Sanmark, Alexandra. "Women at the Thing." In *Kvinner i vikingtid*, edited by Nanna
Løkka and Nancy L. Coleman, 89–105. Oslo: Scandinavian Academic Press,
2014.

Scanlon, Larry. *Narrative, Authority, and Power: The Medieval Exemplum and the
Chaucerian Tradition.* Cambridge Studies in Medieval Literature 20. Cambridge: Cambridge University Press, 1994.

Schwartz, Daniel. *Aquinas on Friendship.* Oxford Philosophical Monographs. Oxford:
Clarendon Press, 2007.

Seidel, Kerstin. *Freunde und Verwandte: Soziale Beziehungen in einer spätmittelalterlichen
Stadt.* Campus Historische Studien 49. Frankfurt: Campus Verlag, 2009.

Sère, Bénédicte. *Penser l'amitié au Moyen Âge: Étude historique des commentaires sur les
livres VIII et IX de l'Éthique à Nicomaque (XIIIe–XVe siècle).* Turnhout, BE:
Brepols, 2007.

Sigurðsson, Jón Viðar. "The Appearance and Personal Abilities of *goðar, jarlar,* and
konungar: Iceland, Orkney and Norway." In *West over Sea: Studies in Scandinavian Sea-Borne Expansion and Settlement before 1300,* The Northern World:
North Europe and the Baltic c. 400–1700 AD; Peoples, Economies and
Cultures, edited by Beverly Ballin Smith, Simon Taylor, and Gareth Williams,
95–109. Leiden: Brill, 2007.

——. "Becoming a Scat Land: The Skattgjafir Process between the Kings of Norway
and the Icelanders, c. 1250–1300." In *Taxes, Tributes and Tributary Lands in the
Making of the Scandinavian Kingdoms in the Middle Ages,* edited by Steinar
Imsen, 115–31. Trondheim: Tapir, 2011.

——. "The Changing Role of Friendship in Iceland, c. 900–1300." In *Friendship and
Social Networks in Scandinavia, c. 1000–1800,* Early European Research, edited by
Jón Viðar Sigurðsson and Thomas Småberg. 43–64. Turnhout, BE: Brepols,
2013.

——. *Chieftains and Power in the Icelandic Commonwealth.* The Viking Collection.
Translated by Jean Lundskær-Nielsen, vol. 12. Odense: Odense University
Press, (1993) 1999.

——. *Den vennlige vikingen: Vennskapets makt i Norge og på Island ca. 900–1300.* Oslo:
Pax, 2010.

——. *Det norrøne samfunnet: Vikingen, kongen, erkebiskopen og bonden.* Oslo: Pax,
2008.

——. "Forholdet mellom frender, hushold og venner på Island i fristatstiden."
Historisk tidsskrift 74 (1995): 311–30.

——. *Frá goðorðum til ríkja: Þróun goðavalds á 12. og 13. öld.* Sagnfræðirannsóknir B. 10.
Reykjavík: Bókaútgáfa Menningarsjóðs, (1987) 1989.

——. "Friendship in the Icelandic Free State Society." Translated by Friendship in the
Icelandic. In *From Sagas to Society: Comparative Approaches to Early Iceland,*
edited by Gísli Pálsson, 205–15. Enfield Lock, UK: Hisarlik Press, 1992.

——. "Fristatens forfatning: et symbol foran sitt fall?" In *Holmgang: Om det førmoderne
samfunn; Festskrift til Kåre Lunden,* Tid og tanke 4, edited by Anne Eidsfeldt, Knut
Kjeldstadli, Hanne Monclair, Per G. Norseng, Hans Jakob Orning, and Gunnar I. Pettersen, 188–204. Oslo: Historisk institutt, Universitetet i Oslo, 2000.

——. "Hugleiðingar um hreppa, bændagildi og goðorð." In *Heimtur: Ritgerðir til heiðurs Gunnari Karlssyni sjötugum*, edited by Guðmundur Jónsson, Helgi Skúli Kjartansson, and Vésteinn Ólason, 243–55. Reykjavík: Mál og menning, 2009.

——. "The Icelandic Aristocracy after the Fall of the Free State." *Scandinavian Journal of History* 20 (1995): 153–66.

——. "Island og Nidaros." In *Ecclesia Nidrosiensis 1153–1537: Søkelys på Nidaroskirkens og Nidarosprovinsens historie*, edited by Steinar Imsen, 121–40. Trondheim: Tapir akademisk forlag, 2003.

——. "Kings, Earls and Chieftains: Rulers in Norway, Orkney and Iceland c. 900–1300." In *Ideology and Power in the Viking and Middle Ages: Scandinavia, Iceland, Ireland, Orkney and the Faeroes*, edited by Gro Steinsland, Jón Viðar Sigurðsson, Jan Erik Rekdal, and Ian Beuermann, 69–108. Leiden: Brill, 2011.

——. "Konur og kvennarán á Íslandi á 12. og 13. öld." *Ný saga* 9 (1997): 71–80.

——. *Kristninga i Norden 750–1200*. Utsyn & innsikt. Oslo: Samlaget, 2003.

——. "The Making of a 'Skattland': Iceland 1247–1450." In *Rex Insularum: The King of Norway and His "Skattlands" as a Political System, c. 1260–c. 1450*, edited by Steinar Imsen, 181–225. Bergen: Fagbokforlaget, 2014.

——. "Noen hovedtrekk i diskusjonen om det islandske middelaldersamfunnet etter 1970." *Collegium Medievale* 18 (2005): 106–43.

——. "The Norse Community." In *The Norwegian domination and the Norse World c. 1100–c. 1400*, Rostra Books Trondheim Studies in History, edited by Steinar Imsen, 59–73. Trondheim: Tapir Academic Press, 2010.

——. *Norsk historie 800–1300: Frå høvdingmakt til konge- og kyrkjemakt*. Oslo: Det norske samlaget, 1999.

——. "Om legender og samfunnspåvirkning." In *Norm og praksis i middelaldersamfunnet*, Kulturstudier 14, edited by Else Mundal and Ingvild Øye, 184–97. Bergen: Senter for europeiske kulturstudier, 1999.

——. "The Role of Arbitration in the Settlement of Disputes in Iceland c. 1000–1300." In *Law and Disputing in the Middle Ages: Proceedings of the Ninth Carlsberg Academy Conference on Medieval Legal History 2012*, edited by Per Andersen, Kirsi Salonen, Helle Møller Sigh, and Helle Vogt, 123–35. Copenhagen: DJØF Publishing, 2013.

——. "Tendencies in the Historiography on the Medieval Nordic States (to 1350)." In *Public Power in Europe. Studies in Historical Transformation*, edited by James S. Amelang and Sigfried Beer, 1–15. Pisa: PLUS–Pisa University Press, 2006.

——. "The Wedding at Flugumýri in 1253: Icelandic Feasts between the Free State Period and Norwegian Hegemony." In *Rituals, Performatives, and Political Order in Northern Europe, c. 650–1350*, edited by Wojtek Jezierski, Lars Hermanson, Hans Jacob Orning and Thomas Småberg, 209–35. Turnhout, BE: Brepols, 2015.

Sigurðsson, Jón Viðar, and Thomas Småberg, eds. *Friendship and Social Networks in Scandinavia, c. 1000–1800*. Early European Research, vol. 5. Turnhout, BE: Brepols, 2013.

Skálholtsbók =*Skálholtsbók: Det Arnamagnæanske Haandskrift 81a Fol. Skálholtsbók yngsta*. Edited by A. Kjær and Ludvig Holm-Olsen. Christiania: Norsk historisk kjeldeskrift-institutt, 1910–86.

Snorra Edda =Edda Snorra Sturlusonar. Edited by Heimir Pálsson. Reykjavík: Mál og menning, 1996.

Spearing, Anthony Colin. Textual Subjectivity the Encoding of Subjectivity in Medieval Narratives and Lyrics. Oxford: Oxford University Press, 2005.

Standen, Naomi. Unbounded loyalty: Frontier crossings in Liao China. Honolulu: University of Hawaii Press, 2007.

Steblin-Kamenskij, Mikhail I. "On the Nature of Fiction in the Sagas of Icelanders." Scandinavica 6 (1967): 77–84.

———. The Saga Mind. Translated by Kenneth H. Ober. Odense: Odense Universitets-forlag, 1973.

———. "Tidsforestillingene i islendingesagaene." Edda 68 (1968): 351–61.

Stefánsson, Magnús. "Frá goðakirkju til biskupskirkju." In Saga Íslands 3, edited by Sigurður Líndal, 109–257. Reykjavík: Hið íslenzka bókmenntafélag, 1978.

———. "Islandsk egenkirkevesen." In Møtet mellom hedendom og kristendom i Norge, edited by Hans-Emil Lidén, 234–54. Oslo: Universitetsforlaget, 1995.

———. "Kirkjuvald eflist." In Saga Íslands 2, edited by Sigurður Líndal, 55–144. Reykjavík: Hið íslenzka bókmenntafélag, 1975.

———. Staðir og staðamál: Studier i islandske egenkirkelige og beneficialrettslige forhold i middelalderen. Skrifter 1. Historisk institutt, Universitetet i Bergen 4. Bergen: Historisk institutt, Universitetet i Bergen, 2000.

Steinsland, Gro. Norrøn religion: Myter, riter, samfunn. Oslo: Pax, 2005.

Stjorn =Stjórn: Tekst etter håndskriftene 1–2. Norrøne tekster. Edited by Reidar Astås. Oslo: Riksarkivet, 2009.

Stordalen, Terje, and Reidar Hvalvik. Den store fortellingen: Om Bibelens tilblivelse, innhold, bruk og betydning. Oslo: Det Norske bibelselskap, 1999.

Sturlunga saga =Sturlunga saga 1–2. Edited by Jón Jóhannesson, Magnús Finnbo-gason, and Kristján Eldjárn. Reykjavík: Sturlunguútgáfan, 1946.

Svare, Helge. Vennskap. Oslo: Pax, 2004.

Sveaas Andersen, Per. Samlingen av Norge og kristningen av landet 800–1130. Handbok i Norges historie 2. Bergen: Universitetsforlaget, 1977.

Sveinbjörnsdóttir, Árný E., Jan Heinemeier, and Gardar Gudmundsson. "14C Dating of the Settlement of Iceland." Radiocarbon 46, no. 1 (2004): 387–94.

Tanner, Heather J. Families, Friends, and Allies: Boulogne and Politics in Northern France and England, c. 879–1160. The Northern World: North Europe and the Baltic c. 400–1700 AD; Peoples, Economies and Cultures. Leiden: Brill, 2004.

Tristram =Saga af Tristram ok Ísönd, samt Möttuls saga. Edited by Gísli Brynjúlfsson. Copenhagen: Det kongelige Nordiske Oldskrift-Selskab, 1878.

Turner, Victor W. "An Anthropological Approach to the Icelandic Saga." In The Translation of Culture: Essays to E. E. Evans-Pitchard, edited by T. O. Beidelman, 349–74. London: Tavistock, 1971.

Tyson, Lois. Critical Theory Today: A User-Friendly Guide. 2nd ed. New York: Rout-ledge, 2006.

Vadum, Kristoffer Mathias. "Bruk av kanonistisk litteratur i Nidarosprovinsen ca. 1250–1340." Hovedfagsoppgave, Universitetet i Oslo, 2015.

Van Deusen, Natalie M. "Sworn Sisterhood? On the (Near-) Absence of Female Friendship from the Íslendingasǫgur." Scandinavian Studies 86, no. 1 (2014): 52–71.

Verboven, Koenraad. *The Economy of Friends: Economic Aspects of Amicitia and Patronage in the Late Republic*. Collection Latomus 269. Brussels: Latomus, 2002.

Vestergaard, Torben Anders. "The System of Kinship in Early Norwegian Law." *Mediaeval Scandinavia* 12 (1988): 160–93.

Vésteinn Ólason. "Norrøn litteraratur som historisk kildemateriale." In *Kilderne til den tidlige middelalders historie: Rapporter til den XX nordiske historikerkongres Reykjavík 1987*, Ritsafn Sagnfræðistofnunar 18, edited by Gunnar Karlsson, 30–47. Reykjavík: Sagnfræðistofnum Háskóla Íslands, 1987.

Vésteinsson, Orri. "The Formative Phase of the Icelandic Church ca. 990–1240 AD." In *Church Centres: Church Centres in Iceland from the 11th to the 13th Century and Their Parallels in Other Countries*, Snorrastofa, Rit 2, edited by Helgi Þorláksson, 71–81. Reykholt, IS: Snorrastofa, 2005.

Vilhjálmsson, Bjarni, and Óskar Halldórsson. *Íslenzkir málshættir. Íslenzk þjóðfræði*. Reykjavík: Almenna bókafélagið, 1991.

Weibull, Lauritz. *Kritiska undersökningar i Nordens historia omkring år 1000*. Lund, SE: 1911.

Wisløff, Carl F. *Norsk kirkehistorie 1*. Oslo: Lutherstiftelsen, 1966.

Wood, Susan. *The Proprietary Church in the Medieval West*. Oxford: Oxford University Press, 2006.

Wærdahl, Randi Bjørshol. *To Serve a King, as All Other Lands in the World: The Incorporation and Integration of the King's Tributary Lands into the Norwegian Realm c. 1195–1397*. The Northern World: North Europe and the Baltic c. 400–1700 AD; Peoples, Economies and Cultures. Leiden: Brill, 2011.

Ysebaert, Walter. "Friendship and Networks." In *Handbook of Medieval Studies: Terms, Methods, Trends*, edited by Albrecht Classen, 580–93. Göttingen: de Gruyter, 2010.

Þorláksson, Helgi. "Er gamli sáttmáli tómur tilbúningur?" In *Þriðja íslenska söguþingið 18.–21. maí 2006*, edited by Benedikt Eyþórsson and Hrafnkell Lárusson, 392–98. Reykjavík: Sagnfræðingafélag Íslands, 2006.

——. "Fé og virðing." In *Sæmdarmenn: Um heiður á þjóðveldisöld*, edited by Helgi Þorláksson et al., 91–134. Reykjavík: Hugvísindastofnun Háskóla Íslands, 2001.

——. *Gamlar götur og goðavald: Um fornar leiðir og völd Oddaverja í Rangárþingi*. Ritsafn Sagnfræðistofnunar, vol. 25. Reykjavík: Sagnfræðistofnun Háskóla Íslands, 1989.

——. Review of *Icelanders and the Kings of Norway*, by Patricia Pires Boulhosa. *Historisk Tidsskrift* 86 (2007): 142–47.

——. "Ríkisvald gegn þingvaldi: Fulltrúar vaxandi ríkisvalds takast á við fulltrúa þingvalds." In *Nordens plass i middelalderens nye Europa: Samfunnsordning, sentralmkt og periferier*, edited by Lars Ivar Hansen, Richard Holt, and Steinar Imsen, 105–23. Stamsund, NO: Orkana akademisk, 2011.

——. "Snorri Sturluson og Oddaverjar." In *Snorri: Átta alda minning*, edited by Gunnar Karlsson and Helgi Þorláksson, 53–88. Reykjavík: Sögufélag, 1979.

——. "Urbaniseringstendenser på Island i middelalderen." In *Urbaniseringsprosessen i Norden 1: Middelaldersteder; Det 17; nordiske historikermøte Trondheim 1977*, edited by Grethe A. Blom, 9–36. Oslo, 1982.

Þorsteinsson, Björn. *Ný Íslandssaga*. Reykjavík: Heimskringla, 1966.

Þorsteinsson, Björn, and Sigurður Líndal. "Lögfesting konungsvalds." In *Saga Íslands* 3, edited by Sigurður Líndal, 19–108. Reykjavík: Hið íslenzka bókmenntafélag, 1978.

Þrjár þýðingar lærðar = Þrjár þýðingar lærðar frá miðöldum: Elucidarius; Um kostu og löstu; Um festarfé sálarinnar. Edited by Gunnar Ágúst Harðarson. Reykjavík: Hið íslenska bókmenntafélag, 1989.

INDEX

Sýslumaðr. *See* District governors
system, 116–23; role of the church, 8

Taxes, 52, 68–70, 122; assembly, 16, 30,
119; church, 75, 77; land, 48; sheep, 22;
temple, 25
Thór, 87–88
Tithes, 77, 82, 121
Tønsberg Concord, 75–76
Treaty of Avaldsnes, 79
Tribute, 67–68, 70–71
Trøndelag, 48, 55–56, 73–75, 125

Unilateral relationships, 47, 125

Valdimar Valdimarsson, 55, 116
Valhalla, 87
Várþing. *See* Spring assemblies

Vestfirðir, 18, 42
Viking period, 12, 87, 103, 108
Vinhollr, 52. *See also* Loyalty
Vinr, 31, 94, 107. *See also* Friendship
Vinsæll, 22, 31, 57, 123, 131

Wisdom: among the elite, 19, 54, 58, 65, 67,
82; in *Hávamál*, 13, 54
Women: at the assembly, 30; friendship for,
34–35, 65, 84, 94, 101, 123, 127; goading,
25, 109; within Christianity, 84, 94,
98–99; within the family, 64, 104. *See also*
Concubinage; Marriage

Þingmaðr. *See* Assemblymen
Þingvellir, 30. *See also* Althing, the
Þórðar saga kakala, 20
Þorgils saga ok Hafliða, 111

Printed in the USA
CPSIA information can be obtained
at www.ICGtesting.com
LVHW090913260124
769958LV00011B/211/J